# Value Development in Higher Education

*Other Books from the Same Author*

Dynamics of Human Management: HR Cases
Educational Technology: Knowledge Assesment
Education for a Global Society: Inter-faith Dimensions
Secondary Education: The Challenges Ahead
Total Quality Management in Education
Governance of School Education in India
Indian Education: Development Since Independence
Education India: The Next Millennium
Open and Distance Education
Open Schooling: Selected Experiences
Optimising Human Learning (Trends in Educational and Training Technology)
Educational Technology: Third Yearbook
Educational Technology: Challenging Issues
Educational Technology: Yearbook 1988
Barriers to Change in Secondary Education: Some Case Studies
Survey of Research in Technical Education

# Value Development in Higher Education

Edited by
Marmar Mukhopadhyay

With an Introduction by
Bart J. McGettrick

Viva Books

New Delhi | Mumbai | Chennai | Kolkata | Bangalore | Hyderabad | Kochi | Guwahati

Author's royalty is dedicated to Gurudev Swami Satchidananda Giri for his project, Yoga Viswavidyalaya in Purulia.

**First Published 2004**
**This Paperback edition published in 2010**

**VIVA BOOKS PRIVATE LIMITED**

- 4737/23 Ansari Road, Daryaganj, New Delhi 110 002
  E-mail: vivadelhi@vivagroupindia.net, Tel. 42242200
- Plot No. 76, Service Industries, Shirvane, Sector 1, Nerul, Navi Mumbai 400 706
  E-mail: vivamumbai@vivagroupindia.net, Tel. 27721273, 27721274
- Jamals Fazal Chambers, 26 Greams Road, Chennai 600 006
  E-mail: vivachennai@vivagroupindia.net, Tel. 28290304, 28294241
- B-103, Jindal Towers, 21/1A/3 Darga Road, Kolkata 700 017
  E-mail: vivakolkata@vivagroupindia.net, Tel. 22836381, 22816713
- 7, Sovereign Park Apartments, 56-58, K. R. Road, Basavanagudi, Bangalore 560 004
  E-mail: vivabangalore@vivagroupindia.net, Tel. 26607409, 26607410
- 101-102 Mughal Marc Aptt., 3-4-637 to 641, Narayanguda, Hyderabad 500 029
  E-mail: vivahyderabad@vivagroupindia.net, Tel. 27564481, 27564482
- First Floor, Beevi Towers, SRM Road, Kaloor, Kochi 682 018, Kerala
  E-mail: vivakochi@vivagroupindia.net, Tel: 0484-2403055, 2403056
- 232, GNB Road, Beside UCO Bank, Silpukhuri, Guwahati 781 003
  E-mail: vivaguwahati@vivagroupindia.net, Tel: 0361-2666386

*www.vivagroupindia.com*



ISBN 978-81-309-1392-6

Published by Vinod Vasishtha for Viva Books Private Limited, 4737/23, Ansari Road, Daryaganj, New Delhi - 110 002. Printed and bound by Sanat Printers, Kundli - 131 028, Haryana.

*Dedicated at the Lotus Feet of*

**Paramhansa Yogananda**
*My Paramguru*

*With the blessings of my Gurudev*

**Swami Satchidananda Giri**

# Contents

# Preface

Growing awareness of the yawning gap between the preaching and practice of values and ethics in life and in organisation has pioneered a new debate on value education. International ranking on corruption and our record card on human rights management do not augur well with the new ambition of a developed nation by 2020. Poor ethics and values in public and private life is seriously obstructing our national development.

Inspired by Richard Feinman's exhortation that irrespective of differences of views one must explore and experiment with new ideas, I decided to take a plunge. I carried out extensive discussion with intellectuals, academicians and thinkers from various fields and walks of life—Vedantic scholars, humanists, leftist intellectuals, management scientists, followers of various religious leaders and schools of thought, educationists, administrators, and the like. There was unanimity regarding need for education in human values for the college and university youth. There was wide divergence, however, in modes and methods of imparting value education. This book brings together results of those consultations over the last two years to share my thrill of learning in this area of human development with my colleagues in education.

There are three sections in the book. Section one presents value education from certain philosophical and conceptual frameworks. The section two, a symposia in print, contains responses to a structured schedule of questions, that were originally recorded on audio; transcribed, edited and vetted by the authors. The third section contains a few life episodes from my unpublished manuscript, "The Life Around". These are all real life events how so ever imaginary they may appear to be. Such episodes can generate debates for value clarification.

I am grateful to Prof Bart J. McGrettick, Professor of Education, Glasgow University, Scotland for magnanimously introducing the book. My thanks are due to all the contributors.

I am thankful to Dr D.N. Khosla for copyediting the manuscript.

MARMAR MUKHOPADHYAY

# Values in Higher Education in India An Introduction

BART J. MCGETTRICK

Education is sometimes seen as a journey—undertaken with exploration in mind, and therefore a limited knowledge of where it will take us, whom we shall meet on the way, and where we shall stop for rest and conversation. In this journey there is sense of feeling that our path is not always smooth. In the modern world the values which people have are uncertain, like the mists swirling around our feet, not allowing us to see the uneven path we are treading and sometimes obscuring the clarity of the way ahead.

There are human values which are constant, and have to be interpreted and re-interpreted in ever new and changing circumstances. There are values which are deeply human, and which are profound in the evolution of any society. The ability to love our neighbour is among the most vital of these. Perhaps the one question which the educationist must always ask is, "*How do I serve my neighbour*?" A country will seek prosperity and it will seek peace. Yet these are the effects of education rather than its primary purposes. The purposes include forming people of love, care, and compassion; who have an appreciation of beauty; and who will serve others by their gifts. It is through this that we can say that we have an educated society. This is a philosophy which lies close to the heart of the Indian culture and the spirituality of its people.

These are often thought of as being troubled times, and times of increasing change, both locally and globally. During these times of change there is a need to know what is constant and what will be subject to change. There is a real danger in believing that everything is in turmoil and can be discarded for the benefit of society. Experience, often a slow teacher, tells us that not all change is progress–and, not all is change. There are some timeless values which remain as significant today as in years gone by. Higher education has to be a student of this, and offer constantly the insights from reading the signs of the times.

So it is across the world there is an awakening of interest in the study of values in our world. There is a real sense of genuine interest in how we are to know better what social and psychological changes there are in society and its individual members. In different countries this is being studied under different subjects or themes. In the United Kingdom, for example the general theme that is being used includes that of "Citizenship"; in the United States there are various themes used, such as "Moral Education", "Ethical Development", "Personal and Social Education" etc. There are also countries where this is being developed as part of studies of spiritual, religious, political, or philosophical aspects of the curriculum. Sometimes this is taught as a single subject, and in other places as part of an integrated approach to the curriculum.

This book offers a range of perspectives which look at the "values crisis" in India from different philosophical perspectives. The significance of this is that there is no one single way of considering values, without these being set within a worldview.

Whatever form this takes in its curricular or institutional setting, it emphasizes the idea that education is never free of values. Nowhere is this more evident than in India. To educate a person is a recognition of the value of that person as a full and free member of our common humanity. It is the birthright of each person to receive a free education, and the duty of each person of dignity and liberty to fight for that right. This is how important education is... and therefore it is a matter to be studied in higher education. This book is a very significant contribution to that debate and movement towards understanding values in education.

There is a very strong need for us to help educators and policy-makers to be "values literate". It is the duty of a university or college of higher education to offer intellectual leadership to society. The contribution to this literacy in values is of profound significance in the modern world. It is therefore a major contribution to this effort to have this book prepared to offer insights into what is happening in India. This has also to be set in a global context, a matter which several authors are at pains to emphasize.

Globally in education there are three areas which we might see being the domains of change in relation to values. These are:

*The Global issues of our time*
*The Institutional issues*
*The Personal issues*

The significant global issues of our time are concerned with liberty, peace, wisdom and equity. To these there are the essential companions of justice and of hope. In Indian society there are some key issues surrounding these aspects of educational provision. The religious, spiritual, social and political character of the country provide a rich and varied backdrop to understanding how these values are played out in Indian society. The place of women in Indian society undoubtedly merits a significant place.

This raises a question about whether women have, or ought to have, different values. From a general point of view, it might be argued that all people share the same rights, the same responsibilities and the same value system, regardless of gender. Culture may be a more discriminating aspect than gender. Men and women may find different ways of expressing these rights, responsibilities and values, but they are not different. They may be distinctive in the ways in which these are expressed in certain cultures, communities and societies. In India, there are incidences of discrimination against women, and this will need positive discrimination to bring justice to all.

For each university there are certain well-defined institutional issues which influence the ethos of the university or college. These have a powerful impact on the values of the students and staff. The ethos of a university is a powerful influence on the nature of the relationships, and its influence cannot be understated. University policy makers have a vital role to play in this regard.

At the heart of education is the person. Education does not reside in the ether of the air, or in the sweet smell of a garden. It is resident in the hearts, minds and hands of each person. It is the personal thoughts, feelings and dispositions of each person which harbours their values. Education gives the opportunity to all people to develop their gifts. It is also the role of a university to give leaders the ethical courage to ensure that these gifts are released and used for the greater glory of all humanity. India has so much to offer a world of discontentment. There is a history of the spirit in India which is a treasure not yet known to the world at large.

Education in India is not only about seeking universal literacy. Universal literacy is a means of encouraging and supporting people to use their gifts and their talents. It is a way of ensuring that the talents of all people are placed at the service of the entire community. It is a way of sharing and communicating the best of what has been thought and known. It is the action and the ability to use talents and gifts "in the common good" which is so important. This concept of "the common good" lies close to the heart of values in society. India is a country which has a store of talent possibly unrivalled in the modern world. This is a matter of justice for each person, and for humanity as a whole.

This book will offer those with a interest in contemporary India the chance to reflect on many of these timeless issues, and will raise some vital questions about issues in a world of social transformation. Social transformation is not only about societies being more open to external influences. It is also about recognising the vital place of the inner self of each person in a world of change. It is about seeing education as the principal way of developing the self. It is about helping reflection on a world of uncertainty, yet striving for peace and for liberty. Above all it is trying to know those companions of justice and hope. It is in the way these impact on the women and men of rural and urban India that the world will benefit.

What is there in a society if we do not know justice or hope?

# Section I

# Education in Human Values: The Premise

MARMAR MUKHOPADHYAY

## INTRODUCTION

The concept of value education is as old as human civilization. The concepts of values, ethics and morality figure both in the western and Indian philosophical traditions. Questions, beyond the realm of material world, searching for higher meanings of life originated in the concept of values, ethics and morality. For example, when erudite scholar Maitreyi refused the material riches offered by her husband Yagyabalka, and asked the most prophetic question: *'ye naham amritasyama tenaham kima kuryam?'*, (what would I do with all that that does not bring me immortality?). Yamaraj offered all material riches to young Nachiketa who, undaunted by Yamaraj's persuasions not to insist on Brahma Vidya, asked for that knowledge with which he could learn everything. Both Nachiketa and Maitreyi were searching for the higher values in life. The search for higher values did not stop at the ancient period. It has been a perennial process through out the corridors of human history.

Value education and inculcation is integral to civilized human society. A parental culture in the early childhood days, carried through schooling during adolescence and through colleges and universities during late adolescence and early youth, importantly, is a social culture throughout life.

Hence, social values differ from one society to another. Value education and inculcation is a natural process of enculturation.

## NATURE OF HUMAN BEING

Human being has been defined as a social being, a psychological entity, a physical being, a cultural being, depending upon the discipline of study from where he/she is seen. Inter-faith literature is probably the single most important original and authentic source for understanding human nature (Mukhopadhyay, 2003); largely because these constitute the revealed wisdom. There is an essential unity of religions (Palkhiwala, 1994). No wonder, there is an interesting convergence on the issue of nature of human beings.

- Human beings are children of God *(Amritasya Putraha)* according to Hindu tradition.
- According to Islam, "Man is God's Viceroy on earth."
- "God is the soul of man, his eternal nature," said Sikhism.
- In Christianity, "Man is God's workman on earth."
- "The Wise One created man to be like Him", contends Zoroastrianism.
- According to the Baha'i, "Man is the supreme Talisman".
- The Jain contention is, "Man is creation of God, made in the likeness of God".
- "Heaven has made man good. His original nature is good, ... " is the contention of Confucianism.

Human beings, thus are defined with reference to and in the image of God. Kahlil Gibran, in his book, *The Prophet* told the parents, "The child is *through* you" and *from the God*. This indicates the essential unity of all religions – *Ekam sad vipraha bahudha vadanti* (*Rig Veda*) *or Wherever you turn, there is the face of God* (*Quran*) (*Karan Singh, 2000*).

The major implication of this proposition is the potential immortality of human beings that is attribute of God. Leonard Orr, the Christian Spiritual Leader, in his interesting treatise, *Breaking the Death Habits,* argued that human beings are basically immortal but develop the habit of dying. This Divinity of human beings is not apparent. Like fire covered in smoke (Gita), it remains covered with habits that hide the propensities. In Baha'i view, "lack of proper education hath, however, deprived him of that which he doth inherently possess".

Thus, in the real world, we experience humans positioned on a continuum between beastliness and divinity. Beastliness is indicated by the habit of acquisition of material wealth and comfort. Religious scriptures also describe hunger, sleep, procreation, fear, anger etc. as indicators of beastliness. Divinity is indicated by renunciation—giving away for the benefit and happiness of others without any expectation in return (Swattvik dana). The saints and seers are known for renunciating all that they have. Sadhu Vaswani gave away his meagre belongings to others in need. The crucifixion of Jesus, the martyrdom of Guru Tegh Bahadur and innumerable instances of saints relieving the sufferings of fellow beings by taking away their diseases on to themselves are some of the outstanding examples. This is a matter of ethics and values. Philosophic traditions of Dewey and others defined ethics and applied ethics in terms of concern for others and selflessness.

Should this inter-faith proposition of the nature of human beings be conceded, the quality of human beings will be determined much more by the values imbibed and practised rather than by the mastery of any amount of information. Inter-faith wisdom is information and knowledge purified on the fundamental values. Carrying the argument forward, human beings are essentially value-configurations, and not knowledge-configurations. Choice of a nuclear scientist to apply his/her knowledge and expertise in creating a nuclear arsenal or nuclear medicine depends upon his/her value system; knowledge is a mere instrumentality. It is education that provides and strengthens values in human's life.

## VALUE EDUCATION

Irrespective of political, religious and socio-cultural convictions, when a parent or a teacher differentiates between right and wrong—what 'should' and what 'should not' be done or between 'desirable' and 'undesirable' behaviours, between 'good' or 'bad', he/she is indeed imparting value education. Even without articulation, parents, teachers and other elders communicate and transfer values to young children through their own behaviour. There is no escape from imparting value education to children and youth. The choices and the debates are between organized efforts and 'letting it happen'.

Organized efforts in value education can be construed as regimentation of the mind. Education itself has been equated with 'shaping of mind' by almost all schools of thought. This is also reflected in the Report to UNESCO by International Commission on Education for the 21st Century (UNESCO, 1996). The post-Marxian philosopher Herbert Marcuse's famous book, '*One Dimensional Man*' propounds the same thesis, although his thesis has larger ramification, for he discusses the issue on a much larger socio-economic canvas.

Values are the hidden determinants of human behaviour, in a way, a behavioural decision support system. There are variations among societies and cultures in expressed forms of behaviour around the common core of values. For example, whenever people meet each other, exchanging greetings is an accepted social value. It could be saying 'Namaskar' with folded hands and a smile, bending and bowing with right hand on the stomach, rubbing noses, shaking hands, offering pecks etc. Similarly, student behaviours in classrooms vis-à-vis the teacher are also guided by values. Indian classrooms receive teachers with 'standing' ovation, as a mark of respect. Such behaviours are not usual in western classrooms. Touching the feet is the token of respect for elders. Such overt behaviours of people that depict values also characterize and give an identity to the society. Values provide the social fabric that holds social institutions like family, marriage etc.

together through time. Industrial, business, educational, political, religious, and such other organizations are also similarly held in place.

Do we need an identity for our Indian society? Is it relevant at a time when information and communication technology are sweeping cultures out of their feet towards globalization? India has been the land of many cultures and peoples for several centuries. The Saks, Huns, Mughals, Pathans and Europeans invaded India through several centuries; they finally settled down and became Indians. In poet-philosopher, Rabindranath's view, India is a pilgrimage; there will be give and take but will not go back. Is that vision still valid?

Even in this age of globalization, a country is not worth its existence without an identity characterized by its heritage and the resilience to subsume variations and new developments. Beyond and besides this macro concern for a cultural identity of nations and role of values therein, there are several implications of values for life at individual, inter-personal, organizational, community and larger socio-economic and political levels. Compatible and responsive behaviour is necessary for meaningful living in all areas of human living. Values being the determining factor for behaviour-options is most significant factor in individual, inter-personal, organizational and social efficiency, effectiveness and total well-being. But why value education?

There are several stages in human development—physical, mental, intellectual and spiritual—from womb to the tomb. Similarly, human values, an element of mental development, also happens through several stages. According to Benjamin Bloom, value is the third level of affective development (Bloom, 1956). Closer examination reveals the roadmap to value development through four stages (figure 1).

The first stage is that of value collection. During the early childhood days, when judgment is yet to develop, children observe and imitate the adult behaviour, particularly, the parents. The similarity of the behaviour brings in positive reinforcement to the child by the adults impressing upon the desirability of the behaviour. This continues beyond

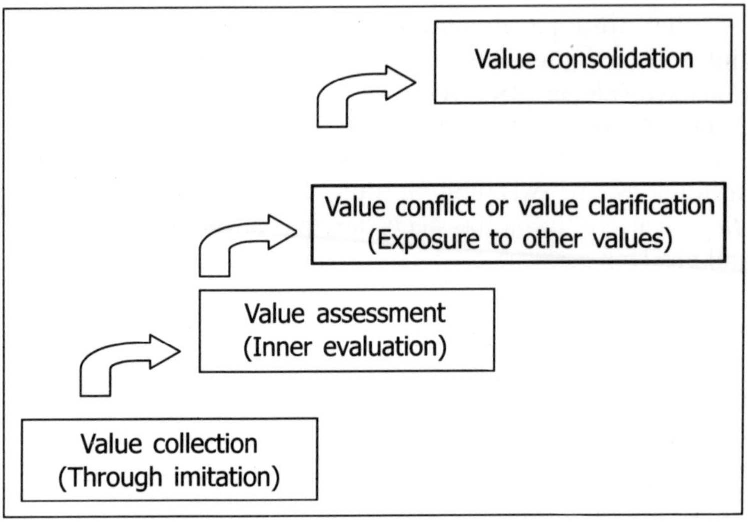


**FIGURE 1**: STAGES OF VALUE DEVELOPMENT

childhood. Values are collected (acquired) from members of the community (interpersonal and community values), teachers (classroom and academic values) and so on. As values are collected, and practised through articulated behaviour, the individual draws approval and disapproval classifying one's behaviour as desirable and undesirable. The process of value assessment within the individual takes place silently that helps the individual learn to choose and imbibe the values one cherishes. With greater and greater exposure to larger number of people, the individuals often get exposed to alternative and contradicting set of values. This leads to value conflict. One of the very subtle dimensions of value conflict is value clarification. There are gaps between practised and preached values, between values as understood by the self and others etc. As one reflects and interacts with others—peers, elders and mentors—the values get clarified. Through these various stages, values are consolidated. It is the consolidated values that provide predictability of human behaviour; and indeed, the very foundation of the personality, described as the style of the man/woman.

Value education is necessary to support value clarification and value consolidation. Let us take an example. The Indian Constitution exhorts every citizen to "renounce practices derogatory to dignity of women" (Article 51A (e)); in other words, upholding dignity of women is a fundamental duty of every Indian citizen. Education offers a weak support to this value compared to the powerful contra-forces of print and electronic media that depict women as unequal and as an object of greed and lust. There are several such examples. Value education, in fact, purports to strengthen positive forces for directing social change to a desirable direction and to strengthen the social fabric that holds the people in a society together.

Value education is imparted in the industrialized capitalist economies in the west, in communist China as well as in the Islamic countries; much though the purpose and framework may be different. In some countries, value education is based on theology; somewhere it is a part of social action programme. As Cheng-Kai Ming, the Chinese scholar-Vice-chancellor puts it, 'in the western world, moral education is needed for individual development, whereas in China, "we need value education for the development of our society". Indian thesis creates a meeting ground for both the goals when it states, "for large-hearted people, the whole world is a family" (*Udaara caritanantu vasudhaiba kutambhakam*). It sees the world as a family, but not unqualified; the world is a family only to the large-hearted people.

Hence, the first goal of value education is to create generous (large-hearted) people who are not self-centered, selfish and exploitative, but are emancipated and magnanimous. Together, they create a family-like-society where people are emotionally inter-related, interdependent, concerned about one another; where they express mutual affection, respect, love and contribute towards mutual well-being. There can, however, be variations in the content of value education, based on behavioural models with certain theoretical underpinnings.

## CONTROVERSY

Value education has attracted controversy in recent years. This is largely due to apprehension of religious education in the garb of value education. The real source of value education should be the heritage of the society—cultural or religious. As a multi-cultural and multi-religious society, the task is far more complicated in India.

First, the division between the believers and atheists on the concept of God as an anchoring point for determining the nature of humans and the value systems. Those who believe in the existence of God are far too large compared to those who do not; even those who subscribe to political philosophies that profess 'religion as opium of the masses' continue to be the practising Hindus, Muslims, Christians, Buddhists, and the like.

The second division arises with respect to schools of religious thoughts—from which religions too derive their inspiration. Religions have two facets—the philosophy and the practice. Inter-faith research indicates essential unity of religions and concurrence on the nature of human beings as in the image of the divine. Hence, at philosophical level, there is no controversy. The difference is in religious practices. In the UN Convention on World Religion in 2000, Sri Sri Ravishankar, the Indian religious leader called upon people to 'love other religion'; he exhorted that tolerance is not enough. Indeed, '*Sarva dharma samabhava*' expects mutual respectability and not just tolerance. For, a Hindu respects Hinduism, not just to tolerate; a Muslim respects Islam, not just to tolerate. *Samabhava*, equality, warrants respect for other religions.

The purpose of education is to exact the full potential within each human being—'manifestation of the perfection already in man/woman' (Swami Vivekananda). Value education is informed not by religious practices but by religious philosophy, and the understanding of human potential.

At an analytical level, even the first, that is, the above-mentioned division is resolvable. The ultimate goal of Marx's and Engel's thesis is socialism where all are equal; from the standpoint of behaviourism, it is the highest form of civility. Purpose of education is reaching that highest form of civility. In the religious philosophy too, self-realization is the final goal that leads to the same highest form of civility[1] . Hence, in the ultimate analysis, both the atheists and the non-atheists can find their meeting ground at the goals of education, in general, and value education, in particular. Keeping the theoretical underpinnings at the backburner for deriving inspiration, value education holds the potential of moving the society towards the goals it has set for itself through the Constitution, and the unwritten socio-cultural conventions that create the identity of the society.

The steady deterioration in human values is indicated by financial corruption in all walks of life, ruthless exploitation of the poor and children, degradation of women—rape, dowry deaths, unequal wages, discriminatory educational opportunities etc., poor work ethics in organization and accountability, poor public behaviour—littering of roads and public places, road rages, unauthorized occupation of public land, honking horns, blaring loud speakers etc.; sexual promiscuity and many others are some of the examples. Education in human values has become more necessary now than ever before at all stages of education. Schools provide the most powerful influence in shaping the mind at the most impressionable years; while higher education contributes leaders and higher level of workers to the organizations, they create organizational values and hence work culture and productivity.

[1] When Ramakrishna Paramhansa cured an incurable patient, himself seething in pains, one of his devotees asked him, 'Why did he do it?' Ramakrishna responded, if religion and self-realization cannot help people in distress what is the use of religion and God? Swami Vivekananda's massive social action programme through Ramakrishna Mission is inspired by the philosophy of service to people is service to God, eventually equating God with people.

Rabindranath in one of his poems wrote, 'Whom are you searching in the temple? He has gone where the cultivator is toiling in the hot sun, where people are breaking stones to create pathways.'

## VALUE EDUCATION PARADIGM

There are several issues in developing a value education paradigm. The most common question is whether education in human values should be integrated with other subjects or it should be taught as a separate subject. Both are possible. Every subject or discipline has its own value system. For example, search for truth is embedded in science. There are, however, certain universal values not necessarily built into the subjects.

The second major issue is the nature of values that need to be developed in the students. There are secular values and religious values; personal values, social values, environmental values, national and global values etc. What are the sources for deriving the list of such values? Religious literature, philosophies, biographies, analytical documents of social institutions, Indian Constitution, national and international declarations on human rights etc. are some of the major sources.

The other issue of the framework is the approach towards developing a curricular framework. The programme can be designed around some live issues. It must expand in steps from self to larger global living. It should begin with an effort to understand and manage the self; and to learn to live together in the family and the community. Transition to work, organizational values, response to fundamental duties as a citizen of independent India, and leadership are other social values to be learnt.

There are to be several alternative frameworks for value education. On the basis of our perception as well as on the basis of extensive search of the literature, I proposed a framework that was discussed and modified in an expert workshop, and in three vice-chancellors' conferences that constitute a seven module curricular structure:

1. Understanding and managing the self
2. Understanding the family and family life
3. Learning to live together
4. Indian constitution and citizenship values

5. Transition to world of work
6. Leadership
7. Indian art and culture

There are several other important issues associated with the curricular framework. One major issue is methodological —whether the conventional way of classroom lectures will develop values among the students; or, there is need to search for alternative pedagogy for value education. Related issues to methodology are the instructional material, instructional aids etc.

Another important issue is that of teachers for value education—who are qualified to teach values? Or should it form a part of all programmes in the colleges and universities? Education in human values is likely to generate sensitivity and awareness among the students exposing the value conflicts and contradictions between the preached and practised values of the teachers, administrators and other employees. This may require a new approach to management; indeed, engineering change in the management for institutions in tune with the values to be inculcated.

## CONCLUSION

In the Gurukula system, Guru's life was an open book for the students. They not only learnt what the teacher taught through discourses, but also learnt through their observation of teacher's life—teacher's own study habits, management of family life etc. They observed teacher's private and public behaviour. Thus, the teacher demonstrated values to the students—he/she walked the talk. This was possible when the number of students was small, and the 'gurus' were not invaded with commercial media preaching consumerism.

The industrial model of education brought in large classrooms, with heterogeneous group of students as well as teachers. The challenge is massive and qualitatively different. The solution is in professionalising teaching and defining minimum basic standards of behaviour. Similar professionalization is also necessary for the management of higher education institutions. Professionalising of management of higher educational institutions warrant changes in the contemporary practices of appointment of people in leadership positions.

## REFERENCES

Bloom, B. *Learning the Treasure Within*, Paris, UNESCO, 1996.

Mukhopadhyay, Marmar (ed), *Education for a Global Society: Interfaith Dimensions*, New Delhi, Shipra, 2003.

Palkhiwala, N.A. *Essential Unity of All Religions*, New Delhi, Bharatiya Vidya Bhavan, 1994.

# Phenomenology of Education in Values: An Exploration

R.P. SHARMA

Human ingenuity lies in cognizing the situation in which one finds oneself and the ways one contemplates or even undertakes to respond to it. Such an endeavour requires not merely colligation of facts but also a judgment of value, approving or disapproving what he is "thrown into". Periscoping the world around yields immense inspectable 'facticity' which constitutes a sizable part of our accumulated knowledge. This knowledge *inter-alia* gets percolated into our curricula which reflect the mood of the age and the needs of the time. Hence an exercise in updating the content, the intent and the instrumentalities of education becomes imperative.

Our response to this obligation might have been spasmodic in the past. However, the present scenario reflects the desired sensitivity on the part of those concerned with education at various levels.

Obviously, in matters of curricular refinement it is the acquisition of knowledge and, to a lesser extent, the attendant skills which occupy the centre-stage. In fact education, as a system, has been serving as repository of knowledge only. The noetic aspect of this human endeavour, at times, leads to the total neglect of other human accomplishments. For various reasons, the qualitative aspect of existence, reflected in behavioural expressions and value judgments, has remained for too long at the periphery of educational dispensation.

The epistemic as well as the epistemological issues have overshadowed the axiological component of education. Never was the need for incorporating value education felt so acutely as in the present context.

There is a growing realization in every civilized society that all talk about development and progress, sans values, is a shallow orchestration of human vainglory. While heralding the triumphant march of man into the brave, new knowledge society, we need to safeguard the 'treasure within' which epitomizes human sensitivities. The hitherto predominant pursuit of knowledge appears inadequate without its complement of value.

While change is inevitable, we are witness to a situation wherein change does not pledge progress. The socio-economic resurgence has not been able to get us any closer to the ethical Elysium or the spiritual *El Dorado*. The grave dangers posed by the eclipse of human sense and sensibilities can be overlooked only by those who opt for self-annihilation.

This state of valuelessness has been variously described as anomie, amorality, anhedonia rootlessness, hopelessness etc. The representative behavioural expression of the so-called highly educated in our society give no assurance of poise, perserverence, prudence and catholicity of views which characterize qualitative excellence in human life.

Responding to this state of 'value-entropy' with all its attendant disorder and its aftermath, it becomes imperative for education to build up appropriate defences against the onslaught of moral, social and psychological degeneration. Jettisoning its self-imposed value-neutrality, the agenda for education has to cater to the needs of the dynamic, vibrant and evolved personalities who can boldly defy 'strident dogmas' and steer clear of ambivalence and 'troubled loyalties'.

Understandably, the forces of change have seriously impacted our perceptions of life—its facticity and preferred pursuits. Education too has not only absorbed the weight and thrust of new knowledge, it has positively responded to its demands. Holding education in quarantine is suicidal for any sane society any time, anywhere. But the revolutionary forces unleashed by information and communication technologies and the emergence of a bewildering array of new branches of knowledge have undoubtedly relegated the context of values to the margins of our ministered enterprises. However, this ought to be treated as a temporary phase. Education, in fact, is well poised to arrogate to itself the challenging task of synthesizing the new with the old, the contingent interests with the perennial concerns, the civilisational variables with the cultural constants.

Advancing this point of thought the newly ascribed function of education could be achieved only when we expose our minds to the diverse, universally acknowledged, humanistic and inclusive ethos that mankind has nourished over the years. And it is possible only when it is assiduously pursued without jettisoning the wisdom that scientific mode of knowledge has proffered. In fact, educational curricula, particularly at higher level, need to straddle the mental scapes with noetic tonality, on the one side, and the cultural axiological perspective, on the other.

While honouring various constraints related to globalisation, education *per se* has to acknowledge and meet its mandated obligation towards a humane society, a task which involves pre-disposition of our vision of a value-based society comprised of enlightened citizenry. However, this discerning course has never been a smooth one, there being many obstacles in the form of dissenting voices, raised with regard to 'why,' 'what' and 'how' of values in education. For explicating this point, a voice, quite vociferous in the beginning, but tenuous these days, was raised against the inculcation of value in education.

The fears expressed pertained to encouragement to indoctrination and conformity hampering free flowering of human personality, a pre-requisite for the creation of a free society. This argument is not tenable on various counts. For instance, education by any definition or description, is a purposive activity. While disseminating knowledge and promoting skills (including life-skills), it transmits certain beliefs, attitudes and values. The nominalistic thin line between knowledge and virtue (to be read as value) had been generating many an animated debate amongst the ancient Greek philosophers. Moreover, an educated person does not play home to inert information: an enlightened person would rather transform information into an idea and an idea into a proposition which involves a judgment. This process of concatenation ends up only as a discerning value.

There are some other contentious issues in the field of value education. The choice of an acceptable typology of values, the face-off between tradition and modernity, the dichotomous claims of faith and reason, individuality and collectivity, are some of the issues considered problematic which need to be looked into not as insoluble controversies but as multi-dimensionality of the theme, reflecting its fecundity.

## DEFINING VALUES

At this juncture any further progress in the study of value education requires adequate acquaintance with the nature of value(s). Any attempt to arrive at a single definition would be too simplistic. Even so the varied meanings and definitional exercises furnish us with substantial database for any theorization about values. Values taken as 'preferential behaviour', 'dominant interest' or motive, 'a master sentiment' are embedded in the psychological endowment of the individual. Expressed in terms such as 'a fashioned will' or sensitivity, a 'cultivated taste', values seem to be the outcome of social interventions — cultural or educational in nature. Values as 'choice' (Dewey) and 'commitment' are the indices of a developed personality, transcending the dogmatic and conventional levels of adherence. Another description reads this way: "value preferences are not simple rational choices between competing, equally plausible alternatives. They also reflect embedded social considerations, structural and institutional restraints and opportunities" (Ramsay). This statement cognizes values as 'artifacts of culture'.

The descriptions of value (judgments) sampled here are pointers to the psychological, socio-cultural and philosophical predilections which thinkers and educationists of different genre have cherished. The presence and availability of the multi-verse of values provides grist to the mill for the theoretical formulations regarding the nature of values and their study at higher level of educational ladder.

## VALUES: THE SUBJECTIVE–OBJECTIVE FACE-OFF

Discussion regarding the nature of values throws up another perspective, as perplexing and engaging as scripting a defensible definition of value. Quite significantly, promoters of education in human values raise the question whether values are objective, subjective, relative or they belong to some other form of theorisation. Aristotle is well recognized as the earliest representative of the objectivistic standpoint on values. According to him each entity is determined by its nature and function. The highest good is attained when a thing realizes its proper function. In the case of man, its his rationality which is the differentiating quality. Hence, it is the realization of this potential which constitutes his value. The intension and application of this principle help us determine the value pattern of the all those that inhabit the world out there, 'objectively' and universally acceptable.

This position on values, held by Aristotle, has been subjected to criticism by thinkers and educationists of different persuasions. A serious objection raised in this regard is that it cannot be demonstrated objectively that one does indeed know the final purpose of life which is often based on intuition or private unverifiable hunches. Another point: values objectively conceived emerge as natural tendencies, thereby depriving one of the 'agency' for one's representative behaviour.

The existentialists too would not support such a theory as it robs them of their freedom of choice and self certitude.

In sharp contrast to objectivism stands subjectivism espoused by the sophists (Protagoras), Bishop Berkely, David

Hume and the existentialists. Their central argument is that values are always a matter of personal preferences. The desire of the individual alone determines the 'desirability'.

Critical of this theory A.J. Ayer and Karl Popper hold that the human factor is 'ultimately uncertain', wayward and volatile and therefore not sound enough to build up a plausible value theory. For Ayer, ethical values as component of axiology are not empirical facts; these are "expression and excitants of feeling". In the absence of any "assertions", they fall short of any judgment and are "un-analyzable". It was perhaps left to Thomas Kuhn "to establish a central place for values in a world of hard facts and number", allocating proportional validity to values.

John Dewey has left a pervasive impact almost on every aspect of educational thought and practice. Spearheading his onslaught on absolutism of any kind, he maintains that values are *relative* and *discovered* by each generation and individual in response to the facts of life that environ it. Values have human origin and must change with the changing time. Dewey terms both social and individual values as "fugitive and precarious" because of their incessant appearance and disappearance in actual experience.

However, Dewey's relativism is not free from flaws. His professed dissociation with knowledge and values transmitted down the ages leaves a person to fend for the thought-constructs thrown up by the person's present experiences and validate his own 'discoveries'. Discarding wisdom of the past and devaluing absolutism, he restricts any generalisation about human values from acquiring universal currency so ubiquitously marshalled by sciences. The 'fleeting' moments become 'frozen' in a timeframe, having validity which has no 'renewability'.

The scenario populated by contrasting dichotomies is nothing short of ideographic presentation. Depending upon certain philosophical (metaphysical as well as epistemological) premises, one could have pot-shots on any other position. The contention of this presentation is not to defend any of the entrenched position but to prepare a case for launching into the study of human values inhabiting education in a way which enjoys credence and relevance.

## THE PHENOMENOLOGICAL WAY

The way suggested for valuation or value theorization is being discussed here under the ruberic of Phenomenology of Education in Human Values. The contention here is that phenomenological analysis can steer us clear of the jamming session of futile wrangling and crippling controversies regarding values and put us in possession of the ideational and affective content that values are conceived of. It is a celebrated method that can help us transcend the world of objects and yield truth of value in all its purity. Before evaluating its appropriateness and effectivity in the study of values, we need to acquaint our-selves with its salient features, its functioning. We need to apprise ourselves how phenomenology could share its insight with us in the present study.

At the outset, it can be stated incontrovertibly that phenomenology, developed by Husserl and others, is neither a school nor a trend in contemporary philosophy. It is rather a movement whose proponents, for various reasons, have propelled it in many distinct directions. Even so 'phenomenology' signifies, first and foremost a methodological conception which has branched into many disciplines and fields of knowledge including education and is being considered suitable for its sub-theme education of values.

Phenomenology has, over the years, acquired the reputation of being a highly technical and sophisticated subject of study and is still developing into a rigorous method of investigation and impartial analysis of problems. It is basically a meaning-bestowing activity. As a philosophical method, it engages in analyzing and unfolding the essential structures of our consciousness about phenomena through reflection and intuition: thereby, phenomenology reduces our percepts into concepts, our experiences into essences. To put it more explicitly phenomenology takes on the onerous task of arriving at the purest form of experience about phenomena, after peeling off layers of pre-suppositions and apperceptions which constitute the essential structures of our consciousness. In fact, our perceptions of the phenomena are invariably tinged with meanings assimilated through our interaction with the milieu. Things are what they mean to us. But phenomenology tries to arrive at things as they are, in themselves, without the adjuncts and trappings imposed on them. It is in this sense that phenomenology is called the study of essences. According to Merleau-Ponty, the existentialist phenomenologist, it "tries to give direct description of our experiences as it is without taking into account its psychological origin or causal explanations."

Phenomenology would not only intuit the 'essences' of the existents but put essences back into existence. It, in a way, returns, after ascertaining essences, to "that world which precedes knowledge, of which knowledge always speaks and in relation to which every scientific schematisation is an abstract and derivative sign language," holds Merleau-Pondy.

As stated earlier phenomenology is, to all intents and purposes, a study of the essences. Essences as the problematic acquire great significance for all of us who are directly associated with issues which are steeped in controversies, as in the case of determining the nature of values. Essences, indeed, provide the most common denominators of human experience. They are the building blocks of value propositions. However, the moot point is as to how to wring out the essences, and this is where phenomenology comes to our assistance.

## THE METHOD OF 'PHENOMENOLOGICAL REDUCTION'

Husserl used the term "phenomenology" for a science of 'ideal meaning' which, he thought, is based on direct intuition, achieved through successive "reduction" of given experiences. This process of 'phenomenological reduction' needs to be understood in its entirety. It is in fact an exercise to isolate mental phenomena in their purity, by setting aside the reality of the objects of experience. This transaction is called "bracketing".

*Phenomenological Reduction* is carried out in two stages: (i) Transcendental Reduction (TR) and (ii) Eidetic Reduction. The TR uses the technique of elimination or bracketing of judgments involving material things. What is left is the stream of pure experiences transcending the given existing world circumscribed by space and time. The next stage in phenomenological reduction is to acquire general or universal knowledge about the intentional structures of the acts in TR—thereby moving from consciousness of the particulars to that of the universals. This second phase is called Eidetic Reduction or Eidetic Variation (E.V.), which directs our experience towards what is common in number of distinct entities—to be termed as essence (Wesen). Eidetic Reduction thus reveals to us the truths about essences. The TR uses the 'bracketing' technique for approaching the pure mental acts whereas E.V. uses the technique of Free Phantasy Free Imaginative Variation to apprehend the essences, the most treasured acquisition in pursuit of any conscious, intentional act, including valuation or value judgments.

Without going into further technicalities of this method, a brief mention of the seven steps elaborated by Spiegelberg would suffice for the present venture which is to ascertain whether phenomenology can be employed to the problematic value—theorisation—in any effective manner. These steps are:

1) Investigating particular phenomenon; (Intuiting, analysis and description)
2) Investigating general essences;
3) Apprehending essential relationship among essences;
4) Watching modes of appearing;
5) Watching the constitution of phenomena in consciousness;
6) Suspending belief in the existence of phenomena; and
7) Interpreting the meaning of phenomena.

Let us be clear about one thing, even though it's being repeated here: Phenomenology does not give us any premises or propositions. Phenomenology is always of something, giving us the tools and the techniques to arrive at the true nature of experience. This applies to the world of values as well.

To clinch this particular issue, it is accepted that phenomenology as espoused by Husserl, Brentano and others makes effective foray into intentional structures through description and interpretative analysis. But there are reasons to believe that not all meaning and expressions of human experience are immediately accessible through the instrumentality of the exalted method of phenomenology. It would be fairly pertinent to mention the import of Yoga and Vedanta (advaita), the Indian school of thoughts, yielding insights which can not only augment the effectiveness of phenomenology of values as an ingredient of educational enterprise but also lead to a realization of the possibilities which are noumenal, beyond empirical notations.

## THE INDIAN CONTRIBUTION

In the ancient philosophical tradition of India if Vedanta serves as a watershed for formulating the context of values, it is Yoga, the Ashtanga Yoga of Patanjali which lights up the pathway for the acquisition of requisite insight into human experience and brings the pursuer to the threshold of pure consciousness which transcends all types of mental, apodictic experiences. Yoga prescribes a distinct methodology of discernment and empowers the practitioner to move from gross forms of experience to the subtle ones. The first five steps of Patanjal Yoga are Yama (the ethical precepts regulating social life), Niyama (ethical principles pertaining to personal observances), Asana (the bodily posture), Pranayama (control of life energy through control of breath) and Pratyahara (withdrawl of the senses from the external world, stimuli). These are preparatory exercises in acquiring control of the psycho-somatic propensities so as to graduate to higher levels of mental and spiritual consciousness (posited in Dharana, Dhyana and Samadhi—comprising the inner journey) which are well beyond our perceptual experiences. In a way, the yogic insights voyage beyond the 'essences' which accrue from the Eidetic Reduction and Free Imaginative Variation—the stock-in-trade of phenomenology. The yogic discipline, when pursued assiduously, helps one intuit the truth with great subtlety. It not only adds to the operational vocabulary of phenomenological analysis but also extends the 'catchment area' of human experiences, espoused by realists (objectivists) of the humanistic genre.

The methodological sophistication achieved by Buddhistic logicians in the form of negative dialectics and the effectivity of the method of Neti Neti (not this, not this), as espoused by Advaita Vedanta, are also potent instruments of getting the quintessential nature of concepts and values and their judgment. Other religious traditions—Judeo-Christian, Islamic, Jain etc.—even while being prescriptive, having canonical undertones, yield wealth of valuational content, the date-base for discussing qualitative excellence.

## IS SCIENCE OF VALUES POSSIBLE?

There is a sub-theme of seminal value which runs in close proximity to phenomenology of value education and that is —whether there can be a science of values? This question itself snowballs into supplementaries—Are there any scientific bases of value theorization? And 'If possible, what would be its nature when juxtaposed to positive or normative sciences'?

The questions posed above are formidable, demanding and deserving a thorough discussion. In fact these are vectors strengthening their claim for inclusion into any formal curricular dispensation on value education. It is not to be construed that study of any scientific bases of values is as plausible an alternative as phenomenology of value education is. However, arguably this discussion itself lifts the quality of debate on the subject under scrutiny. Hence only a conceptual sketch is being essayed here.

We are cognizant of the pervasive and, at times, proselytizing impact of sciences, the positive disciplines of knowledge, in our way of living and thinking. These natural sciences, because of their demonstrable and verifiable attributes (apodicticity) have acted felicitously in inspiring many social and behavioural, even normative sciences in emulating the methodology of the former ones. Such an approach seems to be untenable in the face of the inherent logic which governs their functions. While the content of the natural sciences is governed by inviolable physical laws which are descriptive and explanatory in nature, the normalitive laws are prescriptive and interpretive, arrived at through intuition, intellection, social ascription or 'mandate from heaven'. Any study of values, because of its normative content, would belong to the conglomerate of non-natural sciences, and would be ill-served by the modus operandi adopted by the natural sciences. Robert S. Hartman, in this context, reasons quite incisively: "Descartes, Leibniz, Locke and even Bishop Berkeley failed in their attempt in founding a defensible science of ethics" because they all used the repertoire of natural sciences, in varying degrees, in their endeavour. To Hartman, "naturalists were good hunters of the wrong prey whereas non-naturalists were bad hunters of right prey". Inferentially, fudging the distinction between the two well defined modes of study would show us stranded on an alien soil.

Does this lead to dispensing with the possibility of building an exact theory of value? Perhaps not: there is room for systematic analysis of moral and other normative phenomena as advocated by axiology. Joining the issue, G.E. Moore asserts that 'Goodness', as different from 'good', provides 'the value phenomena.' The axiomatic enunciation that "a thing is good when it fulfills the definition of its concept" furnishes us with a fundamental principle of formal axiology that could adjudicate in controversies tenanting value theorization.

Henry Margenau contributes to this debate somewhat differently. He thinks the natural drives in man's nature provide an obvious criterion for value judgments. However, 'the natural drives' need certain command propositions to be really effective. With the weakening and rejection of the sources that have been traditionally lending certitude to values, he wants the disciplinary value of science to be a potent source of value theorization. In his words, "In this predicament I suggest that we look once more at science, not in repetition of the futile attempt to wring values from science, but in the hope of capturing and perhaps transplanting into value theory that formal feature which imparts universal acceptance and persuasive power to science."

Impressed by this line of thinking, there are scholars who would prescribe logical reasoning and other standard conditions, associated with sciences for ethical formulations, in a way, which is reminiscent of Kants' categorical imperative as also the Karma Yoga of the Bhagavadgita. Any way, no body should harbour any grudge against borrowing of the disciplinary value of sciences by protagonists of value-theory. However such an attempt is fraught with many imponderables, particularly when someone eudemonistically recommends the use of science courses for promoting values. C. Seshadri, well known for rendering pioneering work in promoting value education, very cogently cautions us against treating value development as the additional and overt objective of science teaching. He quite succinctly points out the epistemic as well as the epistemological distortions that could creep into the teaching of science, as a result of such an attempt. Without ever belittling their potential and elasticity for promoting values, what is suggested is that sciences should realize this objective only epiphenomenally.

It is quite interesting, even though perplexing, to find some scintillating minds of our times locking horns on the centricity of human factor so inextricably interwomen with values. Karl Popper (1961), the objectivist, holds that "human factor to be controlled by scientific method is a political suicide." Thomas Kuhn, on the other hand, places human factor and social values at the heart of scientific enterprise. Cushioned by the barbed comments of Lakatos—

"As science grows, the power of the empirical evidence diminishes". Hoffman cautions the social scientists who imagine themselves on the verge of a new science of society in which "human action can be explained and predicted in just the way as the natural events."

## CONCLUSION

For sure, we have not heard the last word on the exalted theme of determining the nature of values. The claims and counter-claims of various academic disciplines in scripting a theory of values have enlivened the pursuit of affectivity to provide balance, if not corrective, to education which has been unabashedly value-neutral, as much by default as by design. Till recently, the scholars found this subject too effete to be placed amongst academic pursuits known for their rigour and profundity. But things have changed for the better. Education for human values is finding increasing articulation and resonance in our policy pronouncements and programmes. It is still a front trench in the siege of affectivity; only the established disciplines represent captured territory.

All through, it has been essayed to explore the contours of the ideational map that should yield the parameters of value theorization at the higher echelons of educational ladder. In this context, science, religion culture, social idioms legislation, jurisprudential commands and commitments have all animated our reflective as well as pre-reflective (intuitive) consciousness. As seminal issues, they, in fact, provide grist to the mill for studying values phenomenologically. Incidentally, no anxiety or constraint has been felt to marshal an argument as a proof of validity of the viewpoint suggested or proposed: no Q.E.D.—quod erat demonstrandum in this case, as done in geometrical theorems.

Finally, this attempt is purely exploratory. Any progress in this pilgrimage is satisfying and humanly ennobling. With its no-nonsense approach phenomenology holds no offence to the scientifically minded and is fairly suited to 'discover' the essence of values and their theoretical bases. Concepts and essences can be misconstrued and misinterpreted: values could be vitiated by whimsical minds. The contingent quite often obscure the absolute. Education needs to develop the dispassion of a scientist and the disposition of a yogin to rise above 'the strident dogmas and troubled loyalties'. And, that is what phenomenology can achieve effectively, in the study of values.

Education as a purposive human endeavour can ill-afford the existing divide between knowledge and values, the noetic and the axiological. What is needed is a synergistic relationship between the two to construct defensible theoretical foundation of value. For all intents and purposes, education for values needs to have differential response to kineticism associated with differed levels of educational ladder. While the lower levels of education would direct their efforts to implement 'approved' ways of individual and social behaviour through the instrumentalities of effective strategies, the higher education must harness its resources to institute vigorous and scholarly analysis of the phenomenological type so as to superintend the fruition of excellence in human existence. Certain agencies 'know' the way, education simply 'feels' the way to the knowledge and realization of values. Values are, indeed, the 'defining metaphors" of education, to be handled with good sense and sensibility.

# Swami Vivekananda on the Science of Values and Education

SWAMI SUPARNANANDA

## INTRODUCTION

Sri Ramakrishna lived a quiet life at Dakshineswar and died a still quieter death in Calcutta in August 1886, leaving behind a few helpless lads under the leadership of a still more helpless Narendranath. And lo! Within six years of his demise could be heard the flappings of the Great Swan (Paramhansa) in the sky across the ocean, which have since been going on unabated. His chosen boy Narendranath, later Swami Vivekananda, worked the miracle. He came back from the West and within four months established on May 1, 1897, the Ramakrishna Mission Association which became the Ramakrishna Mission in 1909, through registration. He was happy beyond measure to give a final shape to his Guru's mission for which he had been commissioned. This is unique in the long history of Hinduism or Sanatan Dharma in that the Hindu monks have so long been taught to free themselves from the shackles of repeated births and deaths. They avoided meticulously all sorts of worldly troubles. Vivekananda inspired his brother monks to emulate the spirit of service in their lives first and then show to the world its efficacy as a means to liberate the embodied self. And his brother monks, liberated souls as they were, took upon themselves this task joyfully and in no time made the mission a vibrant missionary polity in India and abroad. Hundreds of aspiring souls submitted themselves fully to the furtherance of the cause of the Mission.

## PURPOSE OF EDUCATION

Swami Vivekananda's mission was to transform the society through proper education. Education he felt is the panacea for all evils. Swamiji pondered over the widespread difference between the western countries and his own motherland in respect of economic well-being, quality of life etc. Why was this difference? 'Education'—he got the reply. That is why Swamiji's concern for and commitment to education were so total. He wanted to teach values through education. Why? Since through education we must find a way to work within science, technology, industry and even politics. We can ignore none of these since they are the forces that largely shape our destiny. But again, when we become great in the world and try to test our greatness, our pride, hatred, anger etc. are all exposed and we become pygmies. We need then a new kind of strength or greatness to fight them i.e., we have to explore our inner possibility—our divine nature. To know that I and my brothers are one since we are all divine, is what constitutes the realm of spirituality. Swamiji wanted both science and self-control.

*Definition*: He has, therefore, defined education in an emphatic way: 'Education is the manifestation of the perfection already in man (Complete Works of Swami Vivekananda, Vol. IV. 304—henceforth cited as V only); or Education is the nervous association of certain ideas' meaning that even our nerves will stand in protest if we behave not according to our learning. For example, if we learn not to tell a lie, our nervous system will warn us by holding our tongue in check. He saw such a man in Sri Ramakrishna, his spiritual teacher; or again, 'Education is the training by which the current of expression and will are brought under control and become fruitful'. He has also given us important information about what is not education. 'Education may be described as a development of faculty, not of accumulation of words' (V 231). Education is not filling the mind with facts. He said, "Education is not the amount of information that is put into your brain and runs riot there, undigested all your life. We must have life-building, man-making, character-making assimilation of ideas. If you have assimilated five ideas and made them your life and character, you have more education than any man who has got by heart a whole library" (III. 301). Therefore, accumulation of words is a fact; true education will make this fact a faculty. For example, waters of a river drown a man who wants to cross it. This is a fact. But it becomes a faculty when he learns the art of swimming, thus converting waters into an instrument to cross it.

*Aim:* The end of all education, all training should be man-making. By education character is formed, strength of mind is increased, the intellect is expanded (IV. 423).

*What to Study:* We want western Science coupled with Vedanta, Brahmacharya, as the guiding motto and also *shraddha* and faith in one's own self. I look upon religion as the inner-most core of education. Religion is the manifestation of the divinity in man. What we need is to study, independent of foreign control, different branches of knowledge that is our own and with it the English language, western science, technical education and all else that will develop industries (V. 284).

*Method:* There is only one method by which to attain knowledge, that which is called concentration. "The very essence of education is concentration of mind. From the lowest person to the highest Yogi, all have to use this same method." He said, "If I had to do my education again, I would not study facts at all. I would develop the power of concentration and then with a perfect instrument, I could collect facts at will" (V. 282). Therefore, disciplining the mind is the way left to us. Along with it, one must develop the power of detachment.

*Students' Qualities:* Students must be pure and must have real thirst for knowledge and perseverance. "Purity in thought, speech and act is absolutely necessary. As for thirst for knowledge, it is an old law that we all get whatever we want. None of us can get anything other than what we fix our hearts upon. There must be a continuous struggle, a constant fight, an unremitting grappling with our lower nature, till the higher want is actually felt and victory is achieved. The student who sets out such a spirit of perseverance will surely find success at last" (III. 48).

*Role of the Teacher:* One should live from one's very childhood with one whose character is like a blazing fire and should have before him a living example of the highest teaching (V. 285). My idea of education is *Gurugriha-Vasa*. Without the personal life of the teacher there would be no education. You cannot teach a child any more than you can grow a plant. The plant develops its own nature. The child teaches itself. You can take away the obstacles and knowledge comes out of its own nature (V. 324). We have to teach the pupils with freedom because 'liberty is the first condition of growth' (III. 246). Owing to undue domination exercised by parents, our boys do not get free scope for growth. 'Violent attempts at reform always end by retarding reform. If you do not allow one to become a lion, he will become a fox.'

Teachers, therefore, should give only positive ideas. Negative thoughts only weaken men. Swamiji criticized the then system of education as being full of negative ideas. He said, "The child is taken to school and the first thing that he learns is that his father is a fool, the second thing that his grandfather is a lunatic, the third thing that all his teachers are hypocrites, the fourth that all the sacred books are lies! By the time, he is sixteen, he is a mass of negation, lifeless and boneless" (III. 302). The feeling must be modified according to the needs of the thoughts. Past lives have moulded our tendencies and so teachers should give to the pupil according to his tendencies. Take every one where he stands and push him forward. A true teacher will never destroy a single man's special inclinations and give words of hope and encouragement even to the most degraded persons and lift them up. The only true teacher is he who can convert himself, as it were, into a thousand persons at a moment's notice. The true teacher is he who can immediately come down to the level of the student and transfer his soul to the student's soul and see through and understand through his mind. Such a teacher can really teach and none else.

(Vol. IV, p. 22) In fact, the child becomes a man of personality and instead of helping the child to grow we are trying to polish up the outside. What is the use in polishing up the outside when there is no inside?

*Reality vs Science of Yoga:* "The secret of education is to strengthen the personality of the pupil through the science of Yoga which claims that it has discovered the laws and methods for the development of personality. This is one of the great practical things and this is the secret of all education" (II. 14). We shall elaborately discuss it later while developing the idea. Swamiji has taken a practical view of Reality. He would never classify Reality as being physical, mental and spiritual. He said, 'Whatever is, is one'. Reality to him is a tapering existence, the thickest part is physical; it tapers and becomes finer and finer and we call it mental, the finest being called spirit or Atman (II. 16). Power is in the finest, in spirit, in Atman. The Science of Yoga helps us get hold of the finest forces in us like mind, intellect and spirit. Once that being done, we have perfect control over our actions, over our thoughts. It is here where we come to the all-comprehensive issue of the science of values, because to have a controlled mind is to have a sound moral or pure life. More on it, later.

## REALITY VS GOALS OF EDUCATION

The above discussion makes it evident what Swami Vivekananda had to say about education, its role in the society, its relation with Yoga and Reality and, above all, with the Science of values, drawing heavily on Swamiji's own writings on education (compiled and edited from Ramakrishna Mission Vidyalaya, Coimbatore).

Reality, according to Swamiji, cannot be divided into two parts, as it is generally, as being Apara Prakiti (manifested or mutable world) and Para Prakiti (unmanifested or immutable world). Swamiji holds that the same Reality in its thickest part appears as this phenomenal world and when it tapers, it becomes the finest one called unmanifest. We, therefore, do not have two different types of existence. Lord Sri Krishna, in the 7th chapter of the Gita, has also declared His Divine Nature as consisting of two aspects: one, the physical aspect, and the other, the spiritual. The physical aspect is his inferior nature (Apara Prakriti) but his higher nature (Para Prakriti) is the unmanifest one by which all this, that is phenomenal, is sustained. Its import is that nothing outside God remains in the universe.

Corresponding to the two aspects of Reality, education must have two goals in view. One goal is to impart information so that the knowledge of the external world (Kshetra) is complete through the study of the physical sciences. It would confer on man enormous physical comforts leading to his development in the external world (Abhyudaya). The other goal of education is to impart inspiration. Education must see to it that students are inspired to know the other (higher) aspect of Reality. Even now, the western people dealing with physical science consider, in a major way, the one aspect of Reality — the Macrocosm or the objective world known to them through the senses and the mind. Yes, the scientist knows the objective universe. But who is that scientist? Who is it that knows? So, apart from Kshetra, there must be an observer, the witness, the Kshetrajna. It is absolutely impossible to take the observer as a datum. Then the question is asked — what is the nature of this observer? In ancient days the student asked the teacher the most pertinent question: What is that by knowing which we can know everything (*Kasminnu Bhagaban Vijna'te sarvamidam vijnatam sya't?*)? The teacher answered—(*Dve' vidye' veditavye' parachaibaparacha*). Two kinds of knowledge are to be known—Para and Apara. Apara Vidya is the secular knowledge of the universe. It includes Physics, Chemistry, Mathematics, Philosophy etc. and their study. But Para Vidya is that by which that unchangeable Reality is known (*Yaya' tat Aksharam Adhigamyate'*. Mundaka Upanishad 1.1.5).

Education, therefore, will help the students attain both the goals and the teacher will play an important role by teaching the secular subjects and also by inspiring his students to realise their divine dimension. If education means lighting a lamp from another lamp, then the teacher himself has to feel the presence of the Divine Lamp within and then ignite the lamp in the hearts of his pupils. So, it is not enough for the teacher to have faith in the pupils, it is equally important for him to have faith in his own Divine nature. If a teacher has no faith in the theistic philosophy of life and becomes atheistic or agnostic, he is a half-teacher, capable of teaching the secular subjects only, himself remaining totally ignorant about his own real nature, Atman. He may be knowing a lot of the process of evolution from the cosmic level to the organic level and then to the human level. Intellectually he is brilliant no doubt, but spiritually he is bankrupt. In Sri Ramakrishna's words, he has been adding only the number of '0's without adding the most valuable 1 behind them. Unfortunately, our teachers are not made conscious of this all-the-more important task of theirs. We rush to one set of teachers for bread-winning secular knowledge and another set of teachers for knowledge spiritual.

Swami Vivekananda urged that the ultimate goal of education is to make the pupils feel spiritually efficient. But never did he fail to see the immediate goal of education which is the attainment of productive efficiency. Education has to set in motion the process of transformation in man — taking him first, as the crude man, the ordinary man (Nara), then by imparting secular knowledge and education making him the excellent man, the productively efficient man (Narottama) and finally, the God-man (Narayana) through the dissemination of spiritual knowledge. This is the goal before the teacher.

More than anything else, the teacher's role is vital. He is a model, not a guide only. If the students become secularly efficient but spiritually weak, the teacher cannot avoid his responsibility. His task is, as if, to convert the crude oil into the refined one, as is commonly done in an oil refinery. He has to take the student where he stands with all his crudities and refine him gradually till he feels he is Narayana himself. It is a journey on the part of the student from a Nara (crude man) to a Narayana (God-man), acquiring in the process tremendous efficiency of a Narottama in the middle. The point is that students have to feel the urge for removing the animal in him. Swamiji has said, "In the animal the man was suppressed, but as soon as the door was opened, out rushed man. So in man there is the potential god, kept in by the locks and bars of ignorance. When knowledge breaks these bars, the god becomes manifest." (Raja Yoga by Swamiji p. 268).

Revered Swami Ranganathanandaji, the President, Ramakrishna Math, has given a beautiful exposition of this idea while explaining the 15th verse of the 12th chapter of the Gita, Vol. III. The verse says that a man who is not agitated by the world (because he is an all-powerful king) nor is agitating the world (because he is a Rishi) is dear to the Lord. He is free from the excess of joy, anger, fear and anxiety. This man surely has combined in his person the twin qualities of a king and a Rishi. A king has power to control others but he has no power to control his anger, anxiety and fear. He is, therefore, imperfect in a sense. Similarly, a Rishi is weak because he can control himself but he cannot control others. So, both Raja and Rishi are incomplete in isolation. To become a complete man, he has to be a Rajarshi—meaning that he has to be a Raja outside commanding supreme power to control others and a Rishi inside thereby disturbing none but fostering love and brotherhood all around. Rajarshi alone is neither troubled by others nor will he trouble others. So, Kinghood and Sainthood both are to be combined in each of us.

That is the goal of education—to become Rajarshi (Raja + Rishi). If the whole universe is His form then we have to control it or serve it like a Rajarshi. We must work for Dharmyam and Amritam. When we work for the health and stability of the society bringing joy, happiness and welfare to the people we are following Dharmyam. This is the aim of our secular education. And when education takes us towards the realisation of the immortal Atman within, we have Amritam (Nectar). Thus, to acquire a balance between Dharmyam and Amritam, or Kingship and Sainthood, or Secular and Spiritual education is the goal of human life.

## THE CONCEPT OF PERFECTION

Swamiji has defined education as being manifestation of the perfection already in man. But perfection has several facets and expressions. We cannot shake off all our imperfections at a time at a single bounce. It needs preparation, a life-long commitment to the goal. Now-a-days we have manipulation and not education as such. We have excellence and not perfection as our goal. Every body knows—excellence he can reach for, but perfection is God's business, meaning that perfection cannot be attained by personal efforts only. A soul perfects itself through several births. Education helps in bringing out our power which is divine. Now this is a moot point for all of us to recognise how much excellence we allow to penetrate into perfection. The goal of education being the attainment of perfection, can we tone down the goal and work on a balance between man-making and money-making goals? Everybody understands the money-making goal but what about man-making?

After all, all we can do is to teach them the ideals, teach them that the gap between ideals and reality has to be bridged; teach them global responsibility and so on. Suppose, we have been able to find the faculty and administrators who provide role models of integrity, care, thoughtfulness and spiritual power. Could we then hope that the desired goals could be attained? Obviously not. Because everybody knows the limitations of courses taught through lectures. The very process tends to induce passivity among the students. We have to have a pragmatic outlook on the potentials of pupils having different samskaras (mental tendencies) acquired from previous births. That is why through education we do not get, by implication, to the realm of the greatest human goodness.

This is also a fact that higher education itself with its researches etc. depresses the whole scholarly enterprise. The quality of education and quality of life—both are suffering. The more educated a person is, the more ignorant he is of the things he should know to live well. Such ignorance, as it appears, is no longer an easily solvable problem. Therefore, if perfection cannot be attained en masse, can we not then, think of a series of goals leading to the ultimate state of perfection? These are, of course, never substitutes anyway but complementary always. Hopefully, our seniors have thought of a variety of convictions and not merely opinions, about the intermediate goals or milestones lying on both sides of the road to perfection, of which we can list only a few below:

- If the boys are inspired to give up worldly life, embrace monasticism and do good to the world at the same time, we have reasons to have the winners' laugh, forgetting the rest.
- If a large number of students receive initiation and live spiritual life in addition to discharging their duties in the society, they are on the way to perfection.
- If the students appreciate the values the teachers teach them and do not grumble but try to live up to them as best they can we have reason to be complacent.
- If the boys are sincere, honest, hardworking, dutiful in their places of work, they are successfully treading the path of perfection.
- If they are engaged in doing good to others, serving them, looking after them, bringing happiness to all, they are well on their way to unselfishness. Verily, they are on the right track.
- If the students are taught to help those who are helping others and they do really so when they are eligible to serve, they grab the certificate.
- If some brilliant brains are taught to have discriminations in their minds and they make use of them and undertake activities after much thinking, they are definitely on the

road, because it is difficult even for the advanced souls to isolate the grain from the husk, to sift the real from the false. This is a great quality. A man who has developed this capacity to discriminate and appreciate several superior things and reject ordinary ones is a blessed one. Gradually, the flow of discrimination in him will turn out to be of such magnitude that his sacrifice of the inferior becomes natural. No external pressure will then force him to sacrifice and he is always after something profound and deep.

- If they are taught to become strong and protesting and just not to become like jelly fish and they do behave likewise, they are on the right track.
- Even those who are taught the secular subjects are on the road of perfection when they hold ranks in the public examinations; bring laurels to the institute. But for them, the institute is just like one among millions.
- Get they must a high degree but it is bad to get it by foul means. We hold them in high esteem if they learn that it is far more honourable to fail than to cheat.
- We can add one more practical value to the milestones. Students have to be taught not to become traitors because they receive education with the money of the taxpayers among whom are even the poorest of the poor. The boys must be taught to calculate their debt to the society and pay it back when they earn in future and if they do carry this out in their future lives, there is education. They have to be taught, this is their first priority and they must do it not with a hope of praise or glory. They have to do it not even out of compassion, but out of compulsion. Society claims the REFUND.

With these milestones beckoning to the road to perfection, we get a wide range of workable areas. In fact, we have to put the students on the long road of perfection and see how the divine in them ultimately comes out.

## THE SCIENCE OF VALUES AND YOGA

Values and education are inseparable as is evident from the foregoing discussion. Values are normative in nature associated with 'oughtness' as such. As opposed to normative nature there is a positive aspect of statements. Positive statements are those which, when challenged, could be refuted by referring to facts. For example, the positive statements like—the price level of a country has gone up by five per cent—can be put to test and verified. But normative statements like—the Government ought to first check inflation and then tackle the unemployment problem—cannot be tested by appealing to facts, because here the question of value judgment comes to the forefront. The branch of science that studies the values is known as Axiology. Values are classified into two groups: spiritual and secular. Secular values are:

i. Ethical and moral such as duty towards parents, non-violence, truthfulness, kindness etc.
ii. Social values like patriotic fervour, love for service, equality, disgust for untouchability etc.
iii. Aesthetic values like love for art, music etc.
iv. Cognitive values which are purposive, related to the cognition of individuals.

The Spiritual values are humility, purity, steadiness, absence of pride or vanity, service to the teacher, self-control, renunciation of sense objects, reflection on the evils of birth, death, old age, sickness— all helping the knowledge of the spirit. These are indeed the virtues and graces, the mental or other inner transformations, purity and other essential moral values which are conducive to the achievement of the knowledge of the Pure Self. It is very difficult to distinguish between moral and spiritual values. Without moral values the knowledge of the Spirit is impossible. Moreover, we have to distinguish between the absolute or final values and the instrumental values. Values which are an end in themselves are absolute values while those helping to realize other values are instrumental. The Greeks used to regard truth, goodness and beauty as absolute values. The Christians hold that love for God is an absolute value. But the love for man is an instrumental value, being the means to attain the love of God. But the Indian culture has adopted a two-tier system of values known as Purusarthas. The lower tier consists of three values—Kama (sensory pleasure), Artha (Wealth) and Dharma (Morality). Kama and Artha should be governed by Dharma. The upper tier forms the highest value Mukti (Freedom) which is the absolute value, while the lower three values are the instrumental values. *(vide page 20—Values, Yoga and Reality by Swami Bhajanananda in the book entitled 'Values..' published from Ramakrishna Math, Chennai).*

Mere discussion of values won't do. Unfortunately, we have all been doing just this very thing. Swami Vivekananda has warned us strongly about this lapse in us. He said, "'Be Good' and 'Be Good' and 'Be Good', taught all over the world. There is hardly a child, born in any country in the world, who has not been told, 'Do not steal',. 'Do not tell a lie', but nobody tells the child how he can help doing them. Talking will not help him. Only when we teach him to control his mind do we really help him".

Again, "We have to get the power to become moral; until we do that, we cannot control our actions. Yoga alone enables us to carry into practice his teaching of morality. To become moral is the object of Yoga".

By Yoga we mean going beyond the sensory level of life. It refers to a state of mind which can control the sense organs enjoying the sense objects like sound, touch, smell, taste and sight. All the values listed above could be attained only when we accept Yoga as a means. Otherwise, all the discussions will end in utter futility. Students are to be taught Yoga because without Yoga none can become moral. And again, without morality, we cannot control our activities. If our mind is restless, how can we control our actions. So, the most important instrument is the mind, and it has to be controlled through Yoga. Unfortunately, by Yoga people mean only the Raja Yoga and its eight-fold paths and thereby rush towards this yoga-centre and that yoga-centre for some tips to have better heartbeats, controlled blood-pressure etc. But Yoga has a higher purpose to serve. It removes the covering that hides the light of the Self. It transforms our consciousness by making the mind calm and quiet, through Jnana, Karma and Bhakti. Yoga is very comprehensive. It is more than meditation or dhyana even. A housewife attending to her household chores can be a yogi; a cultivator working in the field, a factory worker running his machines can be yogis; a teacher, a lawyer, an officer, everybody doing his duty in his place of work can be a yogi. Even a soldier has to be a yogi. Sri Krishna tells Arjuna, "Therefore be a Yogi, Arjuna" (Tasmat Yogi Bhav Arjuna). "We do good work, help people, serve people, bring happiness and cheer to one and all, develop peace of mind, strong detachment" *(Swami Ranganathanandaji's Bhagavad Gita, Vol. II p. 183).* While working we have to have the detachment of a yogi, the detachment and discrimination of a Jnani, the devotion and compassion of a Bhakta, the heroic enthusiasm and humility of a karmi. When we undertake a venture, we apply all the Yogas together. For example we select a work by applying our reasoning faculty (Jnana). That being done, we begin to work with a steadfast devotion (Bhakti) and efforts (Karma). In all such cases, we take our mind (Yoga) which is peaceful as our guide. Swamiji has given us this comprehensive philosophy of life to be executed by each and everybody for harmonious growth of all the faculties like head, heart, hand and mind in us. He has explained the idea through the emblem of the Ramakrishna Mission.

Waters in the emblem are indicative of activities (Karma), Lotus of Bhakti or emotional aspect, the Rising Sun of the reasoning faculty or Jnana and the encircling serpent indicates the awakened energy, the Kundalini power of Yoga. The idea of the Seal is that when activities (Karma) coupled with emotion (Bhakti) and reasoning (Jnana) are united with mind (Yoga), the vision of the Supreme Swan or Paramahansa is attained. Mind is, therefore, all important. Work itself is neither good, nor sacred or holy. It is the attitude of the mind that makes the work good or bad. A Yogi is a Karmi when he works, but there is no attachment to the fruits of action which he offers to the Lord. A Yogi is a Jnani who works with the knowledge that God alone is true and all else is false and, therefore, his mind is not attached to the world. A Yogi is a Bhakta who worships his God as friend of all beings (Suhridam Sarvabhutanam) and works for the love of God. The problem with us is that we try to get the full results immediately and employ our efforts sometimes beyond our capacity and suffer as a result. We have to take a very modest measure of our capacity and go forward. Maybe, some of my co-travellers are more powerful than I am but I shall follow him and never pull him down. A Yogi feels that the road is long and he sticks to his own pace without harbouring jealousy and hatred towards those who go ahead of him. If all of us work with this high character, high and broad mind, we would surely manifest the power, purity and perfection in us. So, to have proper education, we must take our meditative mind along and undertake activity.

And yet, people want to become Yogis as per Raja-yoga. Basically, there are eight parts of it as propounded by Patanjali and with the help of an efficient teacher, one can learn the process of controlling mind through Pranayama. Before that, the learner has to be equipped with necessary qualities, an exhaustive list of which can be found in the form of 26 divine qualities in the sixteenth chapter of the Gita. The eight parts of the Yoga are:

- Yama: Non-killing, truthfulness, non-stealing, continence and non-receiving are yamas.
- Niyama: Internal and external purification, contentment, mortification, study and worship of God are niyamas.
- Asana: Posture which is firm and pleasant.
- Pranayama: Inhaling (Puraka), restraining (Kumbhaka)

and then exhaling (Rechaka)—they together form one pranayama. The result of this pranayama is Udghata, awakening the Kundalini. The Kundalini once awakened passes through the six centres of consciousness and finally becomes united with Shiva at Sahashrara in the head, the seventh centre (Sat-chakra-veda). A Yogi established in pranayama acquires immense physical and psychic power and can conquer hunger and thirst either completely or with the minimum intake of food or drink can maintain a sound body and mind free from all diseases including lust and other abominable desires if he so likes.

- Our body compared to a city has so many openings leading out into the world. Eyes, ears, nose etc. all are called *dvaras* (gateways). Disciplining these sensory doors or openings, we have character, morality, ethics etc. We have in the spinal system of our body seven centres (Chakras of consciousness). The first Chakra (Muladhara) is located at the organ of excretion; the second located at organ of procreation is known as Swadhisthana; the third (Manipura) at the naval; the fourth (Anahata) at the heart. This is the place for meditation. At the throat is the fifth chakra known as Visuddha; the sixth one known as Ajnachakra is located between the eyebrows, where all the psychic energies are centred.

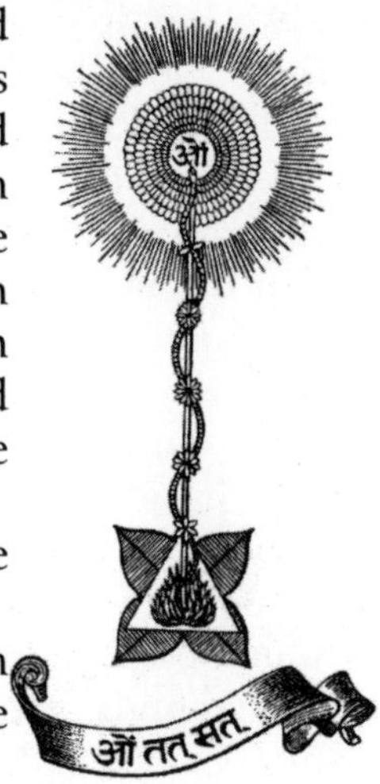


- Pratyahara : The drawing in of the organs (Indriyas) is Pratyahara.
- Dharana : Concentrating the mind on an object either in the body or outside the body for 12 seconds is Dharana.
- Dhyana : An unbroken flow of such 12 Dharanas in that object is Dhyana.
- Samadhi : 12 Dhyanas make for one Samadhi i.e. The Yogi who holds his mind fixed on an object for more than 28 minutes is merged in Samadhi. It is a state of mind when all forms of objects are given up, only the meaning

persists. These three—Dharana, Dhyana and Samadhi—taken together are Samyama.

A Raja-yogi has to be alone free from all hopes and possessions. The goal of the Yogi is to get to the Yogeshwara. He is asked to fix his eyes on the tip of his nose. But the tip of the nose is not the subject of meditation. The subject is Atman, the Self.

## IMPLEMENTATION BY THE RAMAKRISHNA MISSION

People at large expect that Swamiji's educational ideas could better be implemented by the all-renouncing monks of the Ramakrishna Mission through their educational institutions. True. An attempt at setting up educational institutions was made with that end in view by the Ramakrishna Mission nearly a hundred years ago but they mostly came into being in the 1940s and 50s. It is only natural that the public in general should be eager to know about the success rate. It is imperative that by success rate is not meant only academic performance, though boys and girls have been doing fairly well in the public examinations. Students and guardians are satisfied and comforted. So is the society. Students stay on the Ashram campus specially in the residential institutions—a scene reminiscent of the ancient Guru-griha-vasa about which Swamiji said so much. Hostels provide food and lodging, prayer halls for meditation at daybreak and dusk, commonrooms to play in, reading rooms and so on. The Ashram provides them with a sylvan ambience, several pieces of playgrounds, gymnasium and, above all, vast open air to roam about in and inhale. At the schools and colleges, they are taught the essence of our culture and heritage, specially Swamiji's concept of Universal Gospel. At the hostels, they take the test themselves as though in a laboratory through their living a community life with sharing, caring and sacrificing. Living together, in a special family such as this means much to them as they have to forget first the comforts they were used to enjoy at home and then their prejudices with regard to caste, culture and class. Everybody has to respect his fellow brothers, no matter how different their backgrounds are. We have rarely seen such ill-feeling among them as could be ascribed either to their religions or castes. Muslims, Christians, Jains, Hindus, Buddhists, Brahmins, Cobblers, Poor and Rich all consider the place to be sacred for learning and living—all joining the chanting of the Upanishadic hymns or devotional songs from all creeds. We sometimes feel as if in these places only they are all Indians forgetting their credal or racial identities. The feeling of oneness among our pupils is a positive gain to the society torn by so many divisive forces.

If anybody from any corner of the country wants to test a Ramakrishna Mission boy, he will have to ask him three things:

i. How much sacrifice and service and in what exact magnitude and form have you made in your life?
ii. In what way do you help those who help others?
iii. As a result how efficient, pure, powerful have you become?

The answer he would get, barring a few minor aberrations, no doubt, could be in the emphatic affirmative. From the rose plant we do not expect big, fragrant and glossy roses, always blooming round the year, equally alike. There are bad flowers, too. Possibly they are diseased and need treatment. While judging the plant's worth, we pick out the best that it can produce. Similarly, a society has to be judged by one Ramakrishna, one Vivekananda, one Gandhi, one Rabindranath, one Christ, one Buddha, one Mohammed and not by the hooligans in their millions. In general, the Ramakrishna Mission has been sending out hundreds of young and believing men and women to the society every year and they capture the ethos of the Indian life slowly and steadily. In fact, the parents have become more eager than they ever were to protect their children from the onslaught of alien culture and faith. In the Ramakrishna Mission Institutions they find a foothold, a platform to stand on and rest. These institutions constitute a FORUM, so sacrosanct for expressing what is noble and Indian. With the advent of Ramakrishna and Vivekananda, the revival of every aspect of our National life has started and if our students sincerely follow the philosophy of education as enunciated by Swamiji, they can acquire enormous strength in the form of Bahubalam, Buddhibalam and Yogabalam and serve humanity through the spread of the universal gospel of love, sacrifice, tolerance, equity, harmony and peace.

## REFERENCES

*Education:* Compiled and edited from Ramakrishna Mission Vidyalaya, Coimbatore, Tamil Nadu.

*The Bhagavad Gita:* Vols. I, II & III by Swami Ranganathananda, Advaita Ashrama, 5 Dehi Entally Road, Kolkata 700 014.

*Values:* Sri Ramakrishna Math, Chennai 600 004.

**A Syllabus for the H.S. College Students**

1. (a) Sri Ramakrishna Kathamrita: The Gospel of Sri Ramakrishna: General Introduction
   (b) The Life of Sri Ramakrishna, The Holy Mother and Swami Vivekananda in brief.
2. (a) (i) The Concept of Yajna (sacrifice)
   (ii) Civilization Vs Culture
   (iii) Preparation of Balance Sheet — with reference to the modes of living (having & being) [Ref: Swami Bhajanananda's Editorials, May-June, 1982 of the Prabuddha Bharata]
   (iv) Case Study: Kathopanishad & the Gita: Both show how an apparent man is transformed into a real man.
   (b) Unfoldment of power in us (Dualism, Qualified Nondualism, Monism & Vijnanvad — all compared and contrasted). [Ref: Chapter 30, Swami Yatiswarananda's Meditation & Spiritual Life, published by Ramakrishna Ashrama, Bangalore 560019]
   (c) Identification of Faith for a Hindu boy when innumerable alternatives are available to him. Why no such problem for a Muslim or Christian boy? Consequently the basic tenets of Islam, Christianity, Jainism, Buddhism are discussed.
   (d) Six systems of Philosophy & Scriptures [Ref: Hinduism by Swami Mukhyananda, to be had of Advaita Ashrama, Kolkata 700014]
3. (a) The concept of a Universal Gospel: The need for it: It is not the collection of the good elements of all faiths like the preparation of a bouquet, rather it is finding out the elements common to them. These common elements are four in number.
   (b) Four principles of the Universal Gospel by Swamiji.
   (i) Each soul is potentially divine: This is central to Swamiji's teachings. It upholds the most important common element (divinity) in all faiths. The concept of divinity of all life is.

a. An antidote to depression, despair and weaknesses.
b. An antidote to Christian concept of sin and sinner. "It is a sin to call a man a sinner!". Swamiji recognizes errors and mistakes and not sin as an innate nature of man.
c. An antidote to Darwinian concept of evolution. The whole truth of evolution is involution which is the evolution of the involved state of divinity through successive births: The earthworm is the Buddha involved and the Buddha is the earthworm evolved.
d. An antidote to Marxian concept of equality. The method must not be one of coercion, bloodshed but of helping the less-privileged through sacrificing our own privileges and serving the underprivileged. Thus the process helps in levelling up the havenots who may be weak in physique, riches, learning and spirit and not levelling down the haves who have plenty of at least one of these.
e. An antidote to Freudian concept of Libido (sex instincts). Self assertion and self respect, love etc. are the forces we recognize more than we do sex instincts.
f. An antidote to collective evolution of human minds. Each human mind is unique and it has to be taken care of likewise. That is why one should become moral

(ii) The goal is to manifest this divinity within by controlling nature — external and internal (It is a discussion on Science & Religion and also of Microcosm and Macrocosm resulting in *Atman* η *Brahman.* vide, the diagram on Cosmology [Ref: Hinduism by Swami Nivedananda; Swamiji's Jnana Yoga; Vedanta & Modern Science by Swami Jitatmananda]

(iii) Do this either by work (Karma Yoga) or Worship (Bhakti Yoga) or Psychic Control (Raj Yoga) or Philosophy (Jnan Yoga)—by one, or more, or all of these—and be free.

(iv) This is the whole of Religion. Doctrines, or Dogmas, or Rituals, or Books, or Temples, or Forms, are but secondary details: These doctrines etc protect the divine inside as the husk protects the grain. We can remove the husk only when fruit is ripe and not before.

# Education in Human Values: Vision of Rabindra Nath Tagore

ARATI SEN

## BACKDROP

"Life-Skills" and "Human Values" are interrelated concepts, and the context is "Higher Education". "Life-Skills" are the skills required for direct and indirect self-presentation, rearing up of the offspring and enjoying pleasure in the process of living. Herbert Spencer added maintaining of social and political relationship and satisfaction of the artistic and cultural needs. These are the general characteristics of all living beings. To serve life's purpose, there is a need-pattern in every living being that gives rise to a need-cycle – a felt need – drive – tension – action – satisfaction through release from tension until there is the arousal of another felt need. This process goes on continuously. Action patterns are reinforced positively or negatively; some amount of modification of behaviour takes place through learning and experience; and actions are refined and skill development takes place.

Needs of living beings of lower order are limited in variety and simpler in form. Needs of human beings are much more varied, complex, multi-dimensional and are of different categories. Other categorizations of needs are biological, and psychological; moral and aesthetic; philosophical and religious. Some of the needs are manifest in early childhood years while some others appear at a later stage of life. Some of the needs are more fundamental and innate ones, while some others are acquired through learning and also through unconscious cauterization.

Skills are improved modes of action learned by human beings in order to meet life-needs of various categories. In this connection, it should be noted that needs that demand instantaneous satisfaction constitute only a small fraction of the entire need-pattern of a human being; it is often felt that many of the human needs are in conflict with each other—e.g. freedom-need versus security-need. To have fuller satisfaction of needs, a human being should learn skills for self-determination, self-realization, and self-integration. Lack of skills or under-attainment of skills may lead to frustration of needs leading in turn either to an excess of aggressiveness followed by violence, or to anxiety and distress followed by various kinds of physical and mental diseases and disorders.

Life-skills develop during the periods of childhood and adolescence when both the body and the mind are more flexible and more educable. But the process of learning life-skills continues throughout life; the more complex, the more refined, and the higher needs of life appear during the life-process of adults. Hence, emphasis on the necessity for continuing and life-long education for skill-development in adult life also.

## HUMAN VALUES

Values are closely related to needs and skills. We value those objects, emotions and ideas which are useful for the satisfaction of our needs, values develop in accordance with the priority and predominance we give to needs of different domains in our life.

What do we mean by Human Values? In a sense, all values are human values because they appear only in human mind. But in special sense, we use the term to denote particularly those values which deal with human relationship and welfare and progress of the entire humanity. Truth, sympathy, cooperation, inter-racial amity, communal harmony, tolerance, peace etc. are some illustrations of human values.

Also, human needs are in hierarchic order. Abraham Maslow's hierarchy of needs—Psychological needs, Safety needs, Needs for belongingness or love-needs, Need for status and esteem and Need for self-actualization—depicts that relationship. The Upanishads also offer hierarchy of needs in its *panchakosha* paradigm—"*annamaya*" (material), "*pranamaya*"(vital) "*manomaya*" (mental), "*vignanamaya*" (wisdom) and "*anandamaya*" (bliss).

Corresponding to the need-patterns, values also develop in a hierarchical order. There are economic values, recreational values, social values, moral values, aesthetic values, intellectual values, religious and spiritual values and so on. Some of the values are intrinsic, they are important on their own merit, while some others are instrumental, they are helpful in attaining intrinsic values. Generally, values like intellectual, aesthetic, moral, social etc. are considered to be of higher order while material values are considered to belong to lower order, though it depends greatly upon the character of a particular society. Further, value system changes with major socio-economic changes in a society. Life-experience of an individual also may bring changes in his/her value system. During transitional phase of change in a society, we experience what we often describe as value vacuum, erosion of values, value conflict, value crisis and so on. There is no such thing as valuelessness, because we always have one value or the other, as a matter of preference. Preferring one thing over another means valuing.

## HIGHER EDUCATION, VALUES AND LIFE-SKILLS

For the educated genre, higher education is the final stage where individuals enter into adult life at home as well as at work. There is, hence, the necessity of developing new life-skills and values for meeting the challenges of adult life. They will have to develop, with increased vigour, life-skills like:

1. Communicative and self-expressive skills
2. Group participation and teamwork skills

3. Leadership and management skills
4. Skills of self-learning, independent thinking and writing
5. Vocational skills
6. Skills for heterosexual relations and heterosexual adjustments
7. Marital and child-rearing skills
8. Conflict resolution and stress management skills in all types of life situations
9. Introspective and meditative skills
10. Skills of participation in various forms of adult recreational activities.

## RABINDRANATH AND VALUE DEVELOPMENT

It is worth examining Rabindranath's views—philosophy and practice vis-à-vis education and inculcation of human values in higher education. Since the poet-philosopher emphasized on holistic development through life-long learning, it would be difficult to jump on to higher education without looking at the issue of value development at the earlier years. Hence, we would need to look at briefly value education efforts in school education at Shantiniketan. Further, since Rabindranath was an unusual man of action, more than theorizing, he built in value education in the activities of schooling and collegiate education. Hence, we have to take recourse to elaborating on programmes and practices with occasional interspersing of his writings to draw home our agenda of value education in this write-up.

Poet Rabindranath Tagore rejected, in his very boyhood, the system of education established by the British rulers. Afterwards, he expressed his strong repulsion against the system in many of his writings. This repulsion was not against English language or European knowledge as such. In fact, his mind was wide open to European knowledge that made us acquainted with modern schools of philosophy, science and technology etc. What he thoroughly rejected was education that was dull, mechanical, bookish, based on cramming, dominated by examination, lifeless, joyless and useless. In his wonderful story "Tota Kahini" (The parrot training), Tagore described how the bird (read child) with its spontaneity, curiosity, liveliness, freedom and joy of self-expression was killed by being stuffed with irrelevant information into the brain in the name of education in the school, portrayed as the cage of the bird.

Instead Rabindranath reinterpreted the "Tapovana" ideas of education in ancient India and applied them to the present day needs of the country. But his mind did not work in reverse direction. He was not a revivalist. His idea was to form an Indian identity by establishing a link with the forgotten past that was glorious. He did not resist the positive contributions of the Western culture. He emphasized on strengthening our own culture in order to assimilate the western culture and knowledge to make use of it more fruitfully. One of the practices from this tradition was the practice of Brahmacharya. Rabindranath's dream was that learned people from all over the world would assemble in Visva Bharati and form an international community of scholars, engaging themselves in a cooperative pursuit of knowledge as well as welfare of humanity. He had not taken it in a narrow sense. To him, it was to protect the child from a preserved perception of reality and help him/her develop all his/her physical tastes of real freedom. It was to be a self-imposed discipline, not to be achieved through instruction and preaching; but instead, by practising through living a corporate life in a natural surrounding and in close contact with teachers whose personal integrity would be beyond questions.

The school established by Rabindranath Tagore was named "Brahmacharyashram", renamed later as Patha Bhavana. Students here were not engaged in "Tapasya" or "Yajna" in the ancient sense. They would run, jump, climb up the trees, play football and go for excursions. They were encouraged to explore nature and study the life-pattern of the surrounding rural societies. Curriculum in Brahmacharyashram included modern European subjects. To Rabindranath, spontaneity and creative self-expression were of no less importance than discipline and self-regulation. However, hard work including self-sufficiency in daily life, self-reliance, social responsibility and social service, cooperative way of life, close and active relationship with the natural surrounding as well as social surrounding of the Ashram area etc. were some of the most prominent features of Brahmacharyashram.

The fundamental values to be cultivated in the school have been very powerfully described by him in a song sung by the students of schools during the convocation ceremony: "*Mora Satyer Pare mon Aji Koribo Samarpan. . .*".

"We shall dedicate ourselves to the pursuit of truth; we shall not involve ourselves in speaking, thinking or doing anything related to falsity. We shall dedicate ourselves to goodness and shall not speak, think or do evil things. These we shall do at the risk of purity, distress, punishment and even death. We shall remain happy and joyful in all adverse situations of life including sorrows, calamities and humiliation. We shall accept fearlessly the challenges of poverty, distress and death, because we have taken the name of Brahma who is the fear of all fears".

This is like an oath taking.

In this song, truth, goodness, joy and fearlessness were the most significant values that Rabindranath wanted to develop in the students. Aesthetic Value also had a very high place in the Santiniketan System of Education. Rabindranath described Santiniketan as the place of 'Sundara' the supreme beauty, illuminated with "Kalyana"—the supreme goodness ("*Sundarera Padapithatale jekhane Kalyana Deep Jawale*"—it is at the lotus feet of the Supreme Beauty where the lamp of Supreme Goodness is lit). Tagore believed that truth, beauty and goodness are so closely inter-related that their implications cannot be understood in separation from each other.

These lofty ideals had to be concretized through activities in daily life. Rabindranath developed an elaborate scheme for the development of values as well as practical efficiency. In the Ashram Vidyalaya, there was arrangement for the development of physical abilities along with the development of mind and spirit. A hard pattern of life, strenuous physical exercises, participation in games requiring high physical abilities and activities, social work involving hard labour, working in kitchen gardens and fetching water from well—all these were part of education. Students did all these most enthusiastically. Such activities developed their skills in various ways. Some vocational subjects like weavings, carpentry and bookbinding were introduced in the Ashram Vidyalaya. Students took part in village reconstruction work. They have long walks and extensions, took leadership in organizing functions and festivals, hospitality to guests who visited the Ashram, assisted cooks in the kitchen, planted trees and protected them and participated in self-governance for management of their own affairs. These activities provided them ample opportunities for the development of practical skills and human values. Awareness of social surroundings, curiosity of knowing the life-pattern and social customs of the people of the surrounding villages belonging to different castes, tribes and religion and doing some welfare work for the benefit of the downtrodden were highly valued in the Santiniketan School. Opportunities were provided for the development of creativity in children. Art and Music were part of the school curriculum. Students took part in dramatic performances, literary assembly and in festivals like the vasantotsava (spring festival), varsamanagal (welcoming the monsoon) and other seasonal festivals, which were highly aesthetic in nature and demanding a variety to creative abilities. There were other festivals of high social significance like the "Vriksha ropana" (tree plantation), "Hala Karshan"(cultivation) and Silpotsava (craft festival) in Santiniketan. The economic life of the people, the dignity of labour, the protection of eco-balance etc. were highlighted in such festivals. Thus, in Santiniketan and Sriniketan, festivals were not just recreation and fun, although 'joy' was the keynote of the festivals. They were of deep social, moral and spiritual significance. In festivals, participants celebrated the joy of communion with nature, developed a deep-rooted social concern and social awareness. Thus, value inculcation and development of life-skills were built into the Santiniketan system in a variety of ways.

In 1934, the second school, "Siksha Satra" was established. While the general aim of education was same, Siksha Satra was more village oriented, work-oriented, skill-oriented, science oriented and location oriented. All academic subjects were taught in a way directly related to solving a concrete problem of the village, e.g. soil fertility, use of pest killer, manures, pumps, digging latrines, home-gardening etc. The school and it students served as a link between the scientists and the villagers. In Siksha Satra, students were trained in homecrafts like cleaning of rooms, cooking, washing clothes, maintaining personal hygiene etc.; in house-crafts like weaving, mattress-making, paper-making, dying, tailoring, clock repairing, cycle-repairing etc; in out-door crafts like poultry keeping, water-supply and irrigation ; and in the field of human service and citizenship. Thus, in Siksha-Satra, education for attaining human values and life-skills ran hand in hand.

These programmes were made for young children. But adult members of the community and students of higher education, at a later period, also benefited from such programmes. Everybody took part in the activities and festivities of Santiniketan and Sriniketan. .

Rabindranath prepared very concrete and well-formulated programmes to be implemented in the Ashram Vidyalaya in a short essay "Ashram Sikshanaeeti" (education policy). In this essay, his instructions were that the Ashram-life would be organized in a manner that creates opportunity for practising, implementing and testing whatever students have been learning in the classes from teachers as well as from books. The programmes would include development of physical skills, sense-training, development of interest in the objects and phenomena of nature, experience of making things of every day use, developing hygienic habits, beautification of surroundings, learning self-control and disciplined behaviour, self-sufficiency and manners, participating in festivals of the Ashram that would promote creativity, aesthetic appreciation, development of good taste, promptness, organized team work and cooperative attitude; developing awareness of the problems of the country; learning to respect the culture and religions of other countries; awareness of the welfare-programmes of various countries etc.

Rabindranath was a religious, rather a spiritual being. For him religion and spirituality had a larger connotation. According to Rabindranath:

> "Religion is not a fractional thing that can be doled out in fixed weekly or daily measures as one among various subjects in the school syllabus. It is the truth of our complete living, the consciousness of our personal relationships with the infinite, it is the true centre of gravity of our life. This we can attain during our childhood by living in a place where truth of the spiritual world is not observed by a crowd of necessities assuming artificial importance, where life is simple, surrounded by fullness of ample space and pure air and profound peace of the nature, where men live with a perfect faith in the eternal life before them".

Thus, Rabindranath tried to create a total atmosphere and a particular life-pattern that would be conducive to the development of true spirituality. In Santiniketan, a weekly prayer is held in the "Upasana Gruha" (Temple) for about an hour. This is very different from our conventional Mandirs. The Upasana Gruha is made of stained glass with large doors kept wide open during the Upasana. There is no image of any deity. People of all faiths, even of no faith, are welcome to attend the "Upasana"—a very simple prayer reflected from the Upanishad, followed by songs and reading out a passage or delivering a speech of spiritual significance. It has a very beautiful natural surrounding that helps in creating a special feeling among the attendees.

The list of activities of the Ashram-Vidyalaya mentioned above reveals how meticulously Rabindranath chalked out the programme of action for imbibing the desired values among the students and developing practical efficiency in them. Rabindranath's ideas and experiments on education started with education in school. The adult community of the Ashram also took part in those programmes and benefited from them. Later on, the Visva Bharati community also became part and parcel of the Ashram. There was no line of demarcation between the schools and the departments of higher education. The schools (Patha Bhavana and Siksha Satra), the departments of college education (Siksha Bhavana), the departments of research and higher studies (Vidya Bhavana), the department of Music and Art (Kala Bhavana and later on, Sangit Bhavana) and the centres and institutes at Sriniketan—all were included within the framework of Visva Bharati. In fact, the school in Santiniketan developed through a very natural growth into Visva Bharati. All the values, skills and lifestyles developed in the Ashram Vidyalaya were meant for the university also, including all the departments and centres. The educational ladder was not broken by any artificial categorization. It was a continuous whole.

In the multitudes of engagements and activities, the Santiniketan school occupied the core of his heart. Whenever he travelled abroad, he made it a point to visit the schools there, to meet educationists, to get acquainted with educational experiments there, to have exchange of educational ideas and to invite them to visit his own school. The school kept its doors open to receive knowledge, skills, attitudes and values from all sources of the world, although it stood firm on the soil of its own culture. Renowned scholars, artists, architects, philosophers, scientists etc. from different countries of Europe, America, China, Japan etc. and also from different parts of India visited Santiniketan; students had the exposure to a variety of cultures. This broadened their mind at a very early age and lay the foundation for the development of an international understanding.

Visva Bharati as a formal university came into being in 1918 and the first assembly of the registered Visva Bharati was held in 1921. The preamble of Visva Bharati constitution

(Written in Sanskrit) states, "Yatra Visvam Bharatyeka Nidam". Tagore's dream was that people, learned people from all over the world would assemble in Visva Bharati and form an international community of scholars, engaging themselves in a cooperative pursuit of knowledge as well as welfare of humanity. Another song composed by Rabindranath—"*Visva-Vidya Tirtha Prangana karo mahojwalo aajo hey; baro putra sangha virajo hey*"—sung during the convocation, describes Visva Bharati as a pilgrimage (tirtha) where people from various places assemble together with a common holy purpose. This song welcomes in Visva Bharati Jnani (men and women of wisdom), Karmi (men and women of action), Jana-Kalyana-dhyani (men and women deeply engaged in welfare of people) and Dhisaktisampada (men and women endowed with superior intellect). An assembly of such men, he dreamt, would create a "Mukta Bandha Samaj"—a society free from all artificial bondages. These phrases should indicate what kind of values were considered by Rabindranath to be of highest importance in Visva Bharati. They are all human values, as they are above all individual self-interest or sectarian considerations; and take the welfare of the entire humanity as matter of concern.

In an article, Rabindranath wrote: 'Thus gradually, this idea of founding a centre of Indian Culture, with which I started, was enlarged. The full idea of Visva Bharati now included the thought of a complete meeting of East and West in a common fellowship of learning and a common spiritual stringing for the unity of the human race. This stress was now to be laid on the ideal of humanity itself.'

Rabindranath expounded his ideas of the responsibilities of the university community, in general, and its students, in particular, in several essays, like "Visva Vidyalayer Rup", "Shikshar Vikiran", "Vidya Samavaya", Shikshar Milan", Union of Culture, Message to New Education etc. In those essays, he expressed his conviction that a real university should represent the country and the people to which it belongs. This was true to the ancient Indian universities like Nalanda, Taxila etc. and in the Universities of Europe.

It was his conviction that centres of higher learning must have entry into the deeper strata of society. He believed that sustenance of a system of education depends on its acceptance by the larger society. Therefore, higher education institutions should collect and assimilate from all sources and disseminate among the masses. Like The Mandakini, as Ganges is known in Heaven, is hidden from our sight in the disheveled, inter-twisted locks of Shiva; yet she permits her water to come down his divine forehead, and flow on as a common stream in front of the doors of more mortals and never stints her favour but is always pleased to fill our pot and pans to the brim with her sacred water. He contended that modern education should be gracious like her. He says, in the same essay, "The brain is connected throughout with all parts of the human body by a network of rivers. The university will have to play the part of the brain and arrange for a nervous system to broadcast its message throughout the country from one end to the other." Tagore believes that technical knowledge that works in the brains of scholars and popular knowledge enriches the life of common men, differing only in degree, not in quality. Knowledge that is created or collected at the higher level should, like the Ganges, flow down by the side of the habitations of common people so that they can quench their thirst, make their lands fertile and make use of the heavenly water to serve their domestic needs.

Towards the end of his life, Tagore was becoming more and more aware of the necessity of social accountability and social awareness of the students of higher learning. In an address delivered to students in 1937, "Chhatra Sambhashan", he emphatically stressed the following points:

1) Developing the habit of receiving and expressing learning material through the medium of mother tongue. The research has not national or regional sentiment, but he wanted to emphasize that link between the educated elite and the illiterate or semi-literate masses cannot be established except through the medium of mother tongue.

2) His mind was totally open to learn the best elements of European culture; but at the same time, events of the World, specially of the western world, were making him more and more aware that there are many evils in the western civilization against which strong voice of protest should be raised. Students of our universities have a vital role to play in this regard.
3) Students should also try to develop a rational approach towards the grave problems facing the country e.g. the communal conflict, the casteism, starvation, diseases and illiteracy. In his address to university students, he states forcefully, "Cut through the mist of illusion. Acquaint yourself with all the shortcomings, stupidity and shameful ugliness of the country without any exaggeration in a manly way, by means of the bright light of the intellect.

This address delivered in 1937 stares at our face as we witness the same stupidity, the shameful ugliness of the country, probably much more extensively.

## CONCLUDING NOTE

Rabindranath had a philosophy of life; he nurtured a picture of an alternative society in his mind. He wanted to develop Visva Bharati as a model of that society, which had international cooperation at one end, and cooperation at the village level at the other end. Visva Bharati, therefore, is not simply the name of an institution. It symbolizes a humanistic culture of the future, a new social order which alone can save human race from being totally extinct. It is not the fruit of imagination of a lazy, reality-evading, romantic poet. It is based on deep understanding of human civilization, wide acquaintance with various lands and people, deep love for his own countrymen as well as for the whole human race, deep conviction about the goodness of human soul and a strong will to translate thoughts and emotions into action.

It is possible that the ideas of Rabindranath which are more relevant for the present day than ever, may still be sources of new inspiration to the younger students, teachers and workers of Visva Bharati. It may just happen that the original tree may die a natural death here, but the seeds of ideas will get new life somewhere else in the country, and even in the world. Let us, at least, protect the seeds for future.

# Baha'i Philosophy: Education in Human Values for College and University Youth

A.K. MERCHANT

## INTRODUCTION

More and more young people are becoming disenchanted with an education that glorifies knowledge built on the shifting sands of relativism. "Where is the wisdom we have lost in knowledge? Where is the knowledge we have lost in information?" a poet asked.[1] The time has come to devise a system of education that provides a foundation of universality and freedom from intellectual and cultural traditions and superstitions. By means of individually righteous and creative living aimed at developing a world consciousness, as well as through collective activities, young people in our education system must be encouraged to contribute to the betterment of humankind on this planet.

Through education, the youth in our country can and must be brought to realize their sacred obligation to uphold at all cost the cause of universal peace, of world unity and of cooperative fellowship. A new race of human beings, more magnificently endowed and more spiritually attuned to the universe, is waiting to be born. The old values that have dominated human endeavour are destined to be transformed, ambition checked by altruistic motives, ego-centered action replaced by global awareness, the will to succeed transmuted into the will to serve.

How can such a new world community be served by the old curriculum? It must be given a new vision of life, new directives, new knowledge of the Spirit, new conceptions of success. While opportunities for service do exist in some schools it should also be provided in the colleges and universities. Educational institutions must create a climate where students can work together as a learning community, where helping each other is not called cheating, and where service to others is an integral part of the daily life and culture of that centre of learning. An end-of-semester project or an extra-curricular activity is not sufficient. Service activities are, therefore, systematically integrated throughout the curriculum as a distinguishing feature of all Bahá'í institutions.

## SOME ISSUES IN PREPARING A CURRICULUM

In developing a new curriculum world-wide, educators will need to think in terms of curbing the rampant individualism that has come to characterize our culture, and seek instead to nurture the ideals of service and compassion. Unless educational institutions are able to reverse the present-day dangerous trends, our civilization is doomed to perish. "*The principal cause of the suffering, which one can witness wherever one turns, is the corruption of human morals and the prevalence of prejudice, suspicion, hatred and untrustworthiness and selfishness and tyranny among men.*"[2] The increase in crime, the breakdown of the institution of marriage, mental illness, and alcoholism, the dependence upon tranquilizers, the escape from reality into the drug experience, the breakdown of law and order, the corruption of political institutions, and the unethical practices of modern business and industry are all symptomatic of the decomposition of the civilization as we know it.

The specific knowledge and skills that can benefit humankind will vary depending on the requirements of time and problems unique to each country. The disintegration of the old world order and the simultaneous emergence of a new social order founded upon the principle of unity in diversity, Baha'i believe, has begun to effect a radical shift in human consciousness. The description offered above was further analyzed by R.B. Gottlieb,[3] a Bahá'í educationist, as follows:

(1) "The breakdown of traditional family structures, and indeed, of the social fabric at every level. The rising tide of alcohol and drug abuse, unemployment, violent crime, divorce and domestic violence, the flood of migrants, immigrants and refugees, of children abandoned in poverty or orphaned by war—these and other factors have dramatically affected the nature of the young populations around the world.

(2) The shift from agriculture and industry towards an information-based, service-oriented and highly-technical interdependent global economy. In this process, many in the workforce find their knowledge and skills have become obsolete. At the same time, today's children, once essential to the family farm or business, have lost their usefulness to society—a reality that intensifies as they reach adolescence.

(3) The world-wide pattern of massive rural to urban migration with the resulting depopulation of the earth's agricultural regions and the increasing deterioration of its cities.

(4) The unprecedented and ruthless destruction of the natural environment.

(5) The dramatic increase in racial, caste, cultural, linguistic and socio-economic diversity of our communities, effected by the sudden displacement and migration of whole populations due to war and other factors, and a corresponding upsurge in racial tensions world-wide.

(6) The increasingly dangerous hostile interactions between nations, and the seeming inability of statesmanship to resolve international conflict.

(7) The growing influence of the mass media. In the United State, for example, the average high school graduate will have completed approximately 15,000 hours of classroom instruction and watched about 18,000 hours

of television, with its materialistic and often violent messages.[4]

(8) The exponential increase in knowledge and technology and a corresponding moral confusion on all fronts (medical, legal, environmental, religious, political), calling age-old values into serious question and polarizing ever-wider segments of the population.

(9) The accelerating pace of change resulting from communication at the speed of light and transportation at the speed of sound.

These and other trends have profoundly altered the nature of human society, yet educational practice around the world has remained largely unchanged."

Education, then, emerges as an indispensable tool—a tool of active moral learning. There is no other way to raise up positive social actors who are builders of amity and agents of service and probity. "*Regard man as a mine rich in gems of inestimable value*," Baha'u'llah urges, "*Education can, alone, cause it to reveal its treasures, and enable mankind to benefit therefrom*."[5] These "treasures" must be consciously developed because even though nobility, goodness and beauty are innate aspects of our nature, human beings can fall prey to inclinations that corrupt the inner self and quench the light of love.

Educational curricula, whether for the school level or the universities, cannot therefore be solely concerned with the knowledge of physical and social phenomena, but must also be directed toward the goal of moral and spiritual empowerment. As a consequence of the deep connection between individual and social well-being, the Bahá'í programmes of education are designed to instill in every child a twofold moral purpose. The first relates to the process of personal transformation—of intellectual, material and spiritual growth. The second concerns the complex challenge of transforming the structures and processes of society itself. To pursue this dual purpose of individual and collective transformation, specific moral capabilities must be developed. The capabilities of a moral person encompass the concepts, values, attitudes and skills that enable the person to make appropriate moral choices and to promote creative and cooperative patterns of human interaction. Underpinning all such capabilities is a commitment to discover and apply truth in every domain of human endeavour.

## THE NEED FOR CHANGE

In the traditional college and university setting, students are separated in rows, competition is encouraged and talking is generally not allowed. Instruction is dominated by teacher lectures and by readings from textbooks. Students spend most of the college day seated at their desks listening to the lectures, copying from the writing board, answering lecturers' questions and completing assignments given in the textbooks or as instructed by their professors. Students are evaluated by frequent written tests and are assigned letter grades that rank them relative to each other. Traditional grading practices reward individual achievement, where the success of one depends on another's failure—a practice that pits students against one another, often in subtle ways. The curriculum itself is fragmented into brief time periods with little attempt made to integrate the various subject matters into a comprehensive whole.

While this description of traditional practice may not characterize every educational institution or every part of the world, the general pattern is clear. Classrooms everywhere, more often than not, are variations on the same theme. In spite of these similarities however, today's educational systems lack a unity of purpose, a spirit of cooperation, a common vision. Many college going youth feel discouraged by their learning experience; some exhibit problem behaviours in the classroom; and a substantial proportion become misfits in real life. Studies have shown that a significant number of students leave their academic training with poor skills in communication and computation. They lack abilities in problem solving and critical thinking, and acquire only a limited fund of knowledge. Some employers must spend huge sums annually to train entry-level workers in basic business and communication skills. Attempts to deal with these problems have only been partially effective and have not been widely implemented.

If today's students are unprepared to face the present, how will tomorrow's graduates be able to construct a future "*in which all nations, races, creeds and classes are closely and permanently united...*" in a world commonwealth with "*a world legislature... a world executive... a world tribunal... world inter-communication ... a world metropolis... a world language...*", and where "*the enormous energy dissipated and wasted on war, whether economic or political, will be consecrated to such ends as will extend the range of human inventions and technical development, to the increase of the productivity of mankind... and to the furtherance of any other agency that can stimulate the intellectual, the moral and spiritual life of the entire human race.*[6]

As we approach the dawn of a global civilization, a world-wide re-definition of education is required. "*That which was applicable to human needs during the early history of the race can neither meet nor satisfy the demands of this day...*" wrote 'Abdu'l-Baha.[7] In a world already contracted into a neighbourhood and painfully beginning to recognize the interdependence of its nations and peoples, our schools no longer meet the challenge of the age. According to the Baha'i writings the crisis humanity presently faces can be simply stated. Because true religion is dying out, the moral order is collapsing, while science and technology—guided by a profusion of materialistic and secular philosophies—have been permitted to concentrate too many of their powers on developing more efficient ways of destroying man. In other words, the priorities in values are being reversed and are causing widespread disorder in man's relationship to his environment. He has thus entered a period of crisis fraught with many dangers.[8]

## THE CHALLENGE OF THE HOUR

If our youth are to become active and capable participants in the building of a global civilization, they cannot sit passively in rows, day after day, year after year, ingesting and regurgitating the fragmented understandings and mis-understandings of others. They need first, global vision, an understanding of their place in history, a realization of their spiritual nature, a clear sense of purpose, awareness of the needs of the present as well as the future and moral courage necessary to fulfil their mission in life, "the service and salvation of all mankind."[9]

Colleges and universities must create a climate where students can work together as a learning community, where helping each other is not called cheating, where holding a conversation with peers is not considered off-task. Students must be encouraged to strive for excellence as they develop their powers of intellectual investigation, of creative inspiring vision in these words: "Our call is to young India. It is the young who must be the builders of the new world,—not those who accept the competitive individualism, the capitalism or the materialistic communism of the West as India's future ideal, nor those who are enslaved to old religious formulas and cannot believe in the acceptance and transformation of life by the spirit, but all who are free in mind and heart to accept a completer of truth and labour for a greater ideal. They must be men who will dedicate themselves not to the past or the present but to the future. They will need to consecrate their lives to an exceeding of their lower self, to the realization of God in themselves and in all human beings and to a whole-minded and indefatigable labour of the nation and for humanity..."[11]

In some professional circles, a more ecological view of education is beginning to emerge—a vision that is global and integrative, that is based on a fundamental assumption of wholeness and the interconnectedness of all things, that recognizes the transcendence of the human spirit and the nobility inherent in humankind. There is a growing consciousness of the need for a comprehensive curriculum that offers depth, coherence and purpose, and that addresses for the opportunities and dangers in the real world.

Perhaps influenced by the spirit of the age, the new paradigm provides a larger perspective that challenges traditional assumptions and goals of formal education, and may have profound implications for curriculum development, instructional methods, facility design, scheduling, evaluation, administration, and indeed, all aspects of the educational process.

## BAHA'I TRAINING METHODOLOGIES

The Baha'i educational programmes are based on the understanding that students learn better when they are actively involved in experiencing and processing learning activities, given opportunities to practise their learning, when they help each other learn and when they learn in many dimensions at the same time.

The teaching-learning activity, therefore, emphasizes student participation, involvement, reflection, consultation and collective learning. Most teaching sessions in this programme are thus based on the experiential learning design, use of participatory and cooperative learning methods and also involve simultaneous learning in several dimensions. Some of these approaches could be summarized as follows:

### *Experiential Learning Methodology*

The experiential learning methodology is founded on the assertion that in "real life", we learn from our daily experiences. The most profound learning experiences we have had are those that have affected us the most, in which we really "understood" something, and they have usually resulted in dramatic changes of perception about the world, changes of attitude and behaviour or the mastering of new skills.

The real world learning cycle can be illustrated by a simple diagram below.

***Real Life Learning Cycle***

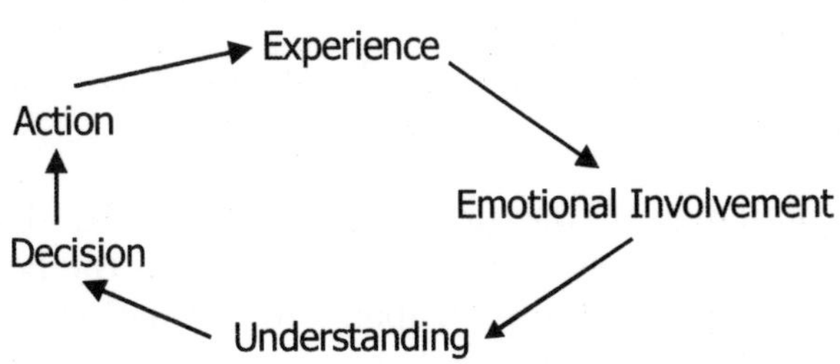

***Experiential Learning Cycle***

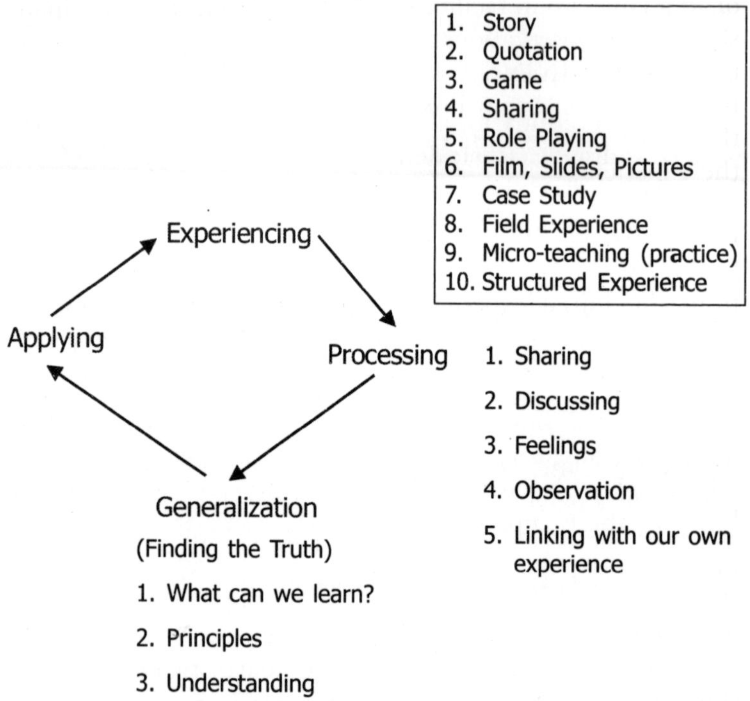


In real life, however, these experiences are often accidental, and due to events, out of our control. Trainers have tried to find out if we could reproduce this learning process in the classroom and make it more systematic, and they have come up with what is known as the *Experiential Learning Methodology.*[12] The purpose of the experiential learning methodology is to create structure experiences in the classroom and then help the students systematically go through this learning cycle.

An experiential learning cycle has four main components illustrated below.

**Experiencing:** In the first stage of the cycle, the teacher creates an experience such as those listed in the box, or any other, which puts the participants in a situation where they experience something together.

**Processing:** In the second stage of the cycle, in small groups or in a large group facilitated by the teacher, the participants share their observations, thoughts and feelings about what they have experienced, how they saw it, what it meant to them and then begin linking this artificial experiences with their own past real life experiences. They begin interpreting the experience.

**Generalizing:** In the third stage, with the help of the facilitator, the participants focus on what they have learned from the initial experience and their own processing and attempt to extract general principles about the subject at hand. Here, the teacher may insert additional principles or theory to complete the participants' learning.

**Applying:** The learning cycle is not complete unless participants make a decision about how this new learning is going to change their behaviour or a decision about how to improve a skill they are trying to acquire, and they are given the opportunity to do so, immediately in the same session, or in another session or in another context.

To understand a concept, change a behaviour or learn a skill, this learning cycle must be repeated several times until the learning is stable. The application phase creates a new experience, that of trying to apply principles or skills learned, and this, in turn, becomes a new experience, which must be processed, generalized and applied again until the experience of applying conforms to the principle.

These cycles can be very short and occur once or more times in the same session or they can be spread over several sessions (where in one or more sessions the experience and processing, generalizing and applying happens in several other sessions), or can even be spread over several situations. For example, the experiences of planting trees, working in groups and serving are intimately related to the learning that is occurring in the classroom, at home and in the community at large.

## TRAINING METHODS

At each stage of the experiential learning cycle, different training methods and techniques can be used to facilitate and enhance learning.

*Participatory Learning:* In participatory learning, an effort is made to increase students' participation and active involvement in their own learning. Participatory learning emphasizes the use of learning activities such as games, songs, role plays, group discussions etc.

*Cooperative Learning:* This is a set of methods that allow as many students as possible to speak at the same time, so that they can participate actively in their own learning, and students working in teams so that they learn to cooperate to find better answers and all gain from the effort, even though each one is accountable for his own learning. There are many different cooperative learning structures, each with its own purpose and characteristics.

*Integrated Learning:* In this approach, learning occurs in several dimensions at the same time. For example, a group doing a service activity together can learn simultaneously about how to remove weeds, about how to work in teams,

**LEARNING TO RIDE A BICYCLE**

Sunil tried to ride a bicycle for the first time. He leaned too much to the left and fell. (Experience). He thought about what happened. He had leaned too much to the left, he had fallen, he had hurt himself, he felt embarrassed and he did not like this at all (Processing). He concluded that leaning to the left makes you fall (Generalizing). He decided that next time, he would not lean to the left (Application). He tried again. This time he leaned too much to the right (Experience). He processed this again (Processing) and concluded that you should not lean to the left or to the right (Generalization) and decided he would try that (Application). His third experience confirmed his learning; he was able to keep his balance and he felt successful... But he did not watch where he was going and he hit a tree... (New Experience).

about planning, implementing and evaluating an activity, about the attitudes and virtues required to perform a service activity and work in groups, and about the effect of weeds on young trees and how this relates to our own spiritual development.

## CONCLUSION

To sum up the Baha'i Faith offers the following as compelling goals[13] in providing an education for the wholesome development of young people at all levels of society:

1. The realization that it is chiefly service to humanity and dedication to the unification of mankind that unlock individual capacity and release creative powers latent in human nature.
2. The understanding that the mere knowledge of principles is insufficient to ensure personal growth and social change, that both require the exercise of volition and application of will.
3. A firm conviction that human honour and happiness lie in self-respect and noble purposes, in integrity and moral equality and not in the mere pursuit of wealth and power for their own sake.
4. A reasonable degree of excellence in at least one productive skill through which individual can experience the truth that work is worship when performed in a spirit of service, and can secure the means of existence with dignity and honour.
5. An adequate understanding of some of the concerns of programming of social progress such as health and sanitation, agriculture, crafts and industry, environment and ecology, at least in the local or regional context.
6. Some development of the individual's capacity for intellectual investigation as a distinguishing power of the human mind and as an indispensable instrument for successful community action.
7. Some capacity to analyze social conditions and discover the forces that have caused them, and a corresponding

ability to express ideas, so as to be able to contribute to consultation on community problems.

8. The capacity to take part in community planning and action as a determined yet humble participant who helps overcome conflict and division and contributes to the establishment of a spirit of unity and collaboration.
9. A disposition to analyze and desire to understand the features of different forms of government law and public administration.

These precepts are not advanced in the abstract, but are based on real experience. Although the Baha'i community cannot claim to have created its desired system of universal education; it feels encouraged by the progress of its several decades of organized educational efforts. Moreover, it is convinced that the principles underlying its approach are applicable universally and can contribute to a global campaign to extend the benefits of education to the generality of mankind. The application of these principles does not necessarily imply a prolonged educational programme, where circumstances do not immediately make this practicable. For children, the process is set in motion in early childhood as a concerned effort to develop character and encourage the emergence of spiritual qualities latent in human nature. This is the contribution we offer humankind in these times of uncertainty tinged with hope for the new millennium. For the spirit that animates the rank and file of the world-wide Baha'i community, is God's immutable purpose at this stage in humanity's glorious evolution and the vision that inspires us all are those poignant words of Baha'u'llah: "Be anxiously concerned with the needs of the age ye live in, and centre your deliberations on its exigencies and requirements."

## REFERENCES

1. Eliot, T.S. *The Wasteland.*
2. The Universal House of Justice, Cited in *Socio and Economic Development – A Baha'i Approach,* (Oxford: George Ronald, Publisher, 1986), p. 38.

3. Gottlieb, Randie Shevin, "Service : Heart of the Curriculum for Global Civilization." (unpublished.)
4. Kagan, Spencer. *Cooperative Learning*, (San Juan Capistrano, CA: Kagan Cooperative Learning Press, 1992), p. 2:2.
5. Baha'u'llah, *Gleanings from the Writings of Baha'u'llah*, (New Delhi: Baha'i Publishing Trust, 1973), No. CXXII.
6. Shoghi Effendi. *The World Order of Baha'u'llah*. (Wilmette, Illinois: Baha'i Publishing Trust, 1969), p. 203.
7. 'Abdu'l-Baha, quoted in *The World Order of Baha'u'llah*. (Wilmette, Illinois: Baha'i Publishing Trust, 1969), p. 165.
8. Cf. Jordan, Daniel C. *In Search of the Supreme Talisman*. (Wilmette, Illinois: Baha'i Publishing Trust, 1970), p. 4.
9. Shoghi Effendi: *Baha'i Education, A Compilation*. (New Delhi: Baha'i Publishing Trust, 1980), p. 67.
10. Kagan, Spencer. Quoted in Randie Shevin Gottlieb, op. cit.
11. Sri Aurobindo. Cited in "29th Convocation Address, South Gujarat University" by Kireet Joshi, 19 January 1998, p. 10.
12. For more information, see David A. Kolb. *Experiential Learning: Experience as a Source of Learning and Development.* (Englewood Cliffs, New Jersey: Prentice Hall, 1984).
13. *Baha'i Education – A Position Paper* by the International Task Force of Literacy appointed by the Universal House of Justice. (New Delhi: Baha'i Publishing Trust, 1988), p. 6.
14. Baha'u'llah. *The Mission of Baha'u'llah.* (Wilmette, Illinois: Baha'i Publishing Trust, 1971), p. 10.

# The Physics of Virtue

SADANAND WARD MAILLIARD

Dr. Leon Kass, who currently serves as the chairman of the United States President's Bio-ethics Committee, made a statement in an interview with Bill Moyers in 1989, which goes a long way to defining the essence of Values Education. He said:

"I regard myself in a way as a teacher, keeping alive certain vital questions about what makes a human life worthwhile, what is good community, what is the human good. ...These are the questions that really bother the young, and if you provide them with the opportunity to think about these things, and if you give them the books that will raise these questions most profoundly, the little candle might stay lit against the barbaric darkness."

My intention as a teacher who has been deeply committed to the process of values education for the past fifteen years is to provide an opportunity in the classroom for students to be exposed to, reflect on, discuss, and eventually integrate positive values into their lives. My goal is to help students learn to think clearly about their lives and the all the conditioning forces that surround them. I believe one of the important goals of education should be to help our young people create a mental framework that will help them understand, interpret and pursue their life experiences in ways that will allow them to attain the happiness and fulfilment that comes from living a life of meaning and purpose.

This idea did not come to me all at once. For many years I have been trying to discover the purpose and essence of true education and how students can truly integrate the important value lessons that will lead them to a life that not only satisfies their own personal needs and inclinations but also nourishes the extended network of their community and the larger society.

## WHAT IS EDUCATION?

The best definition of education, particularly in relation to values, that I have arrived at so far, is "the attaining of knowledge that will allow one to discriminate what is real from what is unreal." Interestingly enough, it is the same definition that I have arrived at with for spiritual attainment. I confess this is not a very new idea. It came to me in large part because of my exposure to India's spiritual philosophy and practice over the last 30 years. This concept has existed as a definition of spiritual attainment in India for thousands of years. Its essence is contained in the well-known Sanskrit prayer:

*Om, asato ma sad gamaya*
*Tamaso ma jotir gamaya*
*Mrityor ma amritam gamaya*
*Om shanti, shanti, shanti*

From unreal lead me to the real
From darkness lead me to the light
From death lead me to immortality.
Om, peace, peace, peace.

The physical and mental processes for achieving the goals of this prayer can be seen very clearly if we look at teachings like those contained in "Patanjali's Yoga Sutras." Here we can discover what the ancient sages of India realized thousands of years ago. The yoga sutras tell us that the highest knowledge we can attain is based on the concept of discriminative wisdom *(viveka khyati)*. At the highest level of discriminative wisdom the mind becomes so concentrated in meditation that it can ultimately discriminate between the essence of spirit and matter and liberation is attained.

What does this have to do with secular values education in modern times? I have come to believe that those who think that education is simply bookish or academic knowledge for the sake of developing professional competence for the accumulation of personal wealth are missing the most important essence of education. True education, when properly understood leads us ultimately beyond the temporary gratification that comes from the pursuit of personal comfort. True education points us to that realm of more lasting joy that comes from living a life that includes a concern for development of one's own positive character and healthy concern for the needs of others.

One of the best formal definitions of education I have seen comes from Professor Tu Weiming, an eminent Confucian scholar at Harvard University who wrote:

> "Education ought to be the civil religion of society. The primary purpose of education is character building. Intent upon the cultivation of the full person, education should emphasize ethical as well as cognitive intelligence. In addition to providing for the acquisition of knowledge and skills, schooling must be congenial to the development of cultural competence and an appreciation of spiritual values."

## WHY IS THIS DISCUSSION IMPORTANT?

At this point a few relevant questions are:

1. Why would a person like me from a country, which is at the apex of material abundance and engaged in its own struggle to reclaim a meaningful value system be discussing the subject of values education in India?
2. Why should any of us as individuals risk looking beyond our measurable material success to this less quantifiable realm of the virtues?

The answers to both questions are somewhat connected. I believe that the answer lies in the realm of physics, which as we know has to do, at least in part, with the laws of cause and effect.

To answer the first question, I would say that I am engaged in values education because I have seen the effects of the loss of meaning and dynamic purpose in my country due to a slow drift away from some of the essential values that bind a society together and give life its meaning and purpose. I am carrying this conversation on in India because I believe India has answers in its philosophical schools of thought that are vitally essential to this discussion on a global level.

I think it is fairly reasonable to say that America is a country that symbolizes for much of the world, both democratic freedoms and material prosperity. However, to the more discerning eye, it is also apparent that our material comfort and wealth has also brought about fragmentation of our family culture and a loss of the dynamic energy that comes from having a clear positive goal. There has been, for many years, a growing separation between the generations that has now become unfortunately an accepted part of our culture. This has created a situation where the positive values, that are the life-blood of a civil society, are not being passed down from one generation to the next as easily and effectively as they once were. As a result there is confusion amongst the young and they are being shaped to an increasing extent by the values that come from the images and messages of the popular media, which is designed to attract their attention by the increasing intensity of the message. The popular media as the famed historian Barbara Tuchman said is appealing to the "lowest common denominator." This means that the content of the media is generally attempting to attract us by appealing to our most fundamental urges rather than to educate and uplift.

For the most part, the essential purpose of the commercial entertainment media and to some extent news media is not to create lasting value but rather to sell products. It is creating a consumer culture, which is addicted to intensity. Addiction here is defined as the need for increasing doses of a substance to produce the same intensity of effect. We can see that, in the increasingly graphic depictions of sex and violence that are required to attract and satisfy, the popular audience, as a result, are becoming gradually desensitized. If stories are the medium by which a society conveys meaning from one generation to the next, then we have to examine the motives and values of those who are telling the story. What do you suppose are the intentions of those who are sponsoring the entertainment you see and to what lengths are they willing to go in order to get your attention?

The USA unfortunately appears to be the leader in this worldwide phenomena, but I am hearing a growing awareness here in India that some of the same trends are also developing in this society. It is precisely because we have this very good case study in the US of what happens to a society when there are few limits to personal gratification that you must reflect and decide if Indian society wishes to travel that same road. Is some way, before it is too late, to gain a better understanding of how over-consumption and the loss of limits on sense gratification ultimately leads to traumatic personal dissatisfaction and a breakdown of the values that promote happiness and unity in a society. It may be entertaining and fun in the short term but what are the consequences in the long term?

In answer to the second question, I would point you to the discussion on the "physics of virtue."

## THE PHYSICS OF VIRTUE

There is an increasingly stronger case that can be made for a study and understanding of the "physics of virtue." That means, to study the laws of cause and effect produced by our value system. I also think we can support our arguments by noticing the many interesting connections between India's great philosophical teachings and the startling discoveries of modern science that now suggest that our thoughts and actions may have more impact and importance than we imagined.

I have come to believe firmly that true wisdom and morality comes from understanding the inter-connectedness of all life. I am not asking anyone to accept any particular set of values. I am asking you to reason with me and see if there are some important connections between ancient wisdom and modern scientific discovery that will encourage you to pursue your own line of inquiry into the "physics of virtue."

We know from physics that all actions create a reaction. This is the primary underlying principle of the physics of virtue. There is also a deeper more philosophical aspect to this simple rule of the chain of action and reaction. Like my earlier definition of education it is not a new concept. This concept is deeply rooted in the Indian psyche and is probably well-known to you as the law of *karma*. *Karma*, as we know, means action. Action creates further action. Our life can be seen to some extent as the result of a series of decisions that we make day by day and the accumulation of those decisions takes our life in a particular direction. Often we cannot see the effects of each action but our character and our lives are gradually and inexorably shaped by our actions. I find it quite intriguing that we are now discovering the scientific equivalent of the ancient laws of *karma* in the astounding new world of quantum physics.

One of the main differences between Newtonian physics and quantum physics has to do with the concept of space. In Newtonian Physics it was believed that space was empty and the atoms and electrons were whirling around relatively vast distances from each other without any discernable connection. Now, quantum physics is telling us something quite different. It is telling us that space may not be empty, that it is "field-rich" meaning that space is full of energy fields and that the electrons and particles that we thought were independent of each other may in fact be inter-connected and inter-dependent. Astoundingly, the universe may be connected not just in the traditional three or four dimensions, but perhaps in as many as ten or eleven dimensions. We may be connected in ways that we have not previously imagined. This is to say that no action takes place independently in a vacuum.

There is a quantum physics metaphor of a butterfly flapping its wings in South America and a hurricane being created in Florida. This metaphorically expresses the idea of local action and distinctly non-local and surprising results. If we apply that idea to our own actions, we begin to discover that every action has a result even if we cannot see it. If the universe is as interconnected as quantum physics suggests, it may just be that our actions have consequences at far greater distances that we previously thought.

Let me take an example. I am a trustee at an orphanage and school called Sri Ram Ashram near Haridwar, where I spend two months each year. The other day I came in for tea at the Ashram and a gentleman was introduced to me, as retired IAS officer who was an advisor to our recent Chief Minister. In the ensuing conversation I discovered that this man who I had never met before had a profound impact on my life due to an action he took 32 years ago.

I discovered that this man as a young IAS officer in Delhi, had kindly written a letter to a Chief Magistrate requesting him to sign the order to allow a silent monk to be given a passport so that he could go to America. He did this action as a simple kindness to a friend and with no other intention or motive. That silent monk, Baba Hari Dass went to the USA in 1970 and brought the teachings of yoga and many of India's other great cultural traditions to America. I met this monk in 1974 and I have been learning from him and working with him for the past 28 years. With his inspiration and guidance, his students have created in Northern California, one of the world's great retreat and seminar facilities, as well as a renowned children's school. They are known as the Mount Madonna Center and Mount Madonna School. His non-profit organization has for the past 28 years produced the largest and longest running production of the Ramayana in the western world. Literally thousands of people in the West have had a positive exposure to Indian culture and spiritual traditions as a result of Baba Hari Dass's presence in America.

When we began to publish Baba Hari Dass's writings in 1975, he asked that all of the proceeds be used for helping needy children in India. The result was the creation of a charitable trust in India that supports the Sri Ram Ashram near Haridwar, which is now an orphanage serving 50 children, a CBSE recognized school up to 12th class for 450 village children, and a free medical clinic, and one important reason I am standing here today speaking to you is because that young IAS officer did a small kindness for a friend 32 years ago. Imagine my delight at being able to thank this man who unknowingly had affected my life and the lives of countless others by one simple gesture.

We cannot truly know or predict such results of our actions, and certainly, I cannot guarantee that any of us flapping our metaphorical wings in India will cause a hurricane in some distant place, but if the concept of this quantum inter-connectedness holds true, then the laws of physics as pertaining to our actions is something we have to consider seriously. Perhaps we should, as a society think more deeply on the possibility that the value system on which we base our actions may have more far reaching effects than we can imagine and is consequently worthy of greater attention throughout our lives.

What an interesting concept to think of ourselves as Neils Bhor, the great physicist, suggests as broadcasting stations where our thoughts and actions are going out continuously to unimagined distances like radio waves. Take a moment and think of what you are broadcasting with your life and what effects it might be having on those receiving your message.

## THE QUANTUM GITA

Again, this is not a new concept. This new awareness that quantum physics brings concerning the surprising inter-connectedness of the universe is also embedded in the teachings of the Bhagavadgita. In the third chapter of the Gita, Krishna who represents universal consciousness *(purusha)* explains to Arjuna who symbolizes the individuated soul *(jiva)*, why even he, Krishna acts in the world as part of his nature (*dharma)*. He says to Arjuna, "I am consciousness itself and there is no action that I need to do, but even I work for the sake of the universe. If I do not work for the good of all, the universe will collapse, because if I do not do action, then others will also not act, and the world will come to an end. So even though I am beyond all action, I work for the good of all."

I am not suggesting that we are ready to act as universally as Krishna who, as I said in the metaphor of the Gita, symbolizes the pure conscious principle *(purusha)*, but I am drawing a parallel, that I think is reasonable. The point is that each of us, at each level of our association must act, to the extent that we can, for the good of the whole, set an example for others, to follow. Otherwise, the fabric of society will begin to break down.

In the inter-connected world of quantum physics every action has it effect and we each exist, as Professor Tu Weiming says, in a "continuously expanding network of relationships" that is affected by our thoughts and deeds. The Gita, written so many years ago, actually foreshadows that the consequences of our actions may be even more profound than that. That our actions may ultimately affect not only the social fabric, but also the ability of nature herself to sustain us.

I have come to believe that in the Gita, Krishna reveals himself to be our first environmentalist when in metaphorical terms he explains the cycle of nature and essence of understanding life as sacrifice *(yajna)*. He tells Arjuna in Chapter 3 that from the gods comes the rain, from the rain comes the plants and animals, and the plants and animals nourish the people, and it is the duty of the people to nourish the gods. He says, everything sacrifices for everything else and we must sacrifice too, or as he puts it, "nourish the gods" because if we do not, the cycle of nature will be broken and the creation will be destroyed. Today, in modern parlance, this notion of the inter-connectedness of creation is called the "*Gaia* Principle" taken from the Greek mythology that anthropomorphizes all of nature as one being, the mother. This idea has been known to the Indian wisdom-keepers for many thousands of years.

The question here is, "What does it mean to nourish the gods?" Perhaps to the devout it means prayer and offerings, but my study of Indian philosophies says that there may be a more universal and modern interpretation. The gods *(devas)* of the Vedas are not just deified personalities, rather they symbolize the various elemental forces of nature. I would suggest that it means that we, as humans, being the beneficiaries of nature's bounty, have the obligation to be responsible in our use of nature's resources that sustain our very existence. We must honour and respect those forces of nature that sustain us by seeing that we do not disrupt or deplete those resources or we risk destroying the foundations of the entire human experiment. Here the laws of physics apply most concretely. We have to know that if we continue to pursue the take, make, waste strategy of 19$^{th}$ and 20$^{th}$ century industrialism, we will dissipate the resources that we depend on for our survival.

Krishna characterizes the take, make, waste strategy in very blunt terms when he says that one who takes from the sacrifice *(yajna)* but does not himself or herself perform sacrifice is verily a thief and will bring about their own destruction and the destruction of those around them. This takes on an aspect of prophesy when one contemplates our growing awareness of how our current strategies in use of nature's resources are leading us to potentially catastrophic consequences such as global warming.

## THE VALUES PROPOSITION

The basic underlying principle being raised here that I am hoping you will consider is that the value system that underlies our actions is something that demands our close attention. Values education should not be simply the preaching of moral precepts and "lip service" to principles that we are willing to talk about but not embody. Values are not a luxury, but an active, essential, dynamic principle that produces real outcomes on scales we cannot envision or foresee. Values education must include introducing our young people to a reflective life and a clear examination of the relationship that exists between our values and the true happiness and meaning that lies within the human potential. Values should not be an "add on" class to an academic calendar, rather it should be in the core curriculum and the core mission of every school in every country of the world.

If we can see that the values system that we hold is actually generating behaviours that are feeding the entire network of the world system at every level, then we must, as rational beings, begin to look more deeply into the cause and effect relationship between our values and the eventual success or failure of the human experiment. Value education is not the preaching of a particular ideology or a set of rules. It is the reasoned observation of the relationship between our beliefs, the value system those beliefs generate, and the kind of life we are creating for ourselves, our families, our community, and indeed our world.

This concept of the physics of virtue is hopefully not just a clever turn of phrase, but a line of inquiry that we as rational thinkers will be willing to consider seriously. Why? Because it suggests that each human life can make a difference, that there are no separate parts, that the entire system of nature and humanity works interdependently. The linear notion that I can throw my metaphorical garbage into the river and it will only affect those below me is being proven to be outmoded, narrow, and a very dangerous way of thinking. Modern science quite recently, and ancient Indian philosophy for centuries, have been telling us the same thing; that life is actually a continuous cycle and ultimately there is no up-stream or down-stream. What we put into the river today will be coming to us in some form or another tomorrow. On deep reflection we see that causing harm to others or acting non-virtuously ultimately will bring harm to ourselves. Modern physics is now suggesting that even the actions that cannot be seen or known by others will still have their effect in the web of life. This adds both to the great potential and the great responsibility of a human life.

Dr. Leon Kass, who I mentioned at the beginning of this talk, makes reference to this point when he said,

> "The moral life, more broadly understood has to do with ordering one's aspirations and trying both in ones family life and communal life for the things that stir the heart and win the admiration of ourselves as human beings."

To be truly moral we must live a reflective life and develop a value system that will guide our actions in a way that will stand up to our own self examination and be worthy of our own admiration, precisely because as the laws of karma so clearly suggest that we are ultimately both the producer and consumer, the sender and the receiver of our thoughts and actions.

## PRESERVING INDIA'S TRUE WEALTH

In this, discussion have been moving back and forth between a few modern scientific concepts and some of the great spiritual traditions of India. Over the past 28 years, in addition to my own search for values in modern thought, as a student of one of India's great teachers, I have been studying some of the classical spiritual philosophies of India. During that time, as you have been reading, I have made some interesting connections between the ancient truths and the so called modern discoveries. I have also witnessed an increasing interest in my own country in the philosophical teachings of the east. The natural need and inclination of the human spirit towards meaning in life has the west looking to ancient cultures like India for guidance. There is a serious study of Indian philosophical teachings going on now in the west.

It is fair to say that in the rush to technical and economic competency in India many thoughtful people are seeing that there is a danger that some of the values that truly make a life worthwhile are being overlooked and forgotten. As a result the philosophical, spiritual and cultural treasure that is the birthright of every citizen of this country may eventually be lost. It is indeed ironic that so many thousands of people in the west are looking to India for spiritual nourishment precisely at the moment when much of India seems eager to reach out to the material values of western democratic capitalism.

Professor Tu Weiming raises a very provocative proposition in his essay on "Multiple Modernities." He puts forth the notion that each country must preserve what is most important of its own traditions and derive its own form of modernity. Otherwise, nations run the risk of the loss of the cultural diversity that is so necessary to the human experiment. Just as the ecologist can prove the vulnerability of an ecosystem that lacks diversity, I think we must also avoid a single interpretation of modernity regardless of its apparent success. I think the value of Indian philosophical thinking will become increasingly more important as modern science rediscovers some of those same truths that heretofore were invisible to the crude instruments of science.

We are on the threshold of a new awareness of the interconnectedness of all life that I believe will be as profound as Galileo's discovery that the earth was not the centre of the universe but that it actually revolved around the sun. Many of you here will be the innovators of tomorrow. You carry the promise of solutions to the many challenges and problems of modernity. It is my hope that your actions will come from a well considered, value rich inward centre where the results of your actions will allow you to be worthy of your own admiration. And that in your professional and personal lives, will continue as Dr. Kass stated, to

> "Keep alive certain vital questions about what makes a human life worthwhile, what is good community, what is the human good. And that you will ensure that the little candle stays lit against the barbaric darkness."

# Education in Human Values and Life Skills: A Conceptual Framework

K.P. PANDEY

It is rightly being argued that sustainable human development, which should be the avowed goal of all true education, has to be understood and explicated as progress through increasing quality in every human activity. Needless to add that for achieving quality, we need better knowledge, we need achievements of science and technology, of social sciences and humanities. This knowledge needs to be integrated into national and local expertise. To recognize quality in human terms, we also need an improved value system. It hardly needs stressing that knowledge interwoven with values creates wisdom.

In implementing the vision of sustainable human development so construed, a new concept and meaning of education becomes inevitable. It is being increasingly observed that the integration of knowledge and values for a more humanistic society, development of high responsibility towards the local, national and global environment, and strengthening the readiness to share an enthusiasm for living together, need special consideration and support. In such a conceptualization, cooperation of leading personalities from the world of politics, production, science and culture in the relevant mass media programmes and communication's network is bound to prove highly catalytic. It is in this backdrop that education in human values and life skills in higher education acquires special meaning and importance for revitalizing the programmes of our universities in the emerging 21st century scenario.

## HUMAN VALUES

As stressed by Education Commission (1964-66) "in the attempt to inculcate values through education, we should draw freely upon our own traditions as well as the traditions of other countries and cultures of the world. The commission verily perceived that 'there are strands within Indian thought itself which can lead to the new outlook appropriate for a modern society and which can prepare the people for a willing acceptance of life with all its joys and sorrows, its challenges and triumphs'. In them, we can find inspiration for social service and faith in the future. Mahatma Gandhi and some other great leaders of thought discovered the inspiration for their idealism and their passionate striving for social justice and social reconstructions largely from these sources. It was wisely visualized by the commission that 'it is such re-interpretations and re-evaluating of the past that are now most needed.' Such a visualization holds a tremendous promise and relevance even after a spell of 40 years now.

It will be in the fitness of things to bear in mind that the question of values is, historically as well as in the modern contemporary setting, of deep concern. It has its roots in religion, in culture, and in the contemporaneous gropings and searches. Certain intrinsic values have been admitted by all cultures in Asia for hundreds of years in the past. Altruism, originating in the love and concern for one human being for another, has been respected as the highest human value, essential for the survival and further evolution of mankind. The Persian poet Saadi wrote about nine hundred years ago in his classic *gullistan* as follows:

> "All men are members of the same body created from one essence. If fate brings suffering to one member, the other cannot stay at rest. You who remain indifferent to the burden of pain of others, do not deserve to be called human."

It may be readily observed that such humanism has been the common thread that runs through all religions and has been preached by ancient and recent thinkers as the only means for achieving unity in the diversity of human cultures and conditions. Related to this value has been the search for 'truth', which is the core of science, of gaining knowledge.

Knowledge has been extolled as a means for overcoming conflicts arising from ignorance. In one of the *Upanishads*, the guru advises his disciple, who desires peace of mind, to take to the threefold path of: (a) *knowledge* to end conflict with nature, (b) *service* to end conflict with other human beings, and (c) *renunciation* to end the internal conflict which goes on in the mind when many pleasures are greedily sought from life.

It is rather distressing to find that this movement of the human spirit which found expression in the visualizations of the sages and seers has not run its course. In the present contexts, it is more like streams of ideas and events merging into each other and defining a collective aspiration. Notwithstanding the cruelties and inhumanities that scarred the previous century—or perhaps out of its very agencies—new value affirmations have crystallized. Even if their roots go back in the past to a range of inspirations, it is now in the new millennium that they are becoming normal tests of societal action—the value relating to human rights and the value relating to individual freedom, dignity and integrity.

It goes without saying that the values order differs from other orders—economic or political or organizational—in the fact that values and all affirmations thereof arise from and relate to the human being; this places education at the core of the value order, and values as the sustaining force in education. Viewed in this perspective, the crisis of values is also in a real sense an educational crisis brought about by trends which seek to empty the educational process of moral sensibility only to expose it to the negative values of indifference, cynicism, foul is fair and fair is foul. Social responsibility and social consciousness, which underlie all lofty values can only be fostered, sustained and developed through education in its broad meaning.

## CONTEXT OF HUMAN VALUES: SPELL OF MODERNIZATION

Mankind lives in two universes of reality, each with its own dynamics of growth. The one 'universe' is the world of objects—externality while the other is centered on the human being—individual or group. These two universes do exist in separation; but there are cross-over points. However, their pace and direction of movement are not the same. Human being would be the poorer if it did not have one or the other. What should change and what has to continue and what continues even in change are issues of judgment and discernment. This is where education has a role to play.

It has been noted that societies, in the course of their development, come to such critical junctures where they have to make choices. There are those who do not only wait to sweep into the future but also wish to be active participants in the choosing and fashioning of the future. For such acts of choice it is necessary to understand what is at stake in the choices. The Indian society, at the present juncture, has to envision for itself the path of choice into the future, which does not have to traverse the wasteland of rootless modernism or, on the other hand, sterile and mindless efforts to duplicate the past. The best in the living traditions of our land, the Asian cultures and the world heritage, their moral loftiness, universality and profound insights into human nature may provide the links of continuity in the flux of the developmental change.

Long back, in one of the Azad Memorial Lectures, Pandit Jawaharlal Nehru, the first Prime Minister of the country, raised a pertinent question. Can we combine the progress of science and technology with the progress of the mind and spirit also? He averred that we could not be untrue to science, because that represents the basic fact of life today. Still less can we be untrue to those essential principles for which India has stood in the past throughout the ages. In the same vein, he observed—"Let us then pursue our path to industrial progress with all our strength and vigour and, at the same time, remember that material riches without toleration and compassion and wisdom may well turn to dust and ashes."

The spell of modernization, which we are currently undergoing, may be a living force if it derives its strength from the strength of the spirit. It is rather axiomatic to say that 'modernization aims, among other things, at creating an economy of plenty which will offer to every individual a larger way of life and a wider variety of choices.' It may be readily perceived that the freedom to choose has its own advantages, it also means that the future of society will depend increasingly upon the types of choice each individual makes. This would obviously depend upon his motivation and sense of values, for he might make the choice either with reference entirely to his own personal satisfaction or in a spirit of service to the community and further the common good.

In this process, the expanding knowledge and the growing power, which it places at the disposal of modern society, must, therefore, be combined with the strengthening and deepening of the sense of social-responsibility-values. The education commission (1964) had rightly remarked that 'while a combination of ignorance with goodness may be futile, that of knowledge with a lack of essential values may be dangerous'.

The growing erosion of social, ethical and moral values in the younger generation, being witnessed today, is bound to result into serious social, ethnic and ethical conflicts. There is now manifest among the various leaderships a desire to balance the knowledge and skills which science and technology engender with the values and insights associated with ethics and religion at its best, viz., a search for the knowledge of the self, of the meaning of life, of the relationship of man to other human beings and to the ultimate reality. In the overall scenario, which is emerging, there appears to be a need to give a proper value orientation to our educational system from the pre-school to the tertiary level, and lay down the true foundation for sustainable development through inculcation of basic life skills.

## VALUES AND VISION

In trying to understand the true import of the concept of value, it may be pointed out, at the very outset, that *values* and *vision* are indicative of doing 'right thing' for the 'right reason'. It may, however, be remembered that 'values' are not hereditary; they are learnt. From a socio-cultural perspective, value is regarded as a key element in the socialization process and is the subject of cultural, religious, political, educational and occupational research. From an individual perspective, value is regarded as a key element in belief systems and attitude formation, and even as a determinant of behaviour and a key component of studies dealing with attitudes, personality and self-esteem.

*Schwartz* (1994) in an article, '*Studying Human Values*' observed as follows:

> "Previous theoretical and empirical programmes of research on values have agreed in defining values as broad, trans-situational goals, varying in importance, that serve as guiding principles in life (e. g, wisdom, health, freedom, security, obedience). Some problems have focused on the values of individuals, others on values of cultures. All view values as playing a central role in the social sciences as key antecedents, consequences and correlates of human action and experience."

In the last four decades, there have been an impressive number of instruments developed to measure values. These instruments represent diverse perspectives and orientations. Braithwaite and Scott (1991) have made a list of 15 multi-item scales that are representative of a variety of perspectives and orientations, which define a value. For example, *The Study of Values* by G.W. Allport, P.E. Vernon and G. Lindzey (1960) and *the Path of Life Survey* by C. W. Morris (1956) define values in terms of preference while V*alue Profile* by R. Bales & A. Couch (1969) and *The East-West Questionnaire* by A.R. Gilgen and J.H. Cho (1979) define it in accordance with agreement. Similarly, *Life Role Inventory Value Scales* by G. Fitzsi Manons, D. MacNab and C. Casserly (1985) and the *Survey of Interpersonal Values* by L. Gordon (1960) articulate value in consonance with importance while the *Morally Debatable Behaviour* by Harding and Philips define it in terms of justifiability. *The Moral Behaviour Scale* by Retting and B. Pasa Marick (1959) stipulates values in accordance with goodness; *The Value Survey* by Milton Rokeach (1967) and *The Goal and Mode Values Inventories* by V.A. Braithwaite and H.G. Law (1985) define it in terms of guiding principle; while *Personal Value Scale* by W.A. Scott (1965) tends to indicate it in accordance with consistent administration.

## VALUE ORDERING

Thus, from the listing of the various measuring tools of values, it is evident that values are conceptualized in multiple perspectives. They are defined as plans, blue prints, generalized ends that guide behaviors towards uniformity in what are otherwise diverse. On close scrutiny it may therefore, appear that there is a central paradox in the definition of values, one with important implications for the study of genesis, evolution and implementation of the important human artifacts (Heffron, 1999).

The definition of values as 'preferences', as choices between equally plausible alternatives suggests that it is possible to rank-order them from the least to the most desired. Economists call this ranking after Bentham's "utility", where the utility assigned to a preferable situation is greater than the utility to a less preferable one. Recently some economists such as *Prof. Amartya Sen* and *Prof. Elizabeth Andersen* have questioned this assumption, suggesting that not all utility or rational choice is a function simply of maximizing one's economic self-interest. Anderson (1993) observes as follows:

> "When National choice is represented in terms of the maximization of value on preference satisfaction, and when intrinsic value and rational preferences are defined independent of expressive norms and contexts, we are tempted to think that the optimizing behaviour of consumer in the market place sets the standards of rationality for all social life"

Thus, an individual may make perfectly rational choice to sacrifice some of his or her welfare for the sake of another or to seek certain non-market goods and aspirations like trust and friendship, for instance. *Sen* contends that when individual preferences take into account altruistic social considerations, they reflect "values", in general, and not simply "preferences". Moreover, the results of social interaction often produce unintended value formulation for which it may be difficult to find a simple economic measure.

This holds good in particular in case of education, which is not simply a teaching and learning activity but plays a social function as well. In so-called *Third World* countries, for instance, educational outreach to child-age mothers has led to a value formation that, over and above reducing family size, puts a premium today on basic education for women, democracy, and free public information (Sen, 1995). These and other externalities may be expected when policies directed at people's well-being produce, sometimes unexpectedly, new modes of individual freedom and agency.

Values are classified in a number of ways. According to John M. Heffrom (1998), "if the social sciences have taught us anything over the last century, it is that we live in stratified societies, stratified by class, race, ethnicity, gender, occupation, family status, religion and education. As a matter of pure economy, relatively few value dimensions constitute the organizing principles for hundreds of specific beliefs and attitudes". The former may be termed the core values of a society; the latter its subordinate or instrumental values. The problem for an empirical classification of values is to identify these penultimate generalities that people judge to be intrinsically satisfying and that anchor all the other desiderata that affect their lives.

In this connection, it will be pertinent to refer to the observations of Harold Fallding (1965) who wrote as follows:

> "The ordering of ends into a hierarchy means that a person will desire not only one thing, but everything he believes its attainment depends upon. Yet it would still be realistic to say that he values only one thing if his other desires include only the things he believes

are necessary for it and are made instrumental to the autonomous end. There is a world of divergence between two persons who desire the same things, if an end which is instrumental to one is self-sufficient to another...."

Thus, values are organizing ends, organizing precisely, because many other satisfactions and actions are subordinate to them. It may, therefore, be seen that a rank ordering of these organizing ends and of the instrumental satisfactions leading up to them is one way of beginning to come to terms with the vast range.and complexity of human values.

Three popular ranking models in respect of value ordering are prevalent. These are from the policy sciences, from sociology and from anthropology. One of the widely reported is Lasswell Value Dictionary (LVD) which has been used to study political behaviour, development performance, jurisprudence, educational policy and of late "positive" human rights. The basic scheme when employed to education refers to the following eight normative principles:

1. Power which implies that education should increase the political capacity of individual citizens to effect change not only in their own lives but also in the lives of others.
2. Enlightenment which envisions that education should create the desire and capacity for further learning. It should help the student in the process of creating value and in pursuing "the good".
3. Wealth which postulates that education should raise capital-generating and income-earning potential through basic education, commercial science courses, job-training, career counselling and professional development.
4. Well-being which sets forth that education should improve the health prospects of all people by introducing them to the fundamental of health and hygiene, including the physical, emotional and psychological sources of wellness.

5. Skill which implies that education should improve the quality of the work-force through job-training and apprenticeship programmes, vocational education, and basic mathematics, and science education.
6. Affections which posit that education should reaffirm family and community values through civics courses, community service requirements and regular parent-teacher conferences. It may be added that affection implies loyalty and commitment. In this connection, McDermoth (1969), quoting Josiah Royce, stated that: "you can love an individual but you can be loyal only to a tie that binds you and other into some sort of unity, and loyal to individual only through the tie".
7. Respect which suggests that education should raise the level of tolerance of diversity through multi-cultural learning and teaching, mainstreaming and "inclusion", and school desegregation policy.
8. Rectitude which lays down that education should provide a moral standard of right and wrong either through religious instrumentation or through more cognitive approaches such as values classification as advocated by Kohlberg (1975).

John M. Heffron (1999) has rightly maintained that the magnitude and direction of these values may vary considerably from one region, one country, one educational system, one university or school and classroom to the other. Equilibrating effects have to be distinguished from dis-equilibrating ones as the effort to maximize one or all these values may lead to either conflict or consensus. It may also be understood that Lasswellian values described in the foregoing exposition imply a fairly consistent and acceptable set of goods, that cannot all be maximized, at least not without jeopardizing what is characteristic and discrete about each of them. For all social choices there are always trade-offs. The important question is what direction these trade-offs take.

## NEED FOR A CREATIVE REVOLUTION

The rapidly developing communications technology in the today's world which has overtaken the globe, seldom uses its tremendous potential to spread global values and foster a more caring, compassionate consciousness. On the contrary, the media are predominantly replete with violence and horror, cruelty and carnage, unbridled consumerism and unabashed promiscuity, a situation that not only distorts the awareness of the young but also dulls our sensitivity to the problems of human pain and suffering. What is urgently needed, therefore, is a creative revolution in our education and communications policies. We need to develop carefully structured programmes on a global scale based unequivocally on the premise that human survival involves the growth of a creative and compassionate global consciousness. The spiritual dimension will have to be given central importance in our new educational thinking (Karan Singh, 1996).

A truly multi-cultural education will have to address simultaneously the requirements of global and national integration, and the specific needs of particular culturally distinct communities, both in rural and urban settings. It will lead to an awareness of diversity and respect for others. To achieve such a truly pluralistic education whose kernel would be the basic human values, it will be imperative to rethink the objectives of what it means to educate and be educated; to remodel the contents and the curricula of formal education institutions; to develop new teaching skills and educational methods; and to stimulate the emergence of new generation of teachers and learners. Thus, a truly pluralistic education will have to be based on a philosophy of humanistic pluralism with an ethos that prizes the social realities of cultural pluralism.

## VALUE EDUCATION: BASIC PREMISES

In this conceptual framework of pluralistic education, the basic function of the university in a modern community acquires a distinct role when re-evaluated in the light of the pressing need for "*Education in Human Values and Life Skills.*" These are more than mere concerns of teaching. *Norman K. Henderson* (1969) in "University Teaching" has identified seven basic functions of the university. These are: to provide a place for pure culture and learning, to conduct research and advance the boundaries of knowledge, to serve as a training school for the professions, to turn out trained leaders for every walk of life, to act as a liaison between the so-called "academic person" and the "good solid practical man", to produce men and women of character and high ideals, and to be the custodian of intellectual freedom safeguarding liberty and unfettered search for truth. It may be observed that the function related 'to producing men and women of character and high ideals' has become specially significant for the 21st century world which is face to face with a rising tide of dehumanizing forces.

The psychological stage of development to which our youth joining college and university level education belongs is marked by a high degree of awareness, of doubts and questionings, of a search, possibly unaware of itself, of meaning and purpose. It is the stage of a growing sense of personal autonomy. It is a stage at which education with a commitment to values and life skills has to participate in the young person's development, directing the questionings to the personal relations and motives and to social responsibilities. The educational commitment is not directed to "implanting" any set of values. Its main purpose, on the other hand, is to develop in the young minds a moral sensibility and discernment, and to help them to deepen their insights so that they may develop for themselves a body of convictions and guiding beliefs. Philosopher Kant once remarked that the proof of an ultimate reality is the "starry heavens above and the moral sense within." That "sense within" is what education in human values is all about. This implies that our young men and women have to be exposed to the great ideas and great expression of values which have lifted humanity to the high ranges of the spirit-ideas of human dignity and freedom, of individuality and social responsibility, of kindness and compassion. It may, however, be remembered that the teaching of moral values in the context of great ideas will not be "instructional"; it can only be dialogic, the conversation between the teacher and the taught and the ideas. Only by dialogic method can the ideas be internalised and made as their own by the young learners, and by that means to make their own lives less unintelligible and more meaningful. This is the learning that makes the soul of the learner capable of defending itself.

It will be pertinent to quote Raja Roy Singh (1991) who observed: "values are the doors of perception through which we look at the world and ourselves and interpret the experience and make it intelligible to ourselves." He asserted that 'to shut these doors on the learners on grounds of "detached view" or "moral neutrality" or "irrelevance of values in the preparation for earning a living" is arguing for education without purpose'. Thus, education that is infused with a constant sense of values should mean deeper moral sensibility and greater human understanding so that the learners, as they have more education can more clearly see the barriers that divide and separate one human being from another.

## PROGRAMMES: UNDERLYING PRINCIPLES

The basic principles and programmes of education in human values and life skills at the tertiary level education may, thus, be derived from and rooted in our concern for helping the youth to understand himself/herself and to manage his/her self, to acquire familial values, to learn to live together, to be able to comprehend the basic tenets of Indian constitution with focus on education in fundamental duties and citizenship values, to imagine and prepare for competent and qualified entry to the threshold for transition to the world of work, to assimilate and cultivate leadership functions by conceptualising leader vs. manager roles, and to bring enrichment through appreciation of various forces of Indian art and culture and empathy.

To fulfil these ends of enabling our graduates to imbibe human values in accordance with the typical cultural ethos of the Indian continent, the modular courses as indicated by Mukhopadhyay in Chapter 1 may be introduced during the three year degree level courses on a credit basis.

In order to effectively transact these modules at the first-degree level, a comprehensive pedagogic plan has to be worked out. The most direct and effective means of fulfilling the objects underlying them have to consist of a variety of strategies—not merely lecturing, but the tutorials, group discussions, brainstorming sessions, projects and role playing. The basic human values can be intellectualised and made clear, illustrated in the context of particular disciplines and subsequently imitated by students. If lecturers have imbued in their teaching relationship these ideals of intellectual rigour and honest enquiry, they will somehow pass them across to their students and the values will persist.

This is why university teaching is so important, why it should be made as effective as possible and regarded as a vital and challenging task. Some, like Dent, state it dogmatically: the primary duty of most university faculty is to teach and to teach well. The ideals the university stands for are expressed most directly and gainfully through the teacher-student relationship. The pursuit of truth is essential to a free and healthy society: it is the right to judge things by standards which reject what is false and second rate in life, to weigh all evidences in the scales of a balance which are not tricked, biased or prejudiced. The ideals of truth and intellectual freedom are not enough without an effective performance of these functions; they are necessary conditions to all forms of worthwhile teaching in the universities. The university programmes have to be invigorated and engineered in such a conceptual frame.

Three principles have to be of vital concern in implementing the programmes of *'Education in Human Value and Life Skills'*. These are: contextualisation, personalisation and adoption of multiple perspectives in the inculcation of human values and development of life skills. Contextualisation implies setting up linkages with man, institutions, issues and cultural characteristics while personalisation stands for bringing home the meaning and messages in personal terms so as to enable the processes of internalisation and assimilation mature into stable schemata. The adoption of multiple perspectives denotes that the presentation of issues, problems, facts and theories should be made in a number of ways ranging from oral to visual and verbal to non-verbal so as to promote heightened awareness of the value-based deliberations leading to correct realisations of personal, social and cultural issues.

In the end, it may be admit ed that the components on '*Education in Human Values and Life-Skills*' should be an integral and prominent part of the various disciplines being formally taught at present and should arise from an 'infusion' approach to course designing as is being contemplated for environment education, human rights and empowerment programmes. In any case, the various concepts and skills have to be synthesised and integrated with a focus on promoting personality traits which will engender basic *sanskars* of national integration, fellow feeling, tolerance, empathy and commitment to the quality of life and living at the local, national and global levels so as to fulfil the truly Indian vision of '*Sarave Bhavantu Sukhinah, Sarva Santa Niramyah*', advocated through the ages.

## REFERENCES

Cheng, K.M. (1990): "*The Culture of Schooling in East Asia*", London: Routledge.

Educational Dilemmas: Debate and Diversity, Vol. 4, *Quality in Education*, ed.

Levine, R. (1982): *Culture, Behaviour and Personality*, 2nd ed. New York: Aldine.

Montgomery, John D. (ed.) (1999): *Values in Education*: *Pacific Basin Research* Centre, Soka University of America.

Mukhopadhyay, Marmar (ed.) (2001), Education in Human Values and Life Skills in Higher Education: A Report of the National seminar-cum-Workshop, New Delhi: NIEPA. (mimeo)

*Report of the Education Commission* (1964-66) Ministry of Education, Government of India.

Singh, Raja Roy (1991): "*Education for the 21st Century Asia-Pacific Perspectives*".

Triandis, H.C. (1989): "The Self and Social Behaviour in Differing Cultural Contexts", *Psychological Review*, 98: 506-20.

UNESCO (1996), L*earning: the Treasure Within*: Report to UNESCO on Education in the 21st Century, Paris: UNESCO.

# A Case for Value Clarification Courses In Higher Education Curriculum

UMA JAIN

Our Society today is affected by many issues and concerns. Some which have roots in values are—pursuit of wealth by people without the desire for adequate contribution, consumerism, terrorism, communalism and violence, widening disparity between rich and poor, environmental degradation, pollution, lack of discipline and civic sense in public settings, widespread corruption even by people in top leadership and absence of role models in leadership. Even at micro level, in organizations, the patterns are visible. There is a perceived impossibility of combining success with desired values. People believe that their career progress is adversely impacted if they practise their cherished values of openness, honesty etc. There are examples of corruption by reputed corporations, competition and struggle for survival determining choices, disappointment amongst people with the lack of practise of values and dissatisfaction even amongst senior professionals in spite of material and career progress.

Paradoxically, with the planned developmental efforts and spread of education since independence, intensity of these issues and concerns can be expected to have declined while actually it seems to be on the increase. To resolve this paradox, it is useful to look at some data about our educational process (AICTE Website).

India has one of the largest 'Higher Education' Systems in the world with approximately 237 Universities, 10600 Colleges with about 70.78 lakh students and 3.31 lakh teachers offering courses covering about 150 different streams as diverse as Science and Technology, Economics to Fine Arts, Religion & Sports.

Education has definitely become more available to many young people today and is providing qualified professionals for the growing requirements of the society. However, the focus in higher education seems to be only on knowledge, tools and techniques. The higher education in the country including the elite management institutes (whose graduates occupy important positions), has more often than not, failed to prepare people as contributors to nation building.

## PROFESSIONAL MANAGEMENT EDUCATION—AN EXAMPLE

There are over thousand management institutes/university departments offering MBA or equivalent courses admitting the cream of Indian youth molding tomorrow's managers. They offer a wide spectrum of courses but seldom give any coverage to values. It is widely believed that values impact decisions. The values upheld by managerial decisions also determine organizational culture. However, values get almost negligible attention in Management Education.

Occasionally, one finds optional courses on ethics, social responsibility, Indian values, etc. which take a prescriptive and normative mode rather than helping the students clarify their own values and build congruence in value practice. It seems that the idea of value clarification is not well known and understood. Any talk about values is perceived as value preaching rather than value clarification.

While the management education makes no contribution towards value-building directly, the process of management education consciously or unconsciously does nurture certain attitudes and values contrary to what people cherish. My sessions with many managers and even management students bring out that their first level of understanding of their own values is honesty, integrity, sincerity, truth, helping, openness, responsibility to the society etc. Process of management education neither validates/supports these values nor does it provide the capacity to bring these values into practise.

Management graduates begin to believe that their values are not relevant in the world of work to succeed. Competition, winning, succeeding, material success, giving priority to personal benefits for survival are some of the attitudes cultivated through the management education process. While professional managers often make choices which uphold such values, they do not acknowledge these as their personal values. In fact, there is a likelihood that some of the managers(not trained by the management institutes) are more governed by at least some of the values they cherish even though they may be lacking in some of the sophisticated management techniques.

The achievement of the management institutes and their graduates is commonly assessed by the average/highest salary which their graduates get, how fast they get placed and how many get placed in MNC's and even more on whether they go preferably abroad. Almost no discussion about the quality of achievement of these professionals in their organizations or the contributions of these organizations to the country takes place.

The above holds true for higher education in all the various areas to a great extent. This educational process has today perhaps resulted in a country which has many more professionally trained people today than three decades ago but is badly managed. Personal success for individuals is not in line with the direction of the growth of the nation—disparities increasing, worst of recessions, many organizations in crisis, increasing unemployment, are some of the symptoms. At the micro level, there are many issues with individuals and organizations viz. a sense of frustration and helplessness, lack of sense meaning and well-being, difficulty in building the desired culture and retaining people etc. If we think that any of these things is something the educational systems should be concerned about, it is worthwhile to look at the curriculum of higher education. Absence of value education is the special area of gap in the curriculum and which I believe is a critical area for professionalisation and can be one important cause of lack of significant contribution of education to society.

## VALUES-RELATED PROCESSES IN ORGANIZATIONS AND SOCIETY

People at all levels of the organization express concern about bringing in certain values in the organization, but also feel quite helpless in doing so. Most often people believe that their intentions to build a desired culture are sincere but their helplessness is also real. Often a gap is perceived between what the organization and leadership states as its values and what they see in practise. At the social level, the phenomenon seems more hazy and associated with greater sense of powerlessness as well as dissatisfaction. The dynamics of co-existence or collision of the traditional family, cultural and spiritual values with the emerging values of the industrial society is complex and neither well understood. It is generally voiced that there is a general degeneration/erosion of "values" in society but there is also an unstated assumption that we are the victim of it and not the cause of it nor can we make a difference. Values are consciously or unconsciously important to people but the energy around the issue of values is focused on getting helpless, frustrated and judgemental towards others' lack of practise rather than enabling themselves to practise what they want.

In the midst of this, some organizations in the industrial and social sector have been concerned about and have initiated training and development interventions for focusing on personal and organizational values. Also, the personal urge to create a sense of meaning and well-being has brought a number of individuals to value clarification workshops/seminars, which I have designed and facilitated. Data from the workshops show:

- The gap between the values people think they hold, what they practise and what others see them as practising.
- There is a tremendous gap between the values wanted, seen as practised and also the values upheld by groups and the desired organizational values.
- There seems to be a tug of war between traditional/

family ideals, emerging values in the changing society and the practises of people. At an individual level, the gap between practises and ideals seems to move towards upholding the self-interest related choices of success, family happiness, etc. and at the group level the traditional concepts of stability, obedience, security, safety, etc.

## THE STORY REPEATS ITSELF

Similar patterns have been observed in work which has evolved and taken place over the last 18 years with over thousand people in many groups, but there is such similarity in the story which repeats itself in every group that even if we gathered a large group of 500 to 1000 people in one place at one time, the picture is not likely to change to any significant extent.

## IMPACT ON ORGANIZATION/SOCIETY

If we juxtapose these patterns with the common concerns and issues in organizations in our society today, a connection can be seen. Individuals' pursuit of wealth and self-interest for example, pursued by a significant section of people forms a social reality which becomes the milieu in which the individuals ultimately have to function. This also becomes a vicious circle which moves from individual choices to the groups, organization and to society with multiplying effect and at any point of time the system finds it difficult to practise values because individuals in it are not doing it and the individuals unable to do it because of the system.

## WHY DOES THIS STORY REPEAT ITSELF?

Why does something, which is of so much concern apparently to so many people, not move in the direction they want? Why does this story occur over and over again? Explorations in the workshops over the years have provided some learnings about repetitive patterns at the root of this phenomenon:

### *Lack of Awareness about One's Own Values and Practise*

Most of the people, almost all of us perhaps, are not fully clear about our own values. Values are often also clouded or covered by the expectations, demands and the need to keep up with the Jones's. People state their values in terms of things which are ideal and look good but are really not aware of what their real values are. Often there is a gap between what people talk and what they practise. This gap partly stems from the lack of clarity of the concept of values itself and partly from a cultivated blindness to their practise. In traditional pre-industrial societies, the values and norms of the society determined behaviour. Today, we have stopped following many of the given norms of the society as they cannot or need not be followed in the current systems, but not clarified our own values or developed the values required today.

### *Choices and Decisions Often Based on Habits, Fears and Expectations of Others, Rather than Values*

In a good part of our life, we do not focus on our values, and even amongst values, our priority values. Many decisions of life are taken as given because that is the way it has been and it is safe or acceptable to others rather than taking the courage to do what we really value.

### *Differing Standards for Self and Others*

While the intellectual concept of values is ideal, this idealism is largely expected to be practised by other people. People tend to judge themselves by their good intentions and excuse their own lack of practise of values with a heart full of helplessness, powerlessness and constraints, but evaluate others' behaviour harshly through the critical eyes of idealism and expectations and feel acutely about the gap between what they want and what is happening.

### *Tendency to Avoid Pain/Loss Rather Than Seek Meaning and Well-being*

It is generally found that people make their choices to avoid the possibility of pain rather than to pursue the values they cherish. They want to practise their values when they will not perhaps have to pay much of a price for it. In this process, they do not pursue what is meaningful and lack a sense of well-being. People seem to lack the clarity and wisdom to prioritize values, to pay the price for their values or to integrate the practise of more than one value.

### *People Making Choices Based on Values Different from Others, Experience Themselves Alone*

Making value choices is risky when they do not match with the prevailing norms of the system. To be able to take the courageous step, people need some support, but more often than not, it is not available or felt. If some people do take the risk of pursuing values different from the norms of the system, they often experience themselves alone, alienated or end up paying a disproportionate price. In this process, people who feel strongly about values, lose their zeal.

### *People Want Others to Change the System, but Their Own Choices Support the Status quo*

People want change in the way things are but expect that someone else rather than themselves should bring out change. They want to start practising the cherished values when it becomes a little safer and it has already become a norm. People generally cherish openness in relationships in organizations, but they are afraid of being open for fear of consequences. They expect others to take the first step and in effect, keep supporting lack of openness.

### *Blindness to Group Processes and Larger Entity*

In group exercises in the workshops, instead of groups adding value to the explorations and coming to decisions with clarity of values, majority prevailed over minority. People are generally unaware of the impact their own behaviour on the group, group processes and lack skills in influencing them. Similarly, people are often unaware of the connection between their actions and the larger system – whether group, organization or society and have a cultivated stance of insignificance, powerlessness and being a victim in the system. This blindness keeps perpetuating the actions which are creating the process of value erosion which no one likes or owns.

### *People Hold Incompatible Values and Often Their Materialistic and Self-related Values Take Priority*

It is not uncommon for people to list all very good things as values. For example, success, kindness, concern for others, family happiness, meaning of life, wealth etc., but they cannot be pursued all together, at least not all at the same time. Most often, when very incompatible values are put together, in decisions and actions, the values related to self-interest and immediate task gain priority over the values related to higher state of human existence. Many times people say that even though they are successful, materially well off, rising up in their careers, they do not feel a sense of satisfaction and well being because they do not see the scope for pursuing their values or they have to do things against their values.

### *End Values not Supported by Process Values and Skills*

For being able to practise a value effectively, we need to cultivate some other values or skills, which support it. More often people are clear about end values, for example, Team work or participative leadership, but they are neither conscious of the process values which will lead towards the accomplishment of this value, for example, trust, openness, respect for others' competence, interpersonal skills etc., nor the skills that will be essential to practise it viz. group observation, listening, facilitating groups etc.

***Unquestioned Pursuit of Materialistic Goals, not Balancing with Spiritual Goals/Values***

There seem to be some unstated goals/end values of success, career growth, wealth etc. which are taken as given without questioning. In the pursuit of the unstated end values, the stated ideals or cherished values are not seen as congruent. Apparently it is believed that success has to be achieved at the cost of values. Being rooted in materialistic goals, values are sacrificed in pursuit of these goals and thus the vicious circle goes on. At higher levels in organizations, pursuit of materialistic goals at the cost of values is not really a survival need but more of a habit or addiction nurtured by lack of clarity of values. If people were even to some extent rooted in spirituality, it could help them in defining the limits of the materialistic goals for their own cherished values.

The above patterns strongly indicate the hurdles and bottlenecks in building the desired culture in organizations as well as personal barriers which people face in pursuing their own values. At the root of the process of value erosion is—lack of clarity about the concept of values, one's own values, inability to prioritize, the lack of courage and willingness to pay the price for one's values, lack of awareness of the impact of one's actions on the system and the lack of skills to pursue one's values. These factors together strengthen each other's impact and it becomes almost impossible for people to recognize where the process began and that they exist in their own attitudes, beliefs and actions.

## VALUE CLARIFICATION COURSES/WORKSHOPS

Value Clarification courses typically address these issues. Typically, in the value clarification workshops, with about 15-20 people, participants go through several steps of individual value clarification. To facilitate Learning Value Clarification Workshops there are various learning events which involve decision-making at individual and group level. The workshops are not about preaching of values, ethics or religion but people clarifying their own personal values, examining the congruence between their cherished and practised values, knowing the impact of their decisions on their own lives and organization culture and developing the courage to practise the values that they cherish. Through these courses, people can also work on developing some of their non-functioning values into fully functioning values and construct some of the values, which they want to have. In these courses at various stages, important learnings emerge for individuals to make a change in their lives as individuals, start relating differently to organizational reality and influencing it. A glimpse of the learnings stated by the participants is given below:

- Not enough to talk also check whether you are practising.
- Gap between stated and practised values was unknown to self.
- Principles are many, values are few.
- Learnt to differentiate between end state and process values
- Shaking out of an existing value is a tough work.
- Affiliation groups are created out of shared values.
- You may have to prioritize, choose. If you seriously prioritize, you can achieve it.
- Cherished values change in a competitive situation.
- It is difficult to achieve all the values you desire, you have to sacrifice something.
- To avoid frustration, you should know your own values.

## BREAKING THE PATTERNS AND THE VISION FOR TOMORROW'S PROFESSIONALS

All the groups that I have met for value clarification workshops at various levels of management as well as young management students have the very similar patterns. If that is so, why wait till they go into organizations and lose time in repeating the same patterns of frustration and disappointment. Why not start creating some perspective, awareness and clarity about values during the educational process itself.

If we did include value clarification as a part of the curriculum, there are chances that there will be a scenario in which a critical mass of young professionals will enter their world of work with a certain degree of clarity of their values and bring them in their practise, the patterns are likely to change and this vicious circle can be converted into a strategic spiral of change in the desired direction. The more widespread we can make value clarification in higher education apart from knowledge, tools and techniques, it will make education applicable to society and congruent with our needs.

The current state of education is caused by the very attitudes and values of the faculty and teachers in higher educational institutions. They themselves seem to believe that tools, techniques and knowledge can be enough to make professionals. Perhaps, the first step to be taken would be a large scale value clarification courses for teachers and faculty who will be opinion leaders and change agents and establish a propagate for the need for the inclusion of value clarification in the curriculum as an integral part of the curriculum rather than optional courses. While all major disciplines may need to specify and make clear the values involved in that discipline, they will be practised only if the person has clarity about his/her own values. Therefore, we need to have separate courses for values to build awareness and skills.

This will not guarantee that all decisions will be value-based or all the socially desirable values will be upheld but there is a greater chance that the people who have clarified their values will:

- More often than not uphold the values, which are the desired ones. Hence there will be greater congruence between stated values and practised values. Some of the cherished values will be actually practised.
- Take clearer decisions congruent with the desired values and culture.
- Find meaning and well-being in work and life and be less in conflict within themselves and with others.

- Respect others' values and support others who want to practise their values.
- Develop the wisdom to prioritise their values, practise their prioritized values and paying the price.
- Choose the profession/organisation in line of their own values and work in it with the values.
- Build organizations around values and for promoting certain values. Instead of being a victim of circumstances, they will see their role in creating some of them and play a role in deciding organisational directions and the direction of the society.
- Nurture a culture in the organization congruent with what is stated and which enhances the emotional and psychological well-being of all.
- Act with responsibility towards organization, society and others.

It seems a tall order looking at the current state and from our existing frameworks but it will be a step in the right direction, which could do no harm at least and set the direction for a significant change. I would like to quote one story (Jaworski, 1996, p.197) in this connection:

> "Tell me the weight of a snowflake," a coal-mouse asked a wild dove.
>
> "Nothing more than nothing", was the answer.
>
> "In that case, I must tell you a marvelous story," the coal-mouse said. "I sat on the branch of a fir, close to its trunk, when it began to snow – not heavily, not in a ranging blizzard – no, just like in a dream, without a wound and without any violence. Since I did not have anything better to do, I counted the snowflakes settling on the twigs and needles of my branch. Their number was exactly 3,741,952. When the 3,741,953rd dropped onto the branch, nothing more than nothing, as you say – the branch broke off."
>
> Having said that, the coal-mouse flew away.
>
> The dove, since Noah's time an authority on the matter, thought about the story for a while, and finally said to herself, "Perhaps there is only one person's voice lacking for peace to come to the world."

I think with all the investment going into higher education and many of the brightest young people availing of it, the least that we can expect is a few of such voices which make a difference to the world but for that we need, not just knowledge, tools and techniques but clarity of one's values and the courage to stand up to them. Hence, the case for value clarification courses in higher education curriculum.

## REFERENCES

Arthreya M.B. (1999). The Mission of the Indian MBA in the 21st Century, pp.1-9. Paper for the IIMAges Special Millennium Edition.

Bargo, M. (1980). *Choices and Decisions: A Guidebook for Constructing Values*. University Associates, San Diego. pp. 164.

Jain, U. (1995). Value Clarification and Visioning for Organizational Renewal". Renewal, Academy of Human Resources Development, Ahmedabad, India, 1:30-31, 49.

Jain, U. (1989). Values of Computer Professionals: Implications for Institution Building. *International Studies of Management and Organization*. 19 (1) : 53-73..

Jain, U. (2002). A Case for Value Clarification Courses in Management Education Curriculum. Presented at Conference of Association of Management Development Institutes in South Asia, Male, Maldives.

Jaworski, J. (1996). *Synchronicity: The Inner Path of Leadership*. Berrett-Koehler, San Francisco, CA, pp. 181-197.

Koikara, F.(1999) Live Your Values. *DB YOUTHAIDS*, Madras, pp. 232.

Kirschenbaum, H. (1977). *Advanced Value Clarification*. University Associates, San Diego. pp. 187.

McCoy, B.H. (1983). The Parable of the Sadhu. *Harvard Business Review*, 83(5). pp. 103-108.

Smith, M. (1977). *A Practical Guide to Value Clarification*. University Associates, San Diego. pp. 322.

Tannenbaum, R. & Davis, S.A. (1969). *Values, Man and Organisations*. Industrial Management Review, 10(2), pp. 67-86.

# Do Women Students Need Special Training Because of Their Gender?

JAYA INDIRESAN

## THE CONTEXT

Education for all is the objective of every society. At the same time, education of women is gaining special attention. It has been observed that various socio-cultural factors have stunted the growth and development of women. It has now been realized that the low status accorded to women in society needs to be corrected and that women need to be empowered so that they can also contribute to society. It is significant to note that the National Policy of Education (1986) has recognized not only the need for the empowerment of women but also the role of education in bringing about social change, a new social order with greater gender equality. The NPE states: 'Education will be used as an agent of basic change in the status of women. In order to neutralize the accumulated distortions of the past, there will be a well-conceived edge in favour of women. The educational system will play a positive intervention role in the empowerment of women. It will foster the development of new values through redesigned curricula, textbooks, the training and orientation of teachers, decision makers and administrators and the active involvement of educational institutions. This will be an act of faith and social engineering."

In the realm of higher education, India perhaps has the largest number of colleges and universities meant exclusively for women students. There are over 1000 women's colleges and five universities. In addition, women have access to the over 10,000 colleges and 200 universities available in the country, as there are no exclusive men's colleges anymore. All are coeducational institutions. Women's enrolment in higher education has crossed the 33% mark. However, it should be pointed out that nearly 55% of women are in the faculty of Arts, 20% in science, 15% in commerce and less than 2% in engineering and technology. While women's access in higher education has gone up, the percentage of women in senior and leadership positions, high profile and high paying jobs is still very small.

The issue is, what is holding back women from achieving significant positions in society? Are there structural barriers and glass ceilings? Is the climate chilly and gender hostile? Are the policies and practices gender insensitive? Are there cultural constraints and societal resistance? Do women themselves lack achievement motivation and desire to excel? Are they diffident and lack self-confidence? Do they have the required skills and competence to overcome barriers? In fact, the low status of women is a complex interactive outcome of these various situational and personal variables.

This raises some critical questions. Is the large system of education that is in place geared to change this situation? Will mere access and academic inputs be enough to bring out the desired changes? Is the education system doing anything to move beyond academics and add value to the education to provide the life skills to empower women students to face the challenges of this complex world that is going through tremendous social transformations?

The focus of this paper is to examine the role and functioning of educational institutions in facilitating women students in this process. Some further questions that arise are:

- Do women students have special needs because of their gender?
- What are the dimensions of development that need to be addressed?

- What are the strategies that need to be put in place?
- What should teachers do for the personal development of women students?
- What are the approaches adopted by teachers in this developmental process?
- Do the teachers have the required skills and competence for carrying out this responsibility?
- What are the driving forces in this effort?
- What are the policy and management implications?

In this paper an effort has been made to highlight the findings based on an extensive national study (Indiresan, 2002) carried out on the Gender Positive Initiatives of Pace Setting Women's colleges in the country. Any programme, project or activity, which is implicitly or explicitly designed to promote any dimension of women's development, is considered as a gender-positive initiative. It could be within or outside the academic or curricular arena. It could be within or outside the classroom. It could be part of the content included in the system of examinations or outside the purview of the grading system. Thus, a gender-positive initiative has a broad definition and includes a variety of happenings in the colleges.

An instrument was developed to quantify the Gender-Positive Initiatives of colleges. Empirical data were obtained from a sample of 136 women's colleges representing various types of government, private, autonomous, urban, rural colleges managed by different Hindu, Muslim and Christian Trusts from all over the country. It was observed that the colleges varied widely in implementing the gender positive initiatives. A large percentage of the colleges had done very little while there were colleges that had put in lot of efforts in implementing highly innovative and successful gender positive initiatives. Based on the survey data 20 pace setting women's colleges who had implemented significant gender-positive initiatives in their colleges were selected. Intensive case studies of these 20 colleges were carried out. Data were collected through specially designed questionnaires and intensive discussions were held with a large number of principals, management representatives, teachers, students, alumni and parents. These yielded rich quantitative and qualitative data on the good practices of these pace setting colleges in their gender positive initiatives.

## DO WOMEN STUDENTS HAVE SPECIAL NEEDS BECAUSE OF THEIR GENDER?

This question becomes relevant when decisions have to be taken about providing special training for women and has been debated extensively. There is one school of thought that argues that men or women, their needs are the same and there should be no distinctions made on the basis of gender. However, there is another school of thought that vehemently argues that men and women are equal but different. Women are not only biologically different but have been brought up differently due to various socio-cultural factors and thus have special needs because of their gender. As part of the national survey referred to above, this question was posed to a large number of students, teachers and principals from various types of women's colleges from all over India. It is interesting to note that over 75% reported that women do have special needs because of their gender and identified several needs that fit broadly into the Maslow model of hierarchy of needs. Some of the salient aspects are highlighted here.

Being vulnerable in this male dominated world, women expressed their physical and security need for protection from sexual harassment. Realizing that the status of women is low in the society, they expressed a desire to meet their social and esteem needs through better interpersonal and communication skills, enhanced self-concept and identity and value clarification. Having been brought up in a protective environment with decisions being taken by parents and significant others, women wanted to develop skills in independent decision making to satisfy their autonomy needs. Women are no more satisfied with their reproductive role.

They have a strong need for self-actualization. They want to feel empowered, liberated from the various societal and patriarchal shackles that have bound them for ages. They want to realize the enormous potential they have, want to take up leadership roles and above all establish an identity of their own.

In addition to the special needs identified by women students, teachers and principals, the NPE document has also spelt out certain specific areas where women need special inputs. They are:

- Enhancing the self-esteem and self-confidence of women
- Building a positive image of women by recognizing their contributions to the society, polity and economy
- Developing the ability to think critically
- Fostering decision making and action through collective processes
- Enabling women to make informed choices in areas like education, employment and health, especially reproductive health
- Ensuring equal participation in developmental processes
- Providing the information, knowledge and skill required for economic independence
- Enhancing access to legal literacy and information relating to their rights and entitlements in society, with a view to enhancing their participation on an equal footing in all areas.

## WHAT ARE THE DIMENSIONS OF DEVELOPMENT THAT NEED TO BE ADDRESSED?

Keeping the overall objective of total development of women students and in view of the identified special needs of women because of their gender, the issue is what are the dimensions of development that need to be addressed. While academic development is the main thrust of any educational institution, it is being increasingly recognized that initiatives and provisions need to be made for the development of other dimensions also. Some broad dimensions and examples of what may be included under these dimensions are briefly presented below.

- Physical development: This would include providing relevant sex education, awareness about reproduction, knowledge on health and nutrition etc. Training in martial arts has been identified as one of the important skills that need to be given to women students.
- Intellectual development: This would include ability to think critically, take independent decisions so that they become self-reliant.
- Emotional development: This would include skills to handle the various stresses and conflicts that women are subjected to at home, in the society, at the workplace etc.
- Social development: This would include skills in handling interpersonal relations and ability to communicate to be assertive and uphold their legal and other rights
- Vocational development: Women are entering the world of work in a big way. They need information and guidance about the wide choice available in the job market and not be constrained by the prevailing gender stereotypes.
- Moral and spiritual development: The rapid social transformations, on the one hand, and the cultural moorings of centuries on the other, push women into intense conflicts and dilemmas. Women need to be helped with value clarifications to provide them the strength required to maintain a balanced view of life.
- Cultural development: This development should not be sacrificed in the modernization process, as women do have a role to play in maintaining and promoting the rich cultural heritage of the nation.

Thus, the dimensions of development are many and varied. Though these dimensions of development are essential for both men and women students, they are particularly salient for women students as they have been socialized differently in this highly patriarchal society. It is imperative that educational institutions should take gender positive initiatives and provide opportunities to women for the proper nurturing and development of all these dimensions.

## WHAT ARE THE STRATEGIES THAT NEED TO BE PUT IN PLACE?

To achieve the total development of women students, special gender positive initiatives have to be put in place. For this to happen, first and foremost, there must be a consciousness about the special needs of women students that go beyond the academics. This awareness is the first step in the process of development. Mere awareness is not enough. There must be a concern that something needs to be done. It should not stop with mere concern but translate into a commitment to initiate action. In addition to the consciousness, concern and commitment the institution needs competence to carry out the developmental efforts. In brief, there is a need for specific gender-positive initiatives to achieve the objective of providing life-skills to women students.

Gender-positive initiatives can be broadly classified into two dimensions, namely, (i) academic interventions, and (ii) extracurricular or co-curricular interventions.

### *Academic Interventions*

It has been observed that women's colleges generally offer courses in the arts and humanities and other "female oriented" courses such as home science, thus perpetuating not only gender stereotypes but also denying women an opportunity to get into the frontier and emerging areas where the high status and high paying jobs are there. Thus, women's colleges should offer courses in the emerging areas like computers, electronics, microbiology etc. Women students should be encouraged to take up job-oriented courses in all emerging areas and not confine themselves to gender stereotyped courses.

Academic interventions should also include courses or topics relating to women and their contribution to society. Gender sensitization may be provided as part of a foundation course or can be incorporated in all the subject areas including arts, science and commerce. Further, any gender bias in any of the texts needs to be carefully eliminated. Incorporating gender issues in the curriculum is not easy for individual colleges that are in the affiliating system. Autonomous colleges have an advantage in this matter. However, under the provision of restructuring of courses gender issues can be built into the curriculum.

### *Co-curricular and Extra-curricular Interventions*

The colleges have total freedom in this aspect. Gender positive initiatives and gender sensitization can be provided through several co-curricular and extra-curricular interventions. These could be done through various activities of the academic associations, clubs and societies. Debates and discussions could centre around women related issues. Cultural activities can be focused on gender issues. Hobbies promoted could be gender neutral like electronics, photography etc. and thus go beyond the gender stereotypes of flower arrangement, rangoli, mehendi etc. Similarly, sports activities can also go beyond gender stereotype. Adventure activities, trips and tours can all provide opportunities for women's overall personality development.

## WHAT SHOULD TEACHERS DO FOR THE PERSONAL DEVELOPMENT OF WOMEN STUDENTS?

The responses of the teachers to this question clearly indicate that teachers have realized that it is not enough just to provide academic inputs but they have to move beyond academics if the objective of overall development of women students is to be assured. Interestingly, the teachers have clearly emphasized the need for the teachers to develop themselves first so that they can help in their student's personal development. As one teacher put it, "teachers should have confidence in themselves and be an integrated person with inner freedom and correct value system". Some of these teacher related aspects include sense of personal worth, sensitivity to student's needs, concept of fairness, being a role model etc. Some examples of these are:

- Accepting one's own self
- Being flexible and open-minded
- Set example by their own behaviour
- Understand the student's background and get sensitized to their needs
- Create a sympathetic, supportive and friendly atmosphere
- Avoid being condescending and judgemental
- Appreciate, encourage and applaud to promote self-esteem, self-actualization, self-image and self-confidence

Several student centered suggestions emerged. Some examples are:

- Help students to discover their potential
- Give personal counselling and career guidance
- Encourage students to ask questions without hesitation or inhibition
- Develop critical thinking ability and provide guidance in independent decision making
- Make the students aware of their rights and responsibilities
- Provide legal education
- Make them aware of current affairs

In addition, several specific gender related dimensions emerged. Some examples are:

- Make them proud of their gender and respect womanhood

- Make women aware of their dignity as women
- Critically evaluate the media and how it depicts women
- Make students aware of the problems faced by women outside the campus
- Raise questions like absence of women in spheres such as decision making
- Help women realize their own discriminatory attitude regards sons and daughters
- Take up burning issues concerning women and discuss them
- Make students present the positive aspects of women through pictures, posters and cartoons
- Prepare them to take a public stand to protest against harassment of women
- Make them realize that they have the same capacity as men and can work on par with them
- Teach women not to take things for granted

## WHAT ARE THE APPROACHES ADOPTED BY THE TEACHERS IN THIS DEVELOPMENTAL PROCESS?

Teachers have reported adopting varied approaches in this endeavour and a brief overview is presented here.

One of the most common initiatives reported is the *academic approach*. Teachers reported taking initiatives in helping the women students improve their academic performance, especially those students who have been lagging behind, by motivating and encouraging them to perform better. These students were provided remedial teaching, taught better methods of learning etc.

Another initiative adopted is the *personal approach*. The focus of this approach is to take the students into confidence, talk to them frankly and freely to understand any personal problems they may have, try to help them with guidance and counselling. Giving positive impetuses, such as appreciating the student's performance and efforts goes a long way in enhancing their self-concept and self-image.

Several *strategic approaches* have been cited, especially for gender sensitization. Raising issues in class, based on newspaper and other media reports, organizing 'facing the class' sessions, providing opportunities for debates and discussions on controversial issues and several other methods have been used by the teachers to go beyond the academics to develop the total personality of the students.

## DO THE TEACHERS HAVE THE REQUIRED SKILLS AND COMPETENCE?

It is to be noted that not all teachers are conscious that it is their responsibility to facilitate the total development of the students. Some of them even argue that their only responsibility is to teach the subject assigned to them and nothing more. There is no concern for the overall development and this is seen as beyond the purview of the institution. With no consciousness and concern, there is no commitment to do anything in this direction. Many teachers are aware of their responsibility, are concerned and committed but have no skills or competence to implement the gender positive initiatives. Teachers, especially men and at times women also, need to be sensitized to the various issues affecting women. The teachers need to be given skills in counselling, in organizing and conducting various programmes and projects, given relevant and useful information that could be passed on to women students. Workshops on gender positive initiatives highlighting the good practices of pace setting colleges and how these could be implemented would be very helpful in equipping the teachers to handle this responsibility effectively.

## WHAT ARE THE DRIVING FORCES IN THIS DEVELOPMENTAL EFFORT?

The study of the pace setting colleges brought out certain distinguishing features that facilitated these colleges in achieving the objective of total development of women students. These are briefly highlighted here.

### *Dynamic Leadership of the Principal*

Whether it was a male or a female principal, the 4 Cs of consciousness, concern, commitment and competence could be seen in all. They were very conscious of the special needs and status of women. They were very concerned about bringing about the desired changes. The principals were not only committed to the cause of uplifting the women but also had the competence to initiate necessary initiatives. All the principals were functioning within the same restrictive, centralized bureaucratic system with outdated rules and regulations and had to comply with the rigid syllabus and centralized examination of the affiliating system. However, all the principals were empowered principals and had clear goals and objectives. Nothing proved to be a barrier for them, as they found ways and means of doing what they wanted to achieve. Finance, time, rules, regulations and resources were no constraints to them. They used a great deal of imagination and innovation to mobilize the resources needed.

### *Supportive Management*

The managements of colleges, especially private colleges managed by Christian missionaries, Hindu and Muslim Trusts were very supportive. The implementation of the principal's ideas and initiatives were greatly facilitated by the support provided by the managements.

### *Availability of Good Infrastructure*

An attractive campus with elegant buildings and playgrounds provides an ambience in which initiatives blossom. A good library and laboratory are essential. A good auditorium, seminar room, facilities for indoor and outdoor games, music room and so on enrich the co-curricular activities. A well-kept garden and clean surroundings also give a sense of beauty and order.

### Committed Teachers

While effective leadership, support from management and infrastructure are important, it is ultimately the teachers who are the real agents of change. The principal's vision, the management's commitment and infrastructure cannot produce results unless the teachers translate these ideas and implement them through their own initiatives. The teachers have to be willing to move beyond academics and invest their time and effort in activities that would promote the total development of students.

### Team Spirit

Gender-positive initiatives cannot be a one-person show. Certain activities can be conducted within the class and others outside the classroom. There is a need for understanding among the teachers so that they are not at cross-purposes with each other, one undoing the efforts of others. This would not only nullify the efforts but would create confusion in the minds of the students.

### Sensitivity to Student Background

Another important feature noticed in the pace-setting colleges was the sensitivity of the management, principals and teachers to the background of the students. In some colleges the parents were invited to the college to talk about their daughters. Remedial coaching was organized, financial assistance was provided where required, psychological support provided to emotionally disturbed students and so on. These colleges showed a personal interest in the overall development of students.

### Awareness of Gender Inequality

Sensitivity to gender inequality was very evident in the pace setting colleges from the types of themes chosen for their various activities like, debates, seminars, poster competitions, workshops etc. For example, these colleges organized workshops on "how to handle eve teasing", organized martial arts classes for the students and so on. In all the pace setting colleges, there was a strong awareness of the low status of women in society. At the same time, there was a faith in the potential and capabilities of women, as well as the belief that they can achieve equality. The gender-positive initiatives were aimed at ushering in greater gender justice.

### *Concern for Community Around*

It was observed that many of the pace-setting colleges laid emphasis on community outreach programmes. They tried to make the students aware of the fact that being privileged enough to study in an institution of higher education, they also have a social responsibility, especially towards the less fortunate women. The development and inculcation of social values was a clear objective.

### *Linkages and Networking*

Another interesting feature of the pace-setting colleges is their capacity to mobilize resources and enrich their own initiatives through linkages and networking. The pace-setting colleges realize that what they can achieve is limited due to paucity of funds and expertise. This is no barrier for them, as they are constantly looking for resources, which they can mobilize to augment their own initiatives.

### *Moving Beyond Academics*

What ultimately distinguishes the pace-setting colleges from the others is their ability to go beyond academics. They have utilized the academic programmes for gender sensitization, going beyond the prescribed syllabus. These colleges have stretched themselves beyond the required mandate of just transacting the given curriculum and have provided opportunities to students for varied experiences.

These colleges have created a gender-positive climate in which women feel free and secure enough to experiment.

## WHAT ARE THE POLICY AND MANAGERIAL IMPLICATIONS?

The study of the pace-setting colleges has clearly demonstrated that there is a need for gender positive initiatives for the overall development of women students. These can be achieved through both academic and non-academic interventions. The management and superstructure has to play a very supportive role in facilitating this process. This requires greater gender sensitivity on the part of educational policy makers and administrators.

The laudable objective cited in the National Policy of Education of utilizing education as an instrument of social change to undo the accumulated distortions of the past will remain a mere rhetoric unless specific gender positive initiatives are put in place. It should be pointed out here that women students are not a homogeneous group. Till a few decades ago, only women from liberated, emancipated, upper caste well-to-do urban families were enrolling in higher education. Now with the tremendous social transformations taking place, women from very conservative and traditional families from socially and economically deprived backgrounds are enrolling in higher education, for education is being seen as a means of social and economic mobility. These women are to a large extent first generation learners and probably the first women in the family to enter the portals of a college.

Women who belong to the first category perhaps can look after themselves. For women who come from the second category, mere academic inputs will not take them far. They need to be provided with additional support to develop the required life skills to cope in this highly male dominated society. It should be acknowledged that there still exist several gender stereotypes, discrimination, inequality and injustice. These cannot be wished away easily. Women need to be empowered to face these challenges effectively. Educational institutions have a responsibility in capacity building of women so that they have an equal opportunity not only for their personal growth but contribute to the societal development. After all, women constitute nearly half the human resources and their potential should not be lost to the society.

## REFERENCES

Indiresan, J. *Education for Women's Empowerment: Gender-positive Initiatives in Pace-setting Women's Colleges*, Konark Publishers, New Delhi, 2002

*National Policy of Education, Programme of Action*, Department of Education, Ministry of Human Resources Development, Government of India, 1986

# Research in Value Education

MADHU PARHAR

There is fairly a long history of education in human values within the formal educational system. In the American continent, education in human values in the school level was found immediately after the World War II, particularly after the dropping of atom bomb in Hiroshima and Nagasaki ("Spirituality in Elementary Schools", published in 1947 by The Principals Association of United States of America, Washington, DC). Education in human values in India can be traced back to the ancient Indian educational system in the Brahmanic period. It was equally visible and prominent during the Buddhist period; since religious education is an integral part of Islamic education, moral education was imparted during the Muslim period as well.

The post-independent India has a different and varied history so far as education in human values is concerned. Because of Constitutional commitment as a secular country, along with religious education, education in human values have largely been excluded from the programmes of large majority of the schools that are supported by the government. However, the denominational and semi-denominational schools in India provide education in human values, under the title moral education. For example, Ramakrishna Mission Institutions, DAV institutions, Sri Aurobindo Ashram Schools, Chinmay Mission Schools and many others offer moral and value education in different forms. Similarly, education in human values is part of the Christian Missionary Schools, and Makhtabs and Madrasas. The evidence of programmes of education in human values in higher education is, however, rather rare. Nevertheless, NCC and NSS type of programmes and activities offer meaningful education in human values in higher education.

Compared to the occurrences of moral education or education in human values, however, research on value education is comparatively recent. Research can provide meaningful support to the design and implementation of education in human values in higher education. In the revised context where education in human values is being considered as an important element of education of the Indian youth, it is relevant and important to scan through the research on value education to assess the knowledge base for developing programmes on education in human values in higher education. Venkataiah and Sandhya (2002) provide a comprehensive review of research in value education. Authors provide a useful framework for reviewing research in value education. An effort has been made, in this paper, to review research on education in human values both in India and outside drawing heavily upon the works of Venkataiah and Sandhya (2002) in structuring this paper.

Many committees, organisations and individuals have contributed to value education which are the main source materials on the subject. The Planning Commission, Government of India in 1992 constituted a Core Group on Value Orientation of Education. The report prepared by the group presents a deep analysis of the current status of the programme of value orientation of education. It synthesizes the suggestions and has described the recommendations of various other committees and commissions on the subject. NCERT (1987) and Department of State Educational Research, Government of Karnataka (1987) published reference material for in-service teachers and school children respectively on value education. Floresca et. al. (1988), Joshi (1986), Rao (1986), Ruhela (1986), Seshadri et.al. (1992), Subramanyam (1990), Usha Sri (1995) are some of the researchers who addressed teachers and students on the issue of moral and value education through their writings.

## TOOLS OF VALUE ASSESSMENT

To measure and evaluate the values, researchers have used various value inventories, tools, instruments, questionnaires, tests, scales, schedules and surveys. Some of the standardized tools to measure values among adolescents and adults in schools and colleges are Rubric Inventory for Expressed Values; Administrative Value Analysis Tool; The Thomas Self-concept Value Test; Kulshreshtha's Test of Democratic Values etc. Analysis of the studies indicate that observation, interview and self reporting are used less frequently to evaluate research in value education. Adhikari and Hasnain (1982), Gandhi (1993), Khare (1968), Mishra (1984), Rama Rao (1986), Seetharam (1990), Usha Sri (1993) also conducted evaluative studies by administering various tools, inventories and questionnaires mentioned above. These studies measured and sought information from teachers, students, trainee teachers on the psycho-social climate of schools, difficulties in evaluating moral education, objectives, content and methodology of direct moral education, methods adopted for inculcating values and the problems involved and suggestions on a better value education programmes.

## CONCEPT AND CURRICULUM

Values are regarded as important and desirable concepts, which guide human beings to do the right things. Values influence our thoughts, feelings, actions and reflect on individuals' personal attitudes and judgments. Value education inculcates a sense of humanism in individuals, especially children. Through value education, social, moral, aesthetic and spiritual attributes of individuals are developed which are often undermined in formal conventional education. Joshi (1986) distinguishes between moral, spiritual and religious values and concludes that morality and spirituality can be independent of any particular religion. Bhat (1996) and Reddy and Reddy (1992), in their studies, elaborated the concept of value education, which is relevant to the elementary, secondary, college and university levels.

Values are considered as the intrinsic component of the overall curriculum. Joshi (1986) proposed syllabus for value-oriented education from classes 1 to 12. In elementary classes, the stress must be given on training the senses and activities to teach basic values. Researchers also analyzed textbooks of different subjects and levels to study how values are dealt in the curriculum. Chaudhari (1974 and 1976), Haq (1973), Pillai (1976) and Susheela (1977) analyzed Hindi, History, Civics, English and Tamil textbooks. It was found that there was neither any systematic pattern, nor any consistency in the presentation of values in the textbooks. Justice, simple living and presentation of religious values were given inadequate representation. Susheela (1977) found that secularism was reflected in the social studies textbooks at the secondary level in Karnataka State. Rajgopal (1989) in his study identified the value awareness and value orientation of 12 standard students in Tamil textbooks. It was found that 40 per cent level of value awareness was there in prose and poetry. Also, it was found that government school students had greater value awareness level than students studying in missionary schools.

## CHANGE IN VALUES

Researchers have studied the changing values in individuals. Findings indicate that values change in individuals themselves and in their physical, social and cultural environments. The results also indicate that the old values of childhood can be strengthened or weakened when they gain adulthood. The change depends upon various types of influences. Inlaw (1972) in his handbook on "Values in Transition", deals with the changes in values. Piaget also postulated that young children of seven to eight years of age reflect the moral values of his or her parents. Home also continues to be the place from where values are strengthened or weakened throughout the child's life. Gordan and Mensh (1962) studied the changing values of medical school students and found a predicted decrease in the benevolence from first through the fourth year.

Researchers have also addressed questions like whether values are different in different professions, and what are some of the background factors, which affect the development of values. Studies have been conducted on both the issues. Studies among various professions reveal that value patterns differ from one profession to another, specially the values in teachers differ from other professionals. Karn (1952) found significant difference among the group of civil, metallurgical, electrical, chemical and mechanical engineers on all the values except theoretical and social values. Medical students, architects and mathematicians were found to be having high theoretical and aesthetic values and low on economic scale scores (Gee 1959, and Mackinnon 1960). Teachers are found to be significantly higher on economic, theoretical and social values than the students and business employees (White 1968, Sandhya 1999). Sandhya (1999) also found that there is no significant difference between urban and rural school teachers in their moral and economic values and their length of teaching experience.

It is not only the profession, but also the background factors like sex, caste, and marital status, teaching experience, religion, birth date and geographical area where a person's life has an impact influenced value development. Kulashrestha (1972) and Prince (1957) found that older teachers and principals are more traditional in value orientation than the younger ones. Roe (1956) contended that persons who had similar values will select similar occupations. Hodgkinson (1971) found that there was little relationship between values and biographic data as age, sex and seniority etc. Shakeela Begum (1959) found that the social values are more important than the individual values in different caste groups like Brahmins, Lingayats, Muslims and Vokkaligas, whereas Shakeela and Haffeez (1964) found no relationship between caste, religion and value orientation.

Studies have been reported on values and socio-economic status, environmental and organizational climate in relation to value education, and knowledge and judgment of value education. Lerner (1937) and Varma and Gupta (1990) found that children of higher status families tend to display more mature forms of moral judgment than their counterparts from the lower social strata. On the other hand, Ratanakumari (1987) found that middle-class background influences value formation. There are studies, which reveal that parental attitudes (Garg 1983), size of the family (Annamma 1984), academic and socio-cultural influences (Lewis 1984), families and friends (Roy 1980) have significant influence on value development. Bhushan and Ahuja (1977) studied the attitudes of parents and students. Values like honesty, obedience and consideration, self-control etc. were given high ranking by the parents and students. Sharma (1975) found a positive relationship between socio-economic status and types of values. In another study, it was found that children raised by educators in better-off homes fare better than the children raised in poverty stricken homes (Bettleheim 1969) whereas Joshi and Poonachand (1994) found that adolescents from joint families have higher scores on moral values than those from the nuclear families.

A number of studies reveal that the organizational climate affects individual's value system and development. Universities and schools like the Dayalbagh Educational Institute, Banasthali Vidyapith, Sri Sathya Sai Institute of Higher Learning, Ramakrishna Institute of Moral and Spiritual Education, Sri Aurobindo International Centre of Education Pondicherry, and Rishi Valley School provide core courses on Indian culture, value based education, Indian Constitution and moral and spiritual education. Teaching of these courses helps in the development of various faculties of observation, judgment, expression and other senses in the students. Several researchers have undertaken studies to find out the effect of environmental and organizational climate on value development. Lobo (1983) found that values need nurturing atmosphere. Sharma (1995) concludes that values are permeated through the conduct of the elders and imbibed by the youngsters. Adiseshaiah (1976), Mittal (1982), Morris (1956), Pillai (1979), and Sahasrabudhe (1977) found in their research that moral development are influenced by the organizational climate of schools and colleges. Teachers' behaviour contributes to generation of open climate and acceptable and conducive students behaviour. Singh (1974) found that teachers' score was high in relation to emotional warmth, fairness and communication and low in trustfulness and status.

Piaget and many others studied the moral judgments of children. Studies indicate that children of different age groups have mainly six types of moral judgment. These are:

- intentionality in judgments,
- relativism in judgment,
- independence of sanctions,
- use of reciprocity,
- use of punishment as restitution, and
- naturalistic view of misfortune.

Kohlberg extended the research of Piaget and traced the steps by which children grow towards making truly moral judgment. Research studies on Knowledge and Judgment in value education have been mostly reported on children in the age group 9 to 17. Sinha's (1979) study on college students and teachers indicated that hero image and models for younger generation are more varied and unstable. Results of the studies conducted by Pachauri and Varma (1981), Suls, Gutkin and Kalle (1979), Varma (1971) and Wellman, Larkey and Somarville (1979) pointed to a positive and significant relationship between the knowledge of values and moral judgment among children.

In India, value education is imparted in schools in the name of moral education or moral instruction. A number of studies are reported under these aspects. Kohlberg (1978) in his work on moral education commented, "in psychology, the study of morality is often regarded as the study of values". Kohlberg has made serious attempts to separate moral values from other kinds and invent techniques of investigation for studying moral values. Studies have been conducted on school teachers, school and college students on different ways of inculcating values (Longstreth, 1971), methods (Proefreidts, 1971), academic and social cultural influences on the development of values (Lewis, 1984), implications of moral education (Sarangi, 1994) and inculcation of different values (Kamnong Keams, 1984). The findings reveal that teachers differed in the ways of inculcation of values; indoctrination, conditioning and affective approaches are the means to inculcate values, school environment influences on the development of moral and religious values. Thompson and Carr (1966) found that students' value systems were of pre-high school period and importance of various values are relatively stray from one age to the next during adolescence (Beech and Schoeppes, 1974).

## TEACHING STRATEGIES AND TEACHERS

A number of teaching strategies were used to teach values among students and teachers. These are Direct Moral Instruction (Seetharamu 1974), Value Clarification Strategies (Singh and Singh 1986), Critical Inquiry Approach (Bhagia 1986), Jurisprudential Inquiry Model (St. Anns College of Education Mangalore), and Value Discussion Model (Dhand et.al. 1993). The findings indicate that these strategies are superior than traditional method of teaching values and improving the moral judgment of the students. Seetharam (1987) found positive impact of moral education course for teachers in improvement in the moral values of teachers. On the other hand, DePetro (1975), Pracejus (1974) and Sklare (1975) found that there was no significant, systematic, demonstrated impact on the students' values by the Value Clarification Strategies.

There are more than 25 studies reported under the theme "Teachers and values". There are studies, which have been conducted on teachers which include both men and women, junior and senior teachers, teacher trainees, and effective and non-effective teachers. Findings reveal that teachers obtain higher scores on political, economic and theoretical values than the religious and social values (Dixit and Sharma

1969, Kakkar 1971, Kaul and Kirpal 1973, Kulshrestha 1972, Kumar and Mutha 1985, Kumari 1981, Pal 1969, Patel 1979, and Roychaudhury 1958). Sinha (1972) reported that younger teachers preferred social values more; and less preference is given to religious, critical and political values. On the age of the teachers, it was found that age influences the religious and political values (Kulshrestha 1972 and Singh 1974). Pachaury's (1973) study, specially on science teachers, indicated that science teachers are creative, objective and open-minded. Findings of cross-cultural and comparative studies reveal that teachers have their own pattern of values (Gage et.al. 1967). They differ on the economic, aesthetic, political and theoretical values (Nelson 1971), age of teachers influences on their value orientation; older the teachers more traditional they are as compared to younger teachers. Teachers felt that values are relative rather than absolute. They just did not believe in planning Value education, and preferred to use examples and discussions for handling values.

## VALUE PREFERENCES

Studies are also reported on students' value preferences. Theoretical values were found to be high among students (Allport et.al. 1960 and Harris 1934) which were followed by social, economic and political values (Agnes 1987, Alavandar 1983, Desai 1974, Reddy et.al 1966, Sandhya 1999 and Singh and Singh 1984). There are studies based on the values imparted by Sri Sathya Sai Baba on students who are studying in Sri Sathya Sai Schools (Nanda 1996, Ramachandran 1988, Sambhi 1989 and Shanthi 1992). It was found in all the studies that children were influenced by the value education imparted in these schools and are aware of human values as stressed by Sri Sathya Sai Baba.

Studies are reported on value patterns of college students (Kundu and Kundu 1983), relation between lower and upper socio-economic class of students on value patterns (Kareem and Kumar 1981, Kumar and Mutha 1986), value patterns among boys and girls (Bhushan and Ahuja 1978,

Chakraborthy and Kundu 1981). Research studies report that girls and boys had differences in order of values. High socio-economic group expressed concern for ambitions, logical and broadminded values. There is significant relation between lower and upper socio-economic class of students. Adiseshaiah (1976) found high scores on social values like justice, courtesy, loyalty and conformity than personal values like truthfulness, self-respect, morality and moderation.

Personal and social factors are also important variables in the growth of moral judgment of individuals. Findings indicate that the most important factor in the moral judgment is the type of schools. Schools provide a wide range of experiences which influence the values. Hartshorne (1928), Piaget (1932), Sinha and Varma (1972) concluded that students who were studying in private institutions have higher academic environment and better judgment.

Research work outside India by Bull (1969), Kay (1968), Kohlberg (1966), and Sears et.al (1957) studied the social class differences in child rearing practices that affect children's moral development. Findings suggest that children who belong to higher social status families show greater maturity in moral judgments than those from lower social class background.

## CONCLUSION

It would be evident from the foregone review that research in value education has covered a large number of issues, particularly, the value development and preferences through age, relationship between value development and a host of socio-economic variables, institution related variables like organizational climate, teacher attributes etc. Research has also covered value related issues among professional course programmes like medicine, engineering, teacher education etc. But majority of the studies, available internationally and through Indian sources are on value education at the school level. There are, in fact, very few studies on value education and development, value clarification and value consolidation among college youth. There is a need to carry out interdisciplinary studies on value development in Indian youth. Nevertheless, studies confirm positive impact of organized value education programmes in schools and colleges on students and teachers.

## REFERENCES

Adhikari, G.S and Hasnain, H. (1982), A Study of Values Among Professional Trainees, *Perspectives in Psychological Researches,* 15 (1),

Adiseshaiah, W.T.V., (1976), Personal and Social Values, *New Frontiers in Education,* 6(3).

Agnes, D. (1987), Value Perception of Post-Graduate Students of Nagarkoil Town, Unpublished M.Phil, Dissertation, Madurai Kamaraj University.

Alavandar, R. (1983), Values of Annamalai University Students, Unpublished M.Ed. Dissertation, Annamalai University.

Allport, G.W., Vernon, P.E. and Lindzey, G. (1960), Study of Values, *Manual for the Study of Values*, Boston: Houghton Mifflin Co.

Annamma, A.D., (1984), Values, Aspirations and Adjustment of College Students in Kerala, Unpublished Ph.D. Thesis, Psychology, Kerala University.

Beech, R.P. and Schoeppe, A. (1974), Development of Value Systems in Adolescents, *Developmental Psychology,* Vol. 10, pp. 644-656.

Bettleheim, B. (1969), *The Children of the Dream.* Thames and Hudson.

Bhagia, Sushma (1986), Approaches to Value-Oriented Education, *in* Ruhela, S.P. (Ed.) *Human Values and Education*, New Delhi: Sterling Publishers.

Bhat, R. K. (1996), Towards A Value Based Education System, *University News.* October 21.

Bhushan, A. and Ahuja, M., (1978), Value Systems and Value Patterns Among Indian Adolescents Belonging to Different Sociometric Levels, *Social Sciences Research Journal,* 3(2).

Bhushan, Anand and Ahuja, Malvinder (1977), Values as a Function of Population Density and Mode of Community Relationships in Rural Urban Areas, *Avagahana,* 1(2), October.

Bull, Norman,J. (1969), *Moral Education*, London: Routledge and Kegan Paul

Chakraborthy, P.K. and Kundu, R.K. (1981), Age, Sex and Type of Education as the Concomitants of Value Pattern, *Journal of Psychological Research*, 25(2).

Chaudhari, U.S., (1974), A Comparative Study of Values Reflected in

National and State Level Hindi Text Books, Unpublished M.Ed. Dissertation, University of Indore.

——— (1976), An Evaluation of Nationalised Hindi Text Books of Madhya Pradesh, Unpublished Ph.D. Thesis, University of Indore.

Depetro, H. (1975), Effects of Utilising Value Clarification Strategies on the Self-Esteem of Secondary School Students, *Review of Educational Research.* 48(3).

Desai, Arvind, N.A. (1974), A Comparative Study of Selected Attitudes, Values and Personality Characteristics of Rural, Urban and Overseas Students, *Journal of Education and Psychology,* 32(1).

Dhand, Harry., Sansanwal, D.N. and Singh, A.K. (1993), Value Clarification of Undergraduate Students - A Cross Cultural Study, *Indian Educational Review,* April-July-October.

Dixit, R.C. and Sharma Deo Dutt, (1969), Incorporation by Students of Teachers Values: A Study of the Student - Teachers Relationship, *Indian Educational Research,* 4(2).

Floresca, Cawagas, Virginia, (1988), Evaluating Values Education Programmes: Concepts and Principles. *WCCI Forum,* 2(1).

Gage, N.L. (1967), *Handbook of Research on Teaching.* Chicago: McNally and Co.

Gandhi, K.L. (1993), *Value Education: A Study of Public Opinion,* New Delhi: Gyan Publishing House.

Garg, R.R. (1983), Children's Conception of Parental Disciplinary Practice and its Relation to the Development of Personality Needs, Unpublished Ph.D. Thesis, Agra University.

Gee, Helen, H., (1959), *Selection and Educational Differentiation,* Report of a Conference, May 25-28. Berkley Field Service Centre and Centre for the Study of Higher Education.

Gordon, L.V. and Mensh, I.N. (1962), Values of Medical School Students at Different Levels of Training", *Journal of Educational Psychology,* Vol. 53.

Government of Karnataka, (1987), *Education in Human Values* (Text Book-cum-Reference Book), Mysore Government Text Book Press.

Haq, E. (1973), Educational and Political Modernisation: An Analysis of School Text Books in Delhi", *NIE Journal,* 7(5).

Harris, D. (1934), Group Differences in the Values within a University", *Journal of Abnormal and Social Psychology,* Vol. 29.

Hartshorne, H. and May, M.A., (1928), *Studies in the Nature of Characteristics in Deception.* New York, MacMillan.

Hodgkinson, C. (1971), Organisational Influence on Value Systems, *Educational Administration Quarterly,* Vol. 7.

Inlaw, Gail M., (1972), *Values in Transition: A Handbook.* New York: John Wiley and Sons, Inc.

Joshi, Kireet, (1986), *Syllabus of Value Oriented Education*, New Delhi: NCERT.

Joshi, Jyothi, and Leena, J. Pooranchand. (1994), Moral Values among Adolescents Belonging to Joint and Nuclear Families, *Journal of Indian Education*, 19(4-5).

Kakkar, S.B., (1971), Values Scores of Teacher Trainees and College Teachers, *Indian Journal of Applied Psychology*. Vol. 8.

Kamnong Keam, Pojanne, (1984), A Proposed Programme of Moral Value Teaching for the Equivalence of Twelth Grades in Secondary Schools in Bangkok, Unpublished Ed.D. Dissertation, Indiana University.

Kareem, A.B. and V.S.R. Vijayakumar. (1981), Value Orientation of College Students in Relation to Socio-Economic Stratification, *Journal of Psychological Research*, 25(1).

Karn, H.W., (1952), Differences in Values among Engineering Students, *Educational and Psychological Measurement,* Vol. 12.

Kaul, G.N. and Prem Kirpal, (1973), *Values and Education in Independent India*. Ambala Cantt: The Associated Publishers.

Kay, William, (1968), *Moral Development*, London: Allen and Unwin Ltd.

Khare, P.G., (1968), Occupational Differences in Life Values, *Indian Psychological Review*, Vol. 4.

Kohlberg, L. (1978), The Cognitive Development Approach to Moral Education, In Schard, P. (ed), *Readings in Moral Education*, Minneapolis, Winston Press.

Kulshreshta. (1972), An Impact of Teachers' Training on Democratic Values, *Haryana Journal of Education*, Chandigarh.

Kumar, P. and Mutha, D.(1985), Teacher Effectiveness as Related with Value Orientations at Secondary Level Teaching. *Journal of Education and Psychology*, 43(1).

Kumari, P. (1981), Personality Needs Moral Judgment and Value Patterns of Secondary Schools Teachers: A Critical Analysis", Unpublished Ph.D. Thesis, Gorakhpur University.

Kundu, R. and Kundu, N., (1983), The Domain of Value Assessment Techniques - A Review, *Bombay Psychologist*, 5(1).

Lerner, E., (1937), *Constraint Areas and Moral Judgement in Children*. Banta: Manasha-Wisconsin.

Lewis, J. T. (1984), Academic and Socio-cultural Influences on Development of Values Among Students in Two Year Colleges, D.Ed. Dissertation, .....

Lobo, Stella Anne Sr. (1983), A Study of Values Manifested in Principals with Reference to Institutional Efficiency, Unpublished *Ph.D. Thesis,* M.S. University of Baroda.

Longstreth, L.E. (1971), Values in the Social Studies Implicit, Explicit or Ignored, *Social Education*, 35(4).

MacKinnon, D.W. (1960), What do we Mean by Talent and How do we Test for it?" *The Search for Talent, College Entrance Examination Board*, New York, Vol. 7.

Mittal, V.K., (1982), A Comparative Study of Attitudes of Primary School Students, *Indian Psychological Abstracts*, 20(4).

Morris, C.(1956), Varieties of Human Value, Chicago: University of Chicago Press.

Nanda, R.T. (1996), A Study of Contemporary Approaches to Value Education and Their Effectiveness in Promoting Human Values, New Delhi: Institute of Advanced Studies, Jamia Millia Islamia.

NCERT, (1985), *National Curriculum for Primary and Secondary Education: A Framework*. New Delhi.

NCERT, (1987), Resource Material Part-1 (General). *National Scheme of Inservice Training of School Teachers*. New Delhi: NCERT.

Nelson, E.Anita., (1971), Value Patterns of Physical Educators in Colleges and Universities of the USA, *Dissertations Abstract*, 31A(10).

Pachauri, A.C. and Varma, M., (1981), Effects of Intensities of Punishment on Moral Judgement in Children. University of Alllahabad, Allahabad.

Pachaury, A.C., (1973), The Ideal and Real Image of High School Pupils, *The Progress of Education*, 47(12).

Pal, S.K., (1969), *Personality Study of Engineering, Law, Medical and Teacher Training of Students*. Allahabad: United Publishers.

Patel, C.K., (1979), A Study of the Prevalent Value System of the Secondary Teachers of the High Schools of South Gujarat, Unpublished Ph.D. Thesis, South Gujarat University.

Piaget, Jean, (1932), *The Moral Judgment of the Child*, London: Routledge and Keagan Paul.

Pillai, J.K. (1979), *Affective Tone in the Primary Classroom*, Madurai: Madurai Kamaraj University.

Pillai, N.T., (1976), An Analytical Study of the Religious Values Imbedded in the Prescribed Tamil and English Text Books for Standard IX in Tamil Nadu, Unpublished M.Ed. Dissertation, Annamalai, University.

Pracejus, E.(1974),The Effect of Value Clarification on Reading Comprehension, *Review of Educational Research*. 48(3).

Prince, R., (1957), Individual Values and Administrative Effectiveness, *Administrator's Note Book*, Vol. 6.

Proefreidt, W.A.(1971), Teaching Value Issues: The Challenge to Rationality, *Dissertations Abstract*. 31(10).

Rajgopal, T. (1989), Identification of values in XII Standard Tamil Textbooks and Value Orientation of XII Standard Students, Unpublished M. Phil. Dissertation, Alagappa University

Rama Rao K.(1986), *Moral Education: A Practical Approach*, Mysore: Ramakrishna Institute of Moral and Spiritual Education.

Rao, R.B., (1986), A Study of Inter-relationship of Values, Adjustment and Teaching Attitude of Pupil-Teachers at Various Levels of Socio-Economic Status, Unpublished Ph.D. Thesis, Avadh University.

Rathnakumari, B.(1987), Studies in Human Values of High School Students in Different Types of Schools of Andhra Pradesh in relation to Their Socio-Economic Status and Mass Media Exposure, Unpublished Ph.D. Thesis, Osmania University, Hyderabad.

Reddy Ravindar, A. and Reddy, Gopal, G. (1992), A Thought for Value Oriented Education, *Journal of Indian Education*, September.

Reddy, K.M. and Parameshwaran, E.G. (1966), Some Factors Influencing the Value Patterns of College Students, *Researches Bulletin,* Department of Psychology, Osmania University, Vol. 2.

Roe, Anne. (1956), *The Psychology of Occupations*. New York: John Wiley and Sons, Inc.

Roy Choudhury, ..... (1958), Allport-Vernon Study of Values in Indian Situations, *The Indian Psychological Bulletin*, 4(1).

Roy, D.K.(1980), A Study of Some Factors and Processes involved in the Development of Values. Unpublished Ph.D. Thesis, Education, Kalyani University

Ruhela, S.P. (Ed.). (1986), *Human Values and Education*. New Delhi: Sterling Publishers.

Sahasrabuddhe, S.A. (1977), Institutional Climate as a Function of Pupil Control Ideology and Student Indiscipline, Unpublished Ph.D. Thesis, M.S. University of Baroda

Sambhi, P.(1989), A Study of the Value Patterns and Some Personality Variables of the Students Studying in Three Institutions - Sri Sathya Sai Higher Secondary School, Missionary School and Central School in Andhra Pradesh, Unpublished Ph.D. Thesis, University of Himachal Pradesh.

Sandhya, N.(1999), An Evaluative Study of Value Education Provided at the S.S.L.C. Level in Mysore District, Unpublished Ph.D. Thesis, University of Mysore.

Sarangi, R.(1994), *Moral Education in Schools: Bases and Implications*. New Delhi: Deep and Deep Publications.

Seetharam, A.R. (1990), An Evaluative Study of the Objectives, Content and Methodology of Direct Moral Education Followed in the

Secondary Schools of Karnataka State, Unpublished Ph.D. Thesis, Mysore University

Seetharamu, A.S. (1974), An Experimental Study of the Problem of Moral Instruction in Upper Primary Schools, Unpublished Ph.D. Thesis, Mysore University.

Seshadri. C., Khader, M.A., and Adhya. G.L., (1992), *Education in Values: A Source Book*. New Delhi: NCERT.

Shakeela, Begum, S. and Haffeez, A. (1964), A Study of Individual and Social Values, *Indian Journal of Psychology*, Vol. 39.

Shakeela, Begum. (1959), A Study of Values and Group Identification, Unpublished M.A. Dissertation, Mysore University.

Sharma, A. P., (1995), Values are Permeated, *University News*, December 11.

Sharma, S. (1975), The Study of Relationship between Socio-Economic Status and Personality Characterestics, Values and Intelligence of Female College students, Unpublished Ph.D. Thesis, Patna University, Patna.

Singh, H.L. (1974), Measurement of Teacher Values and their Relationship with Teacher Attitudes and Job Satisfaction, Unpublished D. Phil. Thesis, Banaras Hindu University.

Singh, L.C. and Singh, P. (1986), Effectiveness of Value Clarification Strategies in Value Orientation of B.Ed. Students, Report of ERIC Funded Research Project, New Delhi: NCERT.

Singh, Rampal, (1974), Teacher Behaviour as Determinant of Pupil Behaviour and Achievement, *Journal of Educational Research and Extension,* 10(4).

Sinha, D., (1972), *The Mughal Syndrome: A Psychological Study of International Differences*. Bombay, Tata McGraw-Hill Publication.

———(1979), The Young and the Old: Ambiguity of Role-Models and Values among Indian Youth, In Kakar, Sudhir (Ed.) *Identity and Adulthood,* Delhi: Oxford University Press.

Sinha, D. and Varma, M., (1972), Knowledge of Moral Values in Children: *Psychological Studies,*17(1)

Sklare, G., (1975), The Effects of Value Clarification Process upon the Values, Clarity of Values and Dogmatism of High School Juniors and Seniors, *Review of Educational Research*, 48(3).

Subramanyam, K. (1990), *Value Education (Socio-Spiritual).* Madurai: Ramana Publications.

Suls, J., Gutkin, D. and Kalle, Robert, J. (1979), The Role of Intention, Damage and Social Consequences in Moral Judgement of Children, *Child Development*, Vol. 50.

Susheela, B.S. (1977), Study of Secularism as Reflected in the Social Studies (Part-1) Text Books prescribed for Secondary Schools in

Karnataka State, Unpublished M.Ed. Dissertation, Mysore Unviersity.

Thomson, Orville, E. and Carr, S.G. (1966), *Values of High School Students*. California: The University of California.

Usha Sri, V. (1995), Restructuring Teacher Education for Value Orientation, *Journal of Higher Education*. 16(4), pp. 601-609.

———(1993), An Evaluation of Value Education Provided at the Secondary Stage of Education in Tamil Nadu, Unpublished Ph.D. Thesis, Annamalai University.

Venkataiah, N. and Sandhya, N. (2002), *Research in Value Education*, New Delhi: APH.

Varma Meera. (1971), Moral Judgement Test for Children, National Psychological Corporation, Agra.

Verma, B.P. and Gupta, C.K. (1990), Effect of Home Environment on Cognitive Abilities of Pre-adolescent Children, *Indian Psychological Review*, 35(11-12).

Wellman, H. M. Craig, L. and Somarville and Susane, (1979), The Early Development of Moral Crisis, *Child Development*, 50-3.

White, T.R. (1968), A Study of the Values and Attitudes of Distributive Education-Teacher Coordinators as Compared to Two Groups of Potential Teacher Coordinators, *Dissertation Abstracts International*, 30(2), July.

# Section II
# VALUE SYMPOSIA

# Value Education for the Global Society

KARAN SINGH

## INTRODUCTION

Contemporary Indian society is passing through a major crisis, a crisis of values in life. We are witnessing a steady erosion of certain traditional values which have sustained the Indian society down through the corridors of time. That seems to be now reversed, inverted or distorted. For example, our national motto *Satyameva Jayatey nanritam* taken from the *Mundakopanishad* means "Truth alone triumphs, not falsehood". And yet, what is actually happening is *nanritam jayate natu satyam*. We are sinking in a morass of nepotism and corruption. Similarly, *Vasudhaiva Kutumbakam,* our great motto inscribed on the first gate of the Parliament House means that "The world is a family" but has become the *Kutumba eva Vasudha*, the family alone is the world. In other words, there is no broader commitment to human values.

We have this long tradition of non-violence inspired by *Ahimsâ Paramodharma*. There is *Shanti Paath* in the Vedas; the *Shanti Parva* in the *Mahabharata*. We have Lord Buddha, Lord Mahavir, Emperor Ashoka, Mahatma Gandhi. And yet we find today *Himsa Paramokarma*, violence spreads at slightest provocation. If there is an altercation between two boys over a cricket ball or a football, and if they happen to belong to two communities or different castes, the whole Mohalla or village goes up in flames. The Vedas pronounced *Bahujana Sukhâya Bahujana Hitâya cha,* encouraging us to work for the welfare of the many, for the happiness of many.

What we find is the reverse; it has become *Swajan Hitaya, Swajan Sukhaya cha*—working only for our narrow personal ends. Indeed, there is a major crisis of values in our contemporary Indian society.

The state of degeneration is all pervasive. We should not hold our youth responsible. After all, it is our generation that has imparted to them the education they have. Also, this is not peculiarly an Indian phenomenon. The wave of modernization is sweeping across the world, almost a typhoon of change. Most traditional societies are facing this sort of crisis. Even in the western societies, with all their liberalism and all their modernism, they also are feeling the brunt of these changes. Hence, in a way, it is a universal phenomenon.

## VALUE TRANSMISSION AMONG YOUTH

There are two ways in which values are transmitted to the youth. One is through education. Our educational system, unfortunately, has become devoid of value orientation. It certainly is intellectually richer and academically broader than it was in our days. Many more subjects are taught now in the schools and colleges; we never heard of computers when we were students. Our youth today know much more than we did; although they read much less than we read. But that is another issue. Value orientation in education is missing.

The second way which the Bhagawadgita says is the example of leaders. The way in which leaders of a society behave, people will follow. But now who are the leaders of society? *Shreshthas* are no longer the *Rishis* and the *Munis*. The leaders of the society are the politicians, and the civil servants; and the way a large number of politicians and bureaucrats behave is too obvious to need any comment. Therefore, both the methodologies whereby value inculcation takes place, have weakened greatly, and it is a fact that value orientation has decreased considerably. But we cannot place all the blame on the youth.

## ROLE OF VALUES IN LIFE

The role of values in our life is very central. If life is to be really worthwhile, irrespective of one's occupation and standing, there has to be a certain value orientation—some family values, values towards society, inner spiritual values, some movement towards love, compassion and helpfulness. A life devoid of values would be very arid, would actually be a life wasted. Values, of course, are intangible. It is difficult to prescribe what value is. Values are melded in our consciousness. According to our great seers, Sri Aurobindo and Swami Vivekananda, if you imbibe certain value orientation, life becomes more meaningful. If the value orientation is positive, then life becomes certainly more worthwhile. So, the role of values in daily life is very real.

This is not simply a philosophical or far off spiritual idea. Whatever one may be doing or whatever the situation of each person's life may be, if those values are transluscent in our consciousness, it will definitely enrich their life. To deny people the opportunity of value orientation is to inflict upon them an entirely unjustified deprivation. They have to be exposed to certain value orientations. How much each individual is able to interiorize them and use them in their own life would of course vary from person to person. But certainly there should be some atmosphere of value orientation in one's life; that helps considerably.

## WHAT VALUES?

There are a variety of values—family value—relations with each other, societal values—cooperation and team work and getting along together, environmental values. But let me take up only the case of Interfaith values, national values and global values.

There are socially desirable values. For example, punctuality is a socially desirable value. It does not belong to any particular religion. It is not a religious value. Or cleanliness, or respect for elders, or helpfulness, or compassion, or love, you can call them universal values.One does not have to be religious to adopt these values. For example in the West, they are meticulously punctual. They may not be religious, but they recognize the importance of time.

In a country like ours, millions of people live in poverty, millions of children go to bed without one square meal everyday; millions of people who get drenched in the monsoons, shiver in the winter, and burn in the summer without a proper place to stay. We are oases of affluence in a vast ocean of poverty in the world. We must never forget that. Particularly those of us who have been born in fortunate circumstances should never forget our debt to society. So, these are what can be termed broadly under the rubric of socially desirable values. Education for Interfaith values, education for environmental values, education for socially desirable values taken together represent education for the global society.

### *Inter-faith Values*

Inter-faith values involve abstracting from the great religions of the world those values which are common. If we look at the deeper moral and spiritual values, we will find a great deal in common. Theologically, there are tremendous differences between the religions. But, should we come down actually to moral values, the way human being should treat each other, and particularly the spiritual values, which the Muslim Sufis like Maulana Jalaluddin Rumi, or the Christian mystics like Meister Eckhart, St John on the Cross and St Teresa of Avila, or the great seers of the Upanishads, the sayings of the Buddha and so on, there is a lot in common. These interfaith values have to be talked about to our youth, because we are essentially a pluralistic society.

We have at least nine of the world's major religions flourishing in India—four were born here, five came from the West Asia. If we do not give any religious education at all, the result is that children will go by the stereo-types. These are very often negative. Hence what we need to do is to try and encourage the educational system to build the awareness of the common elements in different religions.

There have been books published on this in the U.K.; the Temple of Understanding has also published some useful material on inter-faith values.

Talking about secularism as such is not enough, because secularism could also imply an anti-religious attitude, whereas inter-faith values involves a pro-religious, harmonious attitude *Ekam sad viprâh bahudhâ vadanti*, attitude. This is a new element and this needs to be reflected in education.

India is par excellence a land of religion. Swami Vivekananda once said, 'every nation has a genius, and India's genius is religion'. Our people are religious, whether they are Hindus or Buddhists, Jains or Sikhs, Parsis or Muslims. Therefore, religion is not something that can be left to the fundamentalist elements in each religion. We should try and bring about Inter-faith understanding and this, in my view, is a very important factor in much of our value education.

Secularism tends to become sterile if it is negative secularism devoid of any religion. Then every religion is equally redundant, equally absurd. Why respect any religion? Indian secularism is not equal neglect of all religions, it is equal respect for all religions—*sarva dharma samabhâva*. This is an important point and we need to convey it to our youth.

### National Values

Let us take the case of national values—values for national integration. Fundamental Duties as enshrined in the Indian Constitution are important. As you know, there is a chapter in the Constitution of Fundamental Duties. Those ten duties represent a set of values, a truly secular viewpoint. The Government of India appointed a committee on reviewing implementation of these fundamental duties headed by Justice J.S. Verma, of which I was a member. The Committee made an important analysis of the educational scenario vis-à-vis the Fundamental Duties; and also meaningful recommendations that can have significant bearing on developing a programme on value education among the youth of India.

### *Global Values*

We have to inculcate global values. Let us not forget, we are in a new world in a new millennium. We can never stop only with India. The Indian mind is a creative mind—*Aâ no bhadrâh kritavo yantu vishwatah*—Let noble thoughts come to us from every side. We have looked upon ourselves as world citizens—*swadesho bhuvanadwayam* therefore, we cannot accept a narrow chauvinistic nationalism that might have been acceptable at one stage in the fight against the British in India. Today we are part of an emerging global society. We are one-sixth of the humanity; we occupy a central position —geographically, demographically and philosophically.

India can perhaps become a bridge between the East and the West, and between the various religious traditions. Therefore we have to accept and inculcate global values, values for a global society. My contribution as member of the UNESCO's International Commission for Education in the Twenty-first Century is on this issue itself—global values for a global society.

We have to pioneer and propagate a holistic educational philosophy based upon the following premises:

- that the planet we inhabit and of which we all citizens— planet earth— is a single, leaving, all sitting entity; that human race in the final analysis is an interlocking, extended family – *Vasudhaiba Kutambakam* as the Veda has it; and that differences of race and religion, nationality and ideology, sex and sexual preference, economic and social status— though significant in themselves—must be viewed in the broader context of global unity;
- that the ecology of planet earth has to be preserved from mindless destruction and ruthless exploitation, an enriched for the welfare of generations yet unborn; and that there should be a more equitable consumption pattern based on limits to growth, not unbridled consumerism;

- that hatred and bigotry, fundamentalism and fanaticism, and grade and jealousy, whether among individuals, groups of nations, are corrosive emotions which must be overcome as removing to the next century; and that love and compassion, caring and charity, and friendship and cooperation are the elements that have to be encouraged as we transit into our new global awareness;
- that the words direct religion is must no longer work against each other for supremacy but cooperate for the welfare of the human race, and that through a continuing and creative interfaith dialogue, the golden thread of spiritual aspiration that binds them together must be strengthened instead of the dogma and exclusivism that divides them;
- that a massive and concerted drive is needed to eradicate the scourge of illiteracy worldwide by the year 2010, with special emphasis on promoting female literacy, particularly in the developing countries;
- that holistic educational must acknowledge the multiple dimensions of human personality—physical, intellectual, aesthetic, emotional and spiritual—thus moving towards the perennial dream of an integrated individual living on a harmonious planet;"

## HOW SHOULD VALUES BE INCULCATED?

Such questions be better dealt by experts in instructional science and technology. I do not think we can have separate classes for value education. We can perhaps have some Interfaith prayers or meditation classes, but more importantly, what has to be done is to mould and integrate these values in some way into the curriculum. How this is done depends on the subjects. While it may be relatively easier to integrate education in human values in subjects like humanities and social sciences, how would one do that while teaching physics or chemistry? What is needed is perhaps to have these values as an additional input into the whole system. That is the only way we can do it. This is something very technical.

### *Role of Teachers*

The student comes into contact with the teachers only during the class. How will they know what the teacher does in his or her private life? What does the teacher do in the spare time, how much s/he studies, and so on. We are talking about tens of thousands of teachers (nearly 3,50,000 teachers in higher education) around us in the country. College and university teachers cannot really all be expected, to be paragons of scholarships or of virtue. This is unrealistic.

Obviously, teachers have to show their competence, but competence in their subject does not necessarily involve value education. Good teachers will be competent in their subjects. We may have a very noble person who is a lousy teacher; and we may have a very good teacher who is not a very nice person. Should we ask for paragons of virtues in all teachers, we would possibly mix and confuse two different issues. Academic excellence and pedagogic ability is one thing, human values is another. There may not be a direct co-relation between the two. Also, the relationships between the teachers and students at the college stage is different. By then, the students are moving into a broader society. They are exposed to a whole range of other influences. This, however, does not exclude teachers from being influencing forces on the youth. Obviously, the teacher as a role model will always be preferred; but not prescribed.

While we talk of value education, we recognize the contradictions—contradictions between values that are preached versus values that are practised by the teachers in the colleges and elders in the society. There is no magic that will remove these contradictions overnight. It has a long history. It is something that has been going on for thousands of years, between the teachers and students. Let us not hold value-based behaviour of teachers as the only way of value education. For example in distance education, the teacher is not visible, s/he is not there at all. Does that mean there can be no value education in open and distance education? We must overcome our romantic concepts of value education. There is a massive change in the paradigm. Personal contact between the teacher and the student is steadily reducing in modern education. Certainly we need good teachers, noble teachers, teachers who are punctual, competent and well prepared, But should we pin our value education programme upon the assumption that we would have paragons of virtues in teachers, we may not achieve our goals. We have to restructure our curriculum to build certain value orientation.

So far value education has not been looked upon as a major undertaking. If we change our policy and decide to undertake value education as a serious matter, teachers' orientation has to be done as the very first step. Before we press them into value education, they have to be trained. But how do we train them is a big question.

### *Learning Material*

Learning Material is the key to a lot of that we can do. It has tremendous potential. New material needs to be developed; existing materials have to be collected and distributed. A lot has been already done, there are lots of material on value education. The Bharatiya Vidya Bhavan, the Sathya Sai Institute of Higher Learning, the Indian Council for Philosophical Research and others have brought out rich material on value education. NCERT has brought out important volumes on value education. NIEPA has brought out a bibliography. We need to develop a comprehensive information system on such material and disseminate it.

## STRUCTURAL CHANGES

Already the curriculum is heavy. Where do we have the time? Some structural change is really required in the curricula and methodology of teaching. This is still an open issue and needs greater attention.

One of the possible ideas is the integration of vocational activities and value orientation. If the students can be involved in socially productive activities in their villages, in their towns; for example, if they are involved in cleaning up their mohalla, or go where people are ill and help them; help weaker children in the neighbourhood to learn and do better in schools and colleges, and such other activities, values emerge. If these types of activities can be built into the curriculum, it does not matter whether one studies physics or chemistry or any other subject; all are exposed to the practice of a set of values. Reading up on values is meaningless unless it is actualised or operationalised. Unfortunately, the well-conceived National Service Scheme and Socially Productive Work type of programmes with great potential have fallen by the wayside.

## CONCLUSION

Finally, let me refer to Sri Aurobindo's educational philosophy, particularly integral education that proposes integrated development of the human being. We need to ensure physical development, we need mental sharpness to absorb new knowledge wherever it may come from; we need emotional development and balance; aesthetic sensibility—the capacity to perceive beauty; we need social development 'learning to live together'. Finally we need spiritual balance. In our report to UNESCO, *Learning: The Treasure Within* we mentioned four pillars of learning namely—learning to know, learning to do, learning to be and learning to live together. These cover what Sri Aurobindo said in 'integral yoga'. If value education helps to produce an integrated human being, s/he will be able to perform better, in whatever aspect of life. Society is changing much faster than we realise, and a beginning has to be made.

# Helping Students Ascend the Steps of Value Education

AMLAN DATTA

## INTRODUCTION

Much of human suffering has its roots in what is false within us. From this spreads violence and corruption in the society at large. At the same time, it produces pain and poison in the inner life. False values are supported by an unexamined and blindly adopted view of the purpose of life. We need value education to promote a more correct understanding of how life should be lived and social relations framed.

## TRANSACTING VALUE EDUCATION

Unlike other subjects at the tertiary level, transaction of value education requires a different pedagogy. Value education should rely not so much on lectures as on discussions amongst students guided by the teachers. Such discussions will be more effective if the exchange of ideas takes place around live-situations. The situations may not be exact life-situations, but these must be in large measure life like situations that catch the essence of real-life situations. Such participative methodologies would be more effective because of the relevance of the situations and students' active involvement in learning. If situations are so chosen that a student can find some resemblance with life situations, and can identify himself/herself with the situations, it would be easier to attract the attention of the students. Otherwise, most students will tend to pay little attention to the issue of value education; he/she may perceive it as a merely philosophical question. As a matter of strategy, a teacher may introduce the subject and then pass on to the students for discussion.

In fact, students can be asked to write/document a brief case on a life situation when they come to the class next time. There are enough problems among students. Guided properly, students should be able to write and document some of those problems. The student-author need not identify the situation as his/her own life situation. It should be left to him/her to decide whether he/she wants to identify himself/herself with the situation or not. Nonetheless, the situation chosen for documentation must have relevance and reference to life situations as he/she observes among his peers, his/her family and the society at large. That can be the starting point for the discussion. When the whole group sits together and one of the students presents his/her own case, his/her own responsibility in the case, the teacher may ask other students, "what do you think about it?" It is not really important what the teacher thinks about it; what is important is the students' thinking. The teacher should also, from time to time, present his/her views and then ask students to comment on his/her views. Teacher has to learn to accept differences and not impose himself/herself as superior. It is not necessarily true that younger minds are incapable of reacting to situations meaningfully.

The discussion on such relevant incidences and episodes is likely to generate a lively debate leading to either consensus or difference of views. Either way, it opens the way for a clearer understanding of the situations under review. To be aware of differences of views on certain issues is very important. Hence, whether the students arrive at an identity of views or understand the difference of views, both are indicators of success. To be aware of the difference of views is better than having no awareness and just juggling with views. Importantly, the differences can themselves be systematized and organized to develop an understanding of an ongoing debate. My contention is that to have some understanding of an ongoing debate itself is one kind of consensus—'this is what we understand today about the issue, this is the state of the art of the debate at this moment'.

This methodology can be taken to a further level to sharpen the process of conscientization. After the students have arrived at some kind of consensus, they can produce some kind of a drama[1] to give expression to this consensus. A drama is a very good medium for expressing a debate. Perfect identity of views is not necessary. After all debate is also about life; life debates. Our concern is with the differences of views, rather giving creative and tolerant expression to the difference. It will be useful for a student to take a role in a drama. For, in a drama, a student may not necessarily play the role that synchronizes with his/her views; he/she may play the role representing his/her opponents' views as well. That provides a wonderful opportunity of getting into the habit of seeing the views of the other person[2].

Ordinarily, when we take certain positions, we do not realize that there is something to be said in favour of the opposite position also. There are only a few real-life questions

[1] Editor's Note: Drama workshops or creative drama is known educational practice, though rarely used for nurturing creativity and also developing dramatic skills. Prof. Datta's contention is based on sound educational principles that can simultaneously create conscientization on human values, develop life skills and involve students' in a business of learning that is now known as 'learning organization'.

[2] Editor's Note: Long ago, in early 1980's, I conducted a programme on Positive Leadership for Presidents and secretaries of College Unions in Bhopal. In one of the cognitive reorganization exercises, the participants played a drama where one Union leader played the role of principal, another vice principal and two others as student union leaders. The issue was admission to the college from the list provided by the union leader which was not accepted by the college authorities. Little did I realize that it was a live issue in one of the local colleges and the Union leader involved was playing the role of the college principal—it was all incidental. At the end of the programme, the leader approached me and asked for my advice—how to resolve it. What is important is what he told me—'I understand now that what I am demanding as student union leader, the principal cannot do it. Even if I was at his place, I would not do it'.

where there are not two sides; or, there is not really something to be said from either side. Most life situations do demand certain kind of adjustments of opposing considerations. Most life situations are not so simple that there is no opposing consideration to be reconciled. This method will perhaps help students to understand that whatever views they may hold, they need not assume that the opponent is an enemy. The opponent is not necessarily a deadwood, he/she is also another human being, but being placed in a different position, he/she sees the situation in different light. Let us illustrate this with a simple example.

Earning and spending are supposed to be opposite concepts. But they are really the name of the same game seen from two opposing ends. Whatever one spends becomes income for someone else. When you stand at one end, the event is given one name; if you stand at the other end, it is given another name. Thus income and spending are not really two different things, rather two different names given to the same thing. And what name you give depends upon your position—where are you standing, how you are looking at the issue. This is a very simple illustration, not complicated like many other life situations. However, most significant life situations are like that. What is important is to inculcate in the students this awareness that will not complicate the differences and obliterate undue bitterness in discussing the differences.

## TRAINING OF TEACHERS FOR VALUE EDUCATION

This brings us to the question of training and preparation of the teachers for value education. This is an important question if value education has to be implemented properly. This is directly linked to the issue whether value education should be a separate course or it should be a part of, rather integral component of all the regular courses in the colleges and universities. I am inclined to think that it should start as a separate course. I shall prefer to even set aside the question of integrating value education with all other subjects, for the time being.

To start with, value education should be introduced as a separate course for the simple reason that most teachers are not trained in value education. If it is to be taught in conjunction with all the courses, teachers of all the courses have to learn these methodologies. It will not be a valid assumption that all the teachers know how to do it for their own courses. To begin with, we can have a small number of teachers who can effectively take the responsibility and build this new methodology of transacting value education. Value education cannot be kept as part of all courses for all students since these specially trained teachers do not belong to all the courses. Therefore, to begin with, it will be wiser to start value education as a separate course. After experimenting with the methodology for a few years and with sufficient number of teachers, it can then be gradually integrated in all courses. So, I do not propose even to compare at this moment the desirability of these two different approaches to value education; what should draw our attention is the practicability of these two alternatives.

I started with the idea that teaching of value education will be useless unless it is done with a certain amount of skills and competence; otherwise students will only learn to despise the subject. It is better to start with a few teachers who are good at value education than to cast the net very wide. Therefore, my suggestion would be that we attach sufficient importance to training of teachers, and we consider this as a separate course. The course on value education for teachers may find a place in the B.Ed and M.Ed. syllabus as an optional subject. Among other things, it should include relations on comparative religion, ethics and reason, social psychology and some selected areas of mental sickness. It should also draw attention to peace research and environmental studies. Along with these, there should be an extended discussion on methods of imparting value education to students as already suggested.

We certainly do not throw away the idea that value education can be taught integrally with other subjects. Obviously, it can be taught with reference to history and so many other subjects. In fact, it can be taught in connection with almost all subjects, although more effectively in some subjects than with certain others. It will be easier to teach it in connection with botany or zoology than in connection with mathematics. Nature is a great teacher just as the mother is to the child. So it is simpler and more appropriate to start with things that are close to nature before one as scales to greater heights.

One simple way to make the course on values attracted will be to give the students a certificate for attending the course and reward those who show good results. But these are simply material incentives. The reward to students should be made on the basis of some kind of confluence of different methods of assessments. The teachers will make their own assessment. There should also be peer assessment — that is assessment of student by students themselves. These different groups can sit together to arrive at a consensus about the assessment. But a consensus is not essential, only it is useful to try to reach agreement. It must be explained to the students that this method of rewards is not really perfect. The fact that some students are rewarded and some students are not does not present the result of a perfect methodology. It represents partly their own judgment at the moment, and partly the teachers' judgment. The assessment represents the current state of affairs; it cannot be taken as judgment for all time to come. Human beings are dynamic, a static judgment may not be appropriate. Important issue is the temporality of the judgment and assessment. They must know that judgment at some other time may be different, as much as the teacher may also change his/her judgment at some other point of time.

## IDENTIFICATION OF VALUES

The practical side of the issue, rather the basic question is how to identify values. All human beings, students in the instant case, are goal seeking animals. So the first question is selecting a goal. Human being, in order to organize his/

her energy properly, has to have some idea of his goal; otherwise he cannot organize himself properly. Normally, a human being is endowed by nature with a certain store of energy and he/she has also a range of desires; often conflicting desires. With a limited store of energy and so many conflicting desires, it is difficult, if not impossible, to organize and channelize enough energy in a particular direction. We lay waste our powers unless we can set up a goal.

At a certain stage, we may also realize that that the goal we have chosen for ourselves does not really correspond to our deeper aspirations. This happens quite often. For instance, a student decides that he must choose a subject so that he may get a good job. So, a common question is how should a student choose the subjects of his/her study. When a student comes to me and asks my suggestion, they expect me to recommend economics; or a subject that has demand in the market. My normal response is "every subject is good. Question is which subject you are good at? Which subject you are good at, at this stage? And, once you know which subject you are good at and/ you are interested in it is more likely that you do well in that subject. Every subject is good if you do well in that subject. If you choose a wrong subject, a subject that does not correspond to your real talent and interest, you may force yourself to study it and you may not do very badly either. For, if you are intelligent, you can really do reasonably well in any subject. But for the rest of your life, you will be stuck to an area that does not interest you".

Values exist at different levels. The illustration, I gave above, is at a practical level. Metaphorically, there are some stars that give light, and there are some others that borrow light. Similarly, there are derived values, derived from some higher values. Whether a student chooses music or painting or biological sciences, they derive their values from some other higher values. Such higher or ultimate values are the destination; others are really intermediate stations deriving their energy from some other sources.

There is a distinction between ultimate values and instrumental values. As a matter of fact, the same value, or a word signifying that value can have several levels of meaning and significance. Within advocate a value because of the undesirable outward consequences of rejecting it off, again, on account of the positive worth of the inward experience of accepting it. For instance, we can argue against violence pointing out the destruction of material goods that follows the use of violence, particularly in the present stage of high technology. But we can also value nonviolence because of the state of inner peace and freedom that it can achieve by purging our mind of hatred. When one chooses a subject like music, the real question is whether one chooses to learn music just for entertainment or for some higher purpose – 'to lift the heart to a higher level'. For example, court music is often for entertainment, but devotional music is primarily to lift the heart to higher level. Folk music is used in large number of occasions for inspirational purposes. Let us take another example. A young student decides to study medicine and become a doctor. At the medical college, teachers teach him/her certain skills; the college, as such does not teach values. Nonetheless, values are very important for a medical doctor to practice his/her skills. The same set of skills can be used either for advancing personal earning or saving other people's lives. So, it is one thing to be a doctor and learn certain skills, it is yet another thing to practise these skills in the spirit of service.

The spirit of service comes from the ultimate values, skills are at a different level of instrumental values. What is true for doctors is true for all others. It is true for teachers. A teacher may know certain methodologies, but may not necessarily use those for the benefit of his/her students. It is a different thing to learn to love both students and the subject of specialization. That is why and how values are related to life situations. When we say we choose our goals — should one study economics or engineering, these are really goals of the second order.

For any subject that one chooses, there will be a question of relating it to some values. Thus selection of goals gets inspired by certain ultimate values. Discussion on choice of goals must include individual concern—the development and unfoldment of his/her personality. Every person cannot be developed in the same way. Some unfold themselves best through study of physics; others through study of social sciences; yet others who may be through study of fine arts. Hence, choice of goals (subjects, in this example) must be inspired by the understanding of deeper aspirations guided by ultimate values. Further, the unfoldment of self (personality) must be related to the society. After all, society is the essential basis that the individual takes his stand on; he/she cannot become a full human being without the support of society.

## CONCLUSION

I am deeply impressed with what a great philosopher said about man—'man is not man unless social, but he (she) is not much above the brute, if only social'. People with their gregarious instincts, in their own way, are social; they are also useful, but not fully human. To be fully human, they have to be 'more than social'. This is true of creative artists and all those with a deep if message.

Beyond the gregariousness, he/she has to have the capacity of retiring within self to ponder over what he/she really wants to communicate. Merely raising slogans and joining a demonstration may not necessarily communicate what one wants to. One must withdraw. This is evident in the lives of most of the great sages and religious teachers. At some stage of their lives, they withdrew themselves, sometimes in the caves and spent years together in isolation meditating. Then they reappeared in the society with their messages.

One must learn to listen to that inner voice, still small voice within oneself. On the other hand, unless one keeps oneself active and engaged in something larger and higher one may not feel fulfilled. Values have to be looked at, understood and assessed from these two opposite poles—the social and intimately personal. Unless it is intimately personal, it is not authentic. Unless it is social, it cannot be effectively communicated and serve the larger society.

Human beings have their existence simultaneously at different levels, viz., body, mind and spirit. These should not be treated as exclusive and self-contained compartments; they are, in fact, closely inter-related. Take, for instance, the role of sports in education of young men and women. At one level, it is concerned with physical fitness. But it also teaches the art of cooperation in a group organized as a team. However, the sporting spirit aims at something even higher. It teaches us that we have to try your best and then accept whatever comes, victory or defeat, with grace and detachment, a real training of the spirit.

Values ennoble our life and our professions. Without the touch of values, the everyday business of life becomes mere commercial activity. Values inspire a higher level of consciousness where one feels related to the larger scheme of consciousness, larger scheme of life and the universe. This sense can come only from the idea of values. If education is about the full development of the human personality, it remains incomplete without value education.

# Value Inculcation among the Youth

UDAI PAREEK

## INTRODUCTION

There is a value crisis in our country. This is primarily because of a conflict in our culture. We talk about concern for larger cause, concern for the cosmos and so on. This value orientation can be called selflessness, and has been greatly admired and appreciated. The people who personalize such values, become role models. The value orientation of selflessness was primarily promoted by the intellectual elite. On the other side, Indian culture has been highly narcissistic, self-seeking, and self-centered. Self-centeredness has been very prominent. We are concerned more about what happens to us, rather than what happens to others. The conflict is between simultaneous existence of selflessness and self-centredness. This conflict has been further accelerated by two factors. We learned from the learned person and teachers. We admired them; they became our role models. These intellectual elite was generally also from the higher social order. Even those who were poor, were proud of their scholarship and values. This pride came from their social position in the society. They valued scholarship more than money.

The current value crisis is caused by self-seeking orientation that has become more prominent in the society. Two factors have contributed to this new situation. The larger masses of people who were so far outside the elite middle class mainstream are now coming into it. The role of the intellectuals is getting eroded. There is a lot of value confusion. Secondly, the influence of the western model of living and urbanization has promoted self-centeredness in a different way. Amongst the western educated urbanites nuclear family is the norm. This was not true in Indian society. India celebrated living in joint family. People used to sacrifice their lives for their father, brother, sister, sons, daughters, etc. It is not so any more. Western value of individualism has taken its toll. Indian narcissistic psyche (self-seeking) mixed with the western model of individualism has produced a different kind of self-centeredness; and this has produced the value crisis that we experience today. The basic nature of contemporary value crisis is in terms of our lack of concern for larger important social issues.

There is another side of the story. Earlier, by and large, a small section of the society (in the mainstream) were concerned with values. Society cherished higher middle-class values. A larger part of the society was out of the mainstream, exploited and neglected. Increasing democratization and social liberalization, resulting into more and more people coming into the mainstream, is also the cause of confusion and value conflict and crisis. The people from lower socio-economic strata brought in a different set of values which clashed with the values of the elite and the middle class. It will take some time before this process settles down.

## VALUE DEVELOPMENT AMONG THE YOUTH

The social transformation, particularly participation of larger and diverse groups and classes of people in public life has significant bearing in value development among the youth.

There are several issues related to the value development among youth. Compared to earlier period, the youth do not have inspiring social goals and ideals to work towards, and such goals and ideals are important determinants of value development. In the past, there used to be some larger and inspiring causes for which they worked. Those causes are disappearing. For example, the British subjugation offered a visible enemy to fight for freedom. It was not just an abstract idea; this was something very concrete. Probably there is a vacuum of socially desirable ideas that can inspire the Indian youth. This vacuum needs to be eliminated or reduced. They need to be involved in the larger social goals and ideals, which will, inspire them to work beyond themselves. Indian youth have responded magnificently whenever they were involved in some worthwhile ideals and goals. We have witnessed this again and again. For example, *Jai Prakash Narain's* movement attracted and inspired millions of people. At a smaller scale, *Narmada Bachao* or *Chipko* movements inspired youth for a larger cause.

The youth today is as vibrant as those of the past generation. We seem to have a lot of nostalgia for the past, and we seem to enjoy that. When I recollect my own past experiences, I can identify teachers who were role models, but I can also identify teachers who were incompetent and inefficient. We tend to recollect only the positive aspects. We miss a balanced view. Today's youth are intellectually more honest, they are more collaborative, (as reflected in the experience in many of our industries); they are more bold compared to our earlier generations. Exceptions apart, new generation take more risks; they are able to question elders, which we did not. New values are emerging. We need to identify, respect and nurture them. But, simultaneously, we must retain and promote those older values that are needed today to sustain our cultural traditions.

## ROLE OF VALUES IN LIFE

Values are of three types; some are generic personal values that sustain us in a society (e.g. honesty, integrity, fearlessness). The second sets of values are social values, which help others and help the society to be sustained (e.g. compassion, collaboration, empathy). And, the third set of values are organizational values, specific to each organization (e.g. openness, creativity, proaction). Yet, these values are interrelated. Distinction may be made between morality and ethics. While morality emphasizes personal values and behaviour, ethics includes social values and behaviour, which impinges on others. We need to emphasize much more on ethics, and need to develop code of ethics in the various social units. Such social values sustain the society.

## SOURCES OF VALUES

One important issue is sources of values that deserve serious attention for developing any meaningful programme of education in human values in the colleges and universities. There seem to be three main sources that influence and develop values in people.

*Role Models:* Unless there are role models, people do not become aware of the values and are not able to internalize them. We admire some one. Unknowingly, we imbibe his/her behaviours, habits, styles and values. He/she intensely influenced us. We need to reflect on what values he/she practised. We must also recognize that there are role models in different fields; we may have one role model for a teacher, another for a social worker, and yet another, for, say, in the area of sports and games.

*Organizational Experience:* The second source is the experience in the organizational life. People imbibe the values they experience as being practised in the significant groups of which they are members. Family is the first and most critical one. This is immediately followed by schools, colleges and other organizations. Students are influenced by the values experienced not only as practised by the teachers (their role models) but also by the institution as a whole. Values practised in the institution are likely to influence students much more than any lecture on values and didactic teaching of values.

*Readings:* The third important source influencing values is readings, like biographies and auto-biographies of people who stood by great values. Most of the biographies of great men show the values in action. In a way, the great men are also role models, though they are experienced indirectly.

Values can be inculcated by encouraging debates on values and understanding of consequences of one's own behaviour.

The values should be rationally understood and not only emotionally accepted. There should be debate on the consequences of pursuing certain values. For example, why should one be honest? When such a question was raised, for example, with some business people in Gujarat, they responded that this was the best policy to gain confidence of the customers and make profit on a long-term basis. People should be encouraged to debate what are the consequences of pursuing certain values as a result of which personal and social life is enriched or affected. The debate, for example, would be whether a particular behaviour is desirable; the consequences of one kind of behaviour versus another kind of behaviour. If we pursue debates on such issues rather than blindly following the sermons of the elders, values will be better internalized and practised. There should be enough thinking on value clarification – what kinds of values are required and why.

There are certain values which are accepted as tenets, e.g. good of the society, individual growth, individual's freedom to think, act and express, human dignity, and so on. Some of these values are enshrined in our constitution also; there should not be any question on these. But there should be enough opportunity to discuss these also, so that people can internalize them in a cognitive framework.

One aspect deserving serious attention is the methodology of value inculcation, especially in the colleges and universities. Should education in human values be part and parcel of higher education, since it is at this stage that students transit from education to the working life? In my opinion, value education should be much more by modelling and not by any didactic teaching. I am not sure about the utility of a course on value education; but there can certainly be courses on ethics. Such a course should, however, be based on cases. Cases can be collected where certain ethical standards were maintained or they were flouted by some people; and these could then be debated, so that people may begin to evolve their own understanding and, therefore, develop highly internalized commitment to the values. Actually, a meaningful programme of education in human values in higher education can comprise of a theoretical course on ethics adequately supplemented by co-curricular activities, debating on cases of value conflicts, etc.

Further, such a programme should be common to all branches of education, including science. Every discipline has a set of values of its own. Students must realize the values underlying science, and, hence, education in human values must find a special place in science education. For example, science has a set of underlying values like seeking the truth and not taking things for granted by continuously questioning, and, therefore, searching new alternatives and so on. Such an approach would legitimize questioning the authority also. Students should realize that science helps us to move towards a different kind of values—freedom of thought and openness to new thinking, contrasted with authority–oriented system. A meeting of the *Dalai Lama* with the noble laureate scientists in 2002 is an interesting event depicting several values like being open to new ideas and not being dogmatic. Other values are respecting different faiths and different approaches and anti-dogmatic stand.

## ROLE OF TEACHERS

Let us look at the role of the teachers in developing values in education. When we talk of desirability of teaching ethos and developing values amongst students through case studies, debates, etc., the role of teachers is of paramount importance. Are they equipped to deal with value education? If not, how could they be prepared?

Holding on to our argument of values to be lived and the importance of role models in value inculcation among the youth, probably, we need many more programmes for teachers than for students to start with. It is necessary for the teachers to realize and appreciate that life cannot be *"value-free"*. Unfortunately, many teachers are not conscious of the role of values in life and they tend to believe that teaching, say of English, does not require any value. The first step should be to organize programmes for teachers. They should be aware of how important values are in life. The teachers should be involved in programmes to see the role of values in the organizational and personal life, and the ways in which such values can be developed among the students and so on. Some crash programmes or workshops would be useful for teachers. Education in human values should form a major component of the programmes in the Academic Staff Colleges.

For training of teachers in human values, the programme methodologies have to be carefully designed. It could include a basic search of the values people live or practise; then also the desired values in social life. So, some basic research is needed on teachers' present values, desirable values and the process of erosion of certain values, and how the eroded but desirable values can be brought back. Teachers must also debate on cases and episodes that offer opportunities of identifying value erosion and value development. There must be enough opportunities for the teachers for value clarification and exploration.

Further, every profession has its own values. The teachers ought to realize the values that underlie the teaching profession. Teachers as a professional body must be aware of values related to our profession. Some values relate to our own subject matters and what we are teaching. Some relate to the students. Some are application to the society as a whole; others are organizational values. And these probably need to be debated.

## LEARNING MATERIALS

In order to develop a meaningful programme, there must be enough learning material on human values. There must be enough research. There should be enough data on what values people live today and what values people would like to live, though they may not be practising them. There is indeed a major gap between the desired values and values lived. Investigations must document this gap. The second is the kind of dilemmas people are facing while pursing values. Those dilemmas are important to capture; how people get around those dilemmas. Many people have shared the dilemma of practising certain values in the organizational life. For examples, they did not cut corners. If they resisted the temptation of cutting corners; they realized that the path was much better. People may realize that short cuts are not going to help in the long run. Such learning is possible when we analyse and discuss such ethical issues that people experience.

Case studies have been used extensively and intensively in human development programmes. Case studies, in my view, are potential source of learning of human values as well. We need to build a strong repertoire of cases, which involve both individual behaviour and values, and how those values contributed to the sustenance of certain long-term values in the organization. Such cases may be in print as well as in non-print format. There are large numbers of very good films that can provide good material for exploration. For example, the film *Ek Ruka Hua Faisla* which demonstrated that if a person is not cowed down by the opinion of the majority but continues to search and stands up to assert her understanding, s/he can help others to see the truth. Values in the long run are going to help the individuals as well as the organizations.

Autobiographies are also extremely important source of learning. Many of us have been greatly influenced through the reading of biographies. On a personal note, my intellectual life, not only the emotional life, has been significantly enriched by my reading of biographies, including the analysis of consequences of values in sustaining the society. For example, when I read *Gandhji,* he greatly influenced me on the concept of empowerment (see Pareek, 2002,). In fact, Bengali literature, especially the novels of *Sarat Chandra Chatterjee*, influenced me. I internalised many values from the literature, including *Prem Chand's* short stories and novels.

## VALUE ASSESSMENT

Assessment of values is difficult. We have been using several methods, including values scales. Several such scales are available. New scales also need to be developed. Also, one can use peer rating and other techniques. Currently, 360-degree appraisal is very popular. This offers an opportunity to see how one is seen to practise different values.

Unfortunately, there is a big gap between professed and the lived values. In most cases, teachers preach some values (e.g. punctuality) to students, but do not practise. If we are able to bring these contradictions in the open, we will create great opportunities for value clarification and education.

## MANAGEMENT CHALLENGES

We possibly would need some re-engineering of management of higher education institutions. Values are reflected in the practices. One of the roles of the HRD managers is to undertake governance audit, to see what administrative practices reflect what values. Unless people can be helped become aware of the values reflected in the various administrative practices and systems, there will be limited scope of inculcating values. It is not the values that we teach, but those we practise in the institution influence values of its members. Education in human values will generate a positive pressure for governance audit. Even small practices reflect certain values. For example, during meetings, a paper is circulated where people are asked to sign their names as a proof of attending the meeting. Such a practice essentially reflects the value of mistrust. If the chairperson records the names of the persons present and is used as the relevant official record, it would reflect the value of trust. Let me recollect an interesting incidence to illustrate the point.

I was then teaching at the University of North Carolina at Chapel Hill. I had three doctoral students. One of them got 'C' grade in one of my courses. The grades had been sent to the University office. Next day, he came and told me that he had to leave the university, because doctoral students were required to have a minimum of 'B' grade in their courses. I felt bad, because the student had not done so badly. All my education was in India, and I had very little idea of the American educational system. I told him to see me next day. I went to a friend of mine, Sagar Jain, another Indian professor and asked his advice. He told me that I could re-examine, if I liked; or I could give him another assignment and reevaluate him. I gave the student another assignment to be submitted after two months, the student submitted his new assignment, I found it fairly good and deserved 'B' grade. I again went to Sagar for his advice. He told me to go to the examination section and change the grade.

Next day, I went to the examination section where staff clerks were largely young women—wives of the doctoral students. When I reached and found out who deals with the subject, I introduced myself. She asked me, what she could do for me? I told her that I wanted to change a student's grade from 'C' to 'B'. She asked me the name of the student. I told her the name, and waited. She asked me again if she could do anything else for me. I was puzzled that she was not doing anything. Anyway, I left the office. Next day there was a paper on the notice board, announcing the change in the grade.

It was a pleasant surprise for me. She never verified my identity. She never asked me to sign at any place. Everything was based on trust. In such a system no one can even think of cheating. The trust in a system is developed by trusting people.

While dealing with values, we should also have a detailed analysis of what practices we are adopting in organizations and what values do they reflect. If we want to produce counter values, we need to change practices as well. We cannot have teaching of one set of values and practising another set of values. There should be authenticity and genuineness.

## CONCLUSION

To conclude, values are extremely important because values distinguish human beings from animals. If we are not able to establish values in the personal and social life, our life will deteriorate to the animal level. But values cannot be taught. These have to be somehow inculcated and developed. Values have to be evolved in the society. Traditional approaches would not be enough; we need some creative way to meet the challenge of developing human values.

# Value Development among College Youth

ANIL BHATTACHARYA

## INTRODUCTION

Value crisis appears to be a global phenomenon. Such crisis is both at individual as well as at the collective level of the civil society. And, like anywhere else in to-day's world, there is a crisis of values in the contemporary Indian society too. This is especially deplorable in view of the fact that the Indian society, unlike most other societies elsewhere, was structured around a set of traditional values. These traditional values that hold the Indian society together through ages are breaking down and steadily making room for a new set of alternative value systems that contradict the basic ethos of Indian society.

Most of the traditional Indian values that characterized Indian society were derived from spiritual values that had their humane counterparts as well. For example, love of and respect for God leads to love of and service to human beings and all creatures. Many Indian spiritual leaders believed 'service to man is service to God'. There are also a large number of secular values like respect for elders, compassion and empathy for neighbour, truthfulness, chivalry, sharing and co-operation, etc. But among today's youth, especially the urban youth, such traditional values have lost their hold. They are caught in the quagmire of a new set of values that characterize contemporary western traditions and consumerism.

The blame for this is to be shared by the parents as well. For, they have been so allured by the glitter and impact of materialistic prosperity that they deserted Indian ways of life and living in their conception. They set new role models for their children and forgot their role and function to inculcate values in the appropriate manner due; also, they do not teach the younger generation respect for quality of any kind, especially human quality.

## ROLE OF VALUES IN LIFE

As mentioned above, the glittering western materialism that has invaded Indian life and living has quietly convinced the new generation that living a comfortable individual or isolated family life is all that is necessary and important. This isolation and self-centeredness is dangerous for collective living which has become all the more necessary in today's world than ever before. The biggest role of values is in teaching us that living a comfortable life alone is not enough; it is self-defeating as an ideal. This does not accommodate social goals and concerns. What matters is character and quality of living which together ensures happiness in personal life, and harmony in society. Values add that special and all important 'character' to the human personality. Unless a person is conscious of values, the finer expressions of life in art, literature, creative sciences, sports, and the like, life becomes a meaningless existence. The so-called 'standard of living' remains an empty phrase without the content of character and finer aspirations. As a result even materialistic pursuits become a chase for shadows - life ceases to be anything other than a selfish hunt for the gratification of animal cravings. Indeed, life devoid of human values is a burden

A society without values is a jungle where 'ignorant armies clash by night'. It is unnerving even to imagine a society where everyone is aggressively pursuing their own personal agenda without slightest regard and concern for others, particularly the weaker ones. This can only lead to chaos, social strife, tension and crisis.

## LIVING VALUES

To save the society from such a situation, we must inculcate the values. There are a whole range of values that pertain to several domains like secular and non-secular values, individual, social, moral, national, global values, etc. The core minimum values that need to be inculcated among the Indian youth are:

- Unselfish or self-less work, which is service,
- Selfless love both for persons and of ideals,
- Kindness,
- Sympathy,
- Fellow feeling,
- Respect for the good, and
- Reverence for time-tested abstract virtues, etc.

The list is not comprehensive nor exhaustive; it is rather indicative. Nonetheless, these are some of the things to start a value education programme.

But these values cannot be taught just theoretically; values are to be lived. The debate of value education versus value inculcation is genuine. For, values are part of life and not just isles on the cognitive content of the human mind. In other words, values are reflected in an individuals' and a society's life styles. The practical implication is that for developing values in self-less actions, for example, values are to be found in unselfish actions of the elders—parents, teachers and community leaders—that lead to the good of all—especially the poor, under-privileged, and the downtrodden. Only then and through such 'working models' or 'role models', value inculcation can actually happen.

## VALUE EDUCATION: THE MODALITY

I am not quite sure that value education can be imparted in higher education in the form of a formal course with a stipulated curriculum. Perhaps, a feasible alternative would be to sensitize students into values ingrained in various subjects—a deeper insight into sciences and the arts may help acquiring values of accuracy and precision, exploring truth, validation and revalidation of knowledge, aesthetic taste and appreciation, finer dimensions of human life, social relationships and interdependence, etc.; perhaps disinterested enthusiasm for knowledge is a value in itself; perhaps, the day-to-day life in college and universities interacting with other students and teachers, non-academic staff, experiences in classrooms, laboratories and libraries may offer a range of opportunities of value inculcation. An entire value system, in my view, can never be made a curricular exercise to be transmitted through an educational course.

Values are inseparable from life as lived; hence, their inculcation is possible only by effecting changes in style of living and the accompanying social attitude. This calls for a massive comprehensive conceptual framework. Students, the college youth do not acquire values only in colleges; sensitive minds as they are in their youth, they interact with all components of a social system, namely, politics, economy, media, people from all walks of life and professions as much as the educational system. The inculcation of values would mean shifting the focus of education, politics, professional careers and all those that directly or indirectly influence value development among youth. This would also mean a new orientation of the social sub-systems and institutions from narrow sectarian and self-centered goals to wider goals that ensure harmony and improvement of the society at large. This is a massive challenge; for, it calls for re-conceptualization and re-engineering of the society itself.

Though values cannot be taught in classrooms in the conventional manner through a series of course based lectures, they can be inculcated through personal contacts between the right kind of teachers and their students. The implication of the word, 'right kind of teachers' is those teachers who demonstrate desirable values in their living. For example, we mentioned earlier disinterested enthusiasm and persuasion of knowledge itself is an important value in education. The teachers who pursue this value in their life, voracious reader and a life-long learner are likely to inculcate such values of pursuit of knowledge among students. But where and how long do we wait for these 'right kind of teachers' to appear and take charge of value inculcation? We need to enlarge our base. This would mean affecting behavioural changes in the teachers, and also structural changes in the methods and modes of teaching that can demonstrate subject-based values as well as human behavioural values like pursuit of knowledge and excellence, impartiality, concern for students, etc.

## ROLE OF TEACHERS

Teachers are a part of the society. They are also born and brought up within the value framework of a contemporary society. So the teachers also represent the same or similar set of values as are prevalent in the contemporary society. They cannot be expected to be 'odd man out' or the angels in a devil society or the vice-versa. In degenerate societies, teachers are as much contaminated as the taught. This is a vicious circle—teachers inheriting degenerate values from the society and transmitting those to the students.

But then this vicious circle has to be breached at some point. The teachers have to be made conscious of their impact on students—how they consciously or unconsciously act as role models for their students and the students pick up their values from the teachers. Both teachers and the students are to be made conscious of the positive ideals of harmony, unselfish aspiration and non-materialistic attainments. Such awareness and sensitivity may lead to value clarification among both teachers and students.

The best method for securing an insight into values might be the teaching of social, political, cultural and economic history—this would indirectly teach the necessity of tested values in a society oriented towards growth (and also, the link between decay of societies and degeneration of values). For example, the fall of the Roman Empire, and within our own national history, the story of rise and fall of Mughal

Empire provides enormous scope of developing sensitivity towards values and their role in society for both growth and decay.

Besides the methodological issues pertaining to value education among college and university youth, value inculcation cannot be taught in isolation; it must include teachers, students and others at the same time. And, methodologically a sound alternative is to sensitize them in role of values in individual and social life through study of history of societies.

## VALUE DEVELOPMENT OPPORTUNITIES AND ASSESSMENT

Assessment of value development is difficult and must be a subjective affair. It can, however, be attempted if we carefully develop and apply yardsticks for measuring excellence in conduct, attitude and unselfish social work, alongside the yardsticks, we apply for measuring academic excellence. This would necessitate a new range of tools that are not conventional like paper pencil tests used to test academic learning and excellence. This would probably call for careful observation of students' actual behaviour in a variety of situations not only by the teachers but also by peers; for, teachers may not have access to observation of students in all aspects of their behaviour and activities.

The assessment of value development would warrant adequate scope for students to learn/inculcate and demonstrate values in their action in colleges and universities. This would mean some shifting of focus of higher education. There should be more emphasis on group activities and cooperative learning, on individual and group sports and team games, on awareness programmes, etc. A new awareness has to be built up and encouragement has to be given to see academic career as a gateway not only to a brighter financial career for him/herself but also to a position wherefrom the educated can make significant contributions to the society. Shift has to be from living for self to living to help others;

creating a new place of concern for others in the mindset that is otherwise congested with self-interest and self-centeredness.

## SOCIAL WORK FOR VALUE INCULCATION

Some co-curricular activities can, however, be arranged at the level of higher education which may instill a sense of purpose and a secular and scientific outlook among the students. Involving a large number of students in the popular science movement would liberate them from obscurantism, which is the base of a large section of modern Indian polity. Similarly, participation in social action in a large way among the poor and underprivileged, particularly among the tribes, dalits and the minority communities would develop a secular and humane attitude among the students. Such programme would also create an army of dedicated social workers who can involve other sections of the society.

## CONCLUSION

We must concede that contemporary Indian society is facing a value crisis where traditional Indian values are weaning away, creating space for the new self-serving value systems. But this is not just a youth phenomenon; parents and teachers are equally responsible for the shift and the ensuing crisis. Value inculcation and development is the natural antidote to this erosion of values. But a formal course on value education may not be the right response to the challenge. Value is lived; hence, it must be demonstrated 'live' to the students by teachers and elders in the society. This would require new behavioural models in politics, education, social organizations, etc.

Indian society for thousands of years has grown as a vibrant multi-cultural and multi-lingual society. The basic values that Indian society has generated is the tolerance for diverse cultural values, beliefs and mutual respect for each other. Synthesis and harmonization of diverse streams of thoughts and attitudes, rituals, customs and beliefs are the essence of core of Indian culture and tradition. We, Indians, have inherited this great tradition that has been carried through thoughts and preachings of a great number of religious and social thinkers—Gautam Buddha and King Asoka in pre-Christian era, down to Chaitanya, Kabir and Sufi poets and preachers of middle ages. With the beginning of British Rule in India, we got thinkers and reformers like Rammohan, Dayananda Saraswati, Atma Ram Pandurang, Beheramji Merwarji Malabai, Rabindranath Tagore and Swami Vivekananda and many others from different parts of the country who essentially upheld the values of tolerance and need of practising harmony and synthesis.

We can derive lessons from our neighbouring country, China, and see how this great ancient culture has been successful in preserving the basic value of harmony and synthesis inherent in Chinese tradition and cult. The political and economic dynamics of great nation have played an instrumental role in effecting necessary changes in social norms and codes but the basic value of preserving core of Chinese culture has been well preserved.

In the Indian context, efforts should be directed towards preserving the basic value of harmony and synthesis, of mutual tolerance and respect. We certainly do welcome changes in social norms and codes but we have to take care that such changes do not strike a blow against the edifice of values that has been built over the ages.

# Education in Human Values for College Youth

SYED MAHDI

## INTRODUCTION

I remember reading a few interesting sentences on the state of things in the society. Let me quote:

"This is the year of darkness. The children do not obey their parents. The rulers are not fair in their dealings. People do not observe elementary rules of ethics in their transactions, etc."

All these sentences sounded very contemporary. But when I looked at the bottom line, I found that this was a quotation from a Chinese sage and the date was sometime about 2000 years before the Christian era i.e. about 4000 years ago. The lesson that one could draw from such statement is that crisis of values or deterioration of values is not something which is peculiar to our age. There have been innumerable citations of this phenomenon. That is why, I guess, the teacher, the sages have appeared in almost every era. Our own history is replete with that alternating of such resurgence cycles. I do not need to quote examples. Every student of history is familiar with this phenomenon. The deterioration of values and the efforts to counteract such deterioration has been there most of the times. So, to say that the crisis of values is something very peculiar to our contemporary society or contemporary Indian society is rather simplistic.

The value crisis can be ascribed to a host of factors. One hypothesis is the poor value development among the Indian youth. Our debate and discussion can be on a firm ground if we first define the word 'values'—What do we understand by values? Without going into very long philosophical discourse or discussion, one could perhaps take a little pragmatic view and arrive at some kind of a functional definition of value. We can classify values into three categories :

- Individual Values—individual behaviour;
- Values of interaction with other members of the society; and
- National values

If it is limited to this broad definition, one can say that there is a deterioration of values in individual behaviour, social interaction and in public life that we are witnessing around us. But to put the blame on youth only is not fair because the youth is shaped in by the family. There are so many influences on them starting with the values that they imbibe consciously or unconsciously from their elders including the parents, the teachers, the elders with whom they come in contact in their social life, in work place or through the role models that they see in the media. So holding the view that the values rest with our youth will not be getting to the root of the problem. Value crisis is equally visible among adults. The crisis transgresses family life, working life and larger social life. What we see in the youth is at best a minor image of the value crisis in the society at large.

## VALUES AND THEIR SOURCES

An important question is what really is the role of values in life. How the values relate or influence our performance in worldly affairs. Consciously or unconsciously our entire behaviour as individual, as members of larger group like a nation, is influenced and determined by values. The role of values in the life of human beings, which are distinct from other beings because of the inherent facility of making choices, is extremely important. I do not intend to deal with the questions of determinism and free-will here. But for all practical purposes, we must accept that man/woman is responsible for his/her own conduct and behaviours. In that behaviour the values play a crucial role.

But what kind of values are we talking about? We all know that there are certain basic values, which have evolved with the evolution of the societies to this stage. It is possible to contend that certain values were relevant at the beginning of civilization but those are no more relevant and true. These have been embodied in the texts of all the major religions. A comparative study of these values will indicate that almost 90% of the values in their spirit are common. The terminology may be different, but the essence is the same. So, I would put the emphasis on the value, which allow us to

- co-exist peacefully;
- resist exploitation of human beings;
- develop our individual capabilities; and
- support upholding the dignity of man and individual.

These are some of the values that we have to inculcate. The sources of these values exist in almost all the major religious or spiritual or holy traditions whether it is the Ten Commandments or the last address after the last Haj of the Prophet of Islam or the teachings of the ancient Indian sages or the Chinese code of ethics from the times of Confucius. Of course, there may be differences in the emphasis but one could always identify the commonalities. All these values have to be interpreted again and again, and some kind of a common terminology has to be worked out which is very essential in our contemporary world where no civilization or no nation can live in isolation. It is not really identifying the sources, but how these sources are woven into some kind of a consensus. That is an interesting point to ponder. The values, on which the nations have converged, after long deliberations and debates, after lot of give and take, are the values which have a universal validity and application. These are the values enshrined in the various declarations of the United Nations, which the nations have committed themselves by formally signing these documents. So, one way of identification of the values that will avoid controversies would be the values derived from the human rights declarations or the cognates on the social and cultural rights, etc. We should cull out the values from these documents in which there is universal consensus. These values are universal as well as specific. This would serve to be a good guide.

## RELEVANCE TO HIGHER EDUCATION

The need for imparting these values at the pre-higher education level has already been accepted. Value education should have begun much earlier. It should start first at the family and then in the school. Unless we impart directly or indirectly value education at these earlier stages, the effectiveness of value education at the higher education level will be very minimal. In principle, hence, value education should be imparted in higher education. But how? Should it be a separate course or be integrated into the existing subjects and courses? There are certain values implicit in the courses and subjects. Unless we go into the very highest realms of the knowledge structure, values are implicit. For example, in mathematics the implicit value is exactitude; in sciences, the intrinsic value is of arriving at truth; there are certain values implicit in Sociology or Economics. So, the values are already implicit in what we are teaching. Yet, to integrate them into the courses is a very difficult exercise, not very desirable also.

Instead of integrating or mainstreaming in the various subjects, it would be better and practical to impart value education as a supplement. Let me dilate on this a little. For example, let us take the case of a student, who after completing science stream in the +2 stage goes straight into a professional course in engineering and technology; and he/

she does very well in the university. He/she becomes a very good professional in a specific field, be it Information Technology or Biotechnology or whatever else. Technology is an instrument. The choice of use and application of technology is informed and guided by values. Now, the kind of question on the way technology will be used is not taught in these courses. But, such people need to be familiarized with social sciences and humanities so that they develop in themselves human dimensions as well, and do not become intelligent robots. I guess the more we go for narrow specializations, the more it is necessary to have a broader humanistic view of things which provides a context where these narrow specializations can be pursued and be related to the broader issues of facing the humanity. One example could be biotechnology and cloning. Technically, cloning is possible, and we may have human clones. We must recognize that it is not biotechnology, which is going to tell us whether human cloning is desirable, ethical and beneficial for humanity. Neither is it going to inform us of the risks. It is certain broader values that will determine the use of this powerful instrument of change. On a positive note, for example, we are talking of digital divide. Now, this very question would not have arisen unless we had imbibed certain values as a part of our mental and emotional network. It is because of this social consciousness which comes from imbibing certain values that we, at least in India, are trying to find uses of IT which could benefit the disadvantaged classes of our people. For example, the MS Swaminathan Foundation is trying to use information technology for the benefit of the common fisherman by projecting the weather every day so that the fishermen can decide whether to go for fishing or not. Now, this use of information technology would not have been imagined if certain values were not imbibed in our mental and ethical make up.

What I am implying is that the value education should be imparted in higher education. To the extent it does not lead to distortion of the specific subjects, it could be integrated. But a more practical way of doing will be to impart it as a separate programme because certain values cut across various disciplines. They can be imparted in a separate stage.

Having said that education in human values be taught as a separate programme, we need to build up a well considered framework. The report of the National Seminar/Workshop on 24th May 2001, which was held under the auspices of the Educational Administration Unit of NIEPA in New Delhi provides a sound six module framework for education in human values in higher education.

Basically, these six areas provide a broader framework for devising courses for providing value education. The universities should, however, be free to devise their own programmes or courses. This should be left to the collective, creative wisdom of the universities as to how these components of the broad framework are translated into pedagogy or activities.

A related and relevant issue is the methodology of imparting value education? Conventional lectures may not be the right technique. There can, however, be extension lectures. The best way would be to get such people who are practitioners of these values for these lectures.

There should be scope for flexibility. The universities themselves can devise a scheme of courses, lectures and activities depending on their ethos, instead of some kind of uniform/compulsory/prescribed kind of course material or lecture material for this. There can, however, be some kind of broad consensus or guidelines. Such people who are the practitioners of these values can become the role models. For, we must recognize that all of us are much more influenced by the role models than by the theories and by mere words. When a role model speaks to us, the impact is much deeper. In Jamia, we brought a few people who are the living examples of the values they preach.

The second set of methodologies are activities that leave deeper impact on our youth in higher education. Every university has a National Service Scheme. In Jamia, I found that the NSS is doing well and the feedback from the students is encouraging. It creates a sense of social concern. It promotes the human values. We should try to strengthen these schemes, make them more popular, take a look at its content and make it something that becomes attractive among students. Instead of treating NSS as something of a formality, we should develop it as a vibrant living institution for the students. This NSS, and to certain extent NCC also, which inculcates the spirit of self-help, helping each other, living together more seriously as means for inculcation of human values needs special consideration. These schemes should be strengthened and conducted in such a way that the students feel proud of being part of it and take more interest in these schemes.

A related question in value education is assessment of value development among the college youth. It is a tricky issue. Right at the very beginning, working out a formula for assessing the value development will not be a very useful exercise. It will reduce the impact into formula or index. The effect of the value education among college youth in the society will become manifest or tangible only after a long time. Moreover, there are just about 7% of the relevant age group in the colleges and universities. Leave alone those who are not in the colleges and universities, many of the graduates, in real life, face frustration of unemployment or the non-fulfillment of their aspiration. So, to put the burden of transforming the society through what they have learnt through value education in the universities will not be very realistic.

## CONCLUSION

Value education in higher education must begin at home through role modelling. The colleges and universities must demonstrate the ethos, values and ethics they propose to develop among the students. The leadership in the university itself has to set an example. It starts from the vice chancellor and his team, the senior faculty, specially the heads of the departments or the dean. Any artificial means of social engineering may not be very productive. On the contrary, this can be achieved to a great extent by introducing transparency in the management; whether management at the head of the institution, chief executive level or at the faculty or the department level. By transparency we mean fairness adhering to rules and regulations, which also implies integrity in terms of the selection process, etc. If these things can be established, practised and seen to be practised, we should be able to demonstrate values. The university administration at the central, faculty, and, department level should not only seem to be fair but also should be seen to be fair. That can create ethos in which value education will be effective.

# Education in Human Values among University Youth

MARMAR MUKHOPADHYAY

## INTRODUCTION

Indian society has been in a state of steady transition, with three distinct phases since independence. The first phase from 1947 till the middle of 1960s, characterized by patriotism, nationalism and associated euphoria of freedom from the British rule, is largely the aftermath of the struggle for independence that naturally generated strong sentiments for the country against the British rule. Swadeshi, more in the form of exclusion of foreign goods, and use of Indian material irrespective of their quality, Indian values characterized by austerity as opposed to consumerism were very much in the air. The Russian planned development model, and the Indian community development movement had significant contribution to this transitional phase. Indeed, the country was struggling to establish a new social identity distinctly different from the humiliating colonial identity.

The second phase in this transition is largely the period between middle of 1960s till the middle of 1980s. During this period the patriotic fervour steadily came down; political turmoil characterized by splitting of political parties on leadership issues gripped the nation; a steady decline in the quality of role models among public men and women; new ambition of westernization—consumerism, nuclearization of families, etc. became steadily the new set of values of Indian society. Although Indian television began in 1960s, there was a quantum jump with the Asiad in 1982 that ushered in a new era in television and mass communication in India; immediately followed by a boom in cable television. That brought the world into the Indian households—into the drawing room, the bedroom and the kitchen, particularly of the middle class. The Indian society—middle and upper middle-class in particular—was immediately exposed to the western consumerist traditions, as well as western culture and ethos. The search for the new Indian identity with traditional native cultural values was replaced by a new cultural script where national public ambition was identification with western traditions and life-styles.

The third phase is about two decade old, beginning primarily with the leadership of Rajiv Gandhi in the mid 1980's. The National Policy on Education of 1986 is one of the important articulations of the mood of the new nation, 'India to be'. In fact, neo-Indianism—searching for a distinct identity for India as a modern nation—was born during this period. This new search for identity was substantially different from the first phase search; it was characterized by futurism and global competitiveness based on new found confidence as compared to nostalgic and 'looking-back' version of the Indian identity. This mood and national resurgence found a natural ally in the rightist political parties in the late 1990s. Regional aspirations in the form of regional parties, on the one hand, aggravated the leadership struggle, while, on the other hand it started nurturing federalism. Social transition gave India a combative mood to take the challenge of development in the new global order.

This three-phase transition has resulted in a significant shift in the social and individual values. New cultural and sub-cultural scripts with new set of values have been authored. Indeed, there is a phenomenal value confusion, if not value crisis, in the contemporary Indian society. This is a common cry among academicians, administrators, politicians, bureaucrats and people from all walks of life. The situation raises a series of fundamental questions.

- Is this crisis peculiar to India alone?
- Does it mean that the Indian society had never had value crisis?

- How does one know whether the society is indeed under crisis of values? What are some of the indicators to decide whether the society is in crisis or not?
- Is it the crisis of individual behaviour that collectively constitutes social crisis or is it the societal functioning and governance that indicates the crisis of values in a society?

The evidences are in favour of believing that the crisis is universal. It is a question of looking at the issue and labeling it the right or wrong values. For example, massive military campaigns are victimizing millions of people in Vietnam, Iraq, Afghanistan, Cuba, Chechnia by the developed nations, where human rights are cherished with all sincerity. It is the same society where individuals cherish compassion, truthfulness, value time, empowerment, etc. and still children play game of killing in schools. Is there a value crisis in such societies? As Dalai Lama said, 'values and ethics are the way a particular set of behaviour is chosen, and the logic behind it'. The western societies are equally confronted with problems of drugs, AIDS, violence, etc. There are several instances where the leaders of the multi-national companies have been handcuffed and put behind bars. Thus, value crisis is universal.

The second issue is whether the Indian value crisis is a recent development. Again, it cannot be labeled as a contemporary phenomenon alone. For example, when a few were fighting against the British Empire for freedom, large number of Indians not only served the British rulers but brutally killed their own countrymen as Royal Police and Army. Further peep into the history will reveal despicable casteism where Brahmins did not even walk over the shadows of the Shudras; Brahmins justifying polygamy in the name of Kaulinya. The landlords not only exploited their subjects but also brutally treated them. Women were substantially discriminated against in social and public life. Without such moral turpitudes and value degradation, Sri Krishna would not have to pronounce, "*yada yada hi dharmasya glanirbahavati baharata, .... Smabahavami yugey yugey".* Thus, value crisis has been a universal phenomenon across time in the Indian society?

An important question is how do we decide whether there is a crisis of values. What are some of its indicators? It is natural that we will refer to things like corruption, dishonesty, violence at slightest provocation, nepotism, disregard for parents and elders, selfishness and self-seeking behaviour at the cost of public good and such other events in the social life. It is within the reach of our experience and known research that none of them are necessarily a contemporary development. The question is much more on the extent of the spread of these dis-values. I guess, the basic indicator of value crisis is the massive spread of counter-values that were earlier restricted to small number. More than the spread, it is the growing favour for counter-values, particularly among the educated genre.

Also, this perception of crisis is aggravated due to the nostalgic single-minded monopolistic view about human values. For example, we often quote, '*Vasudhaiba kutumbhakam*'—'world is a family' as the core of Indian philosophy. Reality is slightly different. It professed, '*Udaracharitanantu Vasudhaiba kutumbhakam*' meaning 'for the large-hearted people, the world is a family'. The implied meaning is the existence of a large number of chicken-hearted people as well. Both chicken-heartedness and large-heartedness are universally true. Sister Nivedita, Annie Besant, Mother Teressa, The Mother (Sri Aurobindo Ashram), and many others who not only settled in India but also served the community as their own family. This nostalgia has inhibited Indian mind to adopt a rational approach to value development that is so very necessary in the present context of a globalized world. Similarly, we claim the Indian wisdom and its supremacy with *Satyameva Jayate*—it is the Truth that triumphs and not the falsity. This is universally true and practised in all societies. When Jesus Christ was brought back to the king, he proclaimed that he had told the truth knowing fully well that he will be crucified.

Socrates is another important example who stood by truth and accepted death. There are many such instances.

Such glorification and nostalgia restrain us from taking a scientific view at the Indian society that housed, along with the values, all the dis-values that we see today. Over and above, the society was highly structured into classes and castes. The values that were admired and appreciated belonged to the elite class, elite not necessarily in terms of material riches, but also in terms of social standing and education. The Brahmins or the Brahmanic mentality were characterised, for example, by learning and scholarship—attaching higher value to scholarship than material riches. But education or scholarship itself was restricted to only few in the society. At times, they were restricted only to the Brahimns. The tribal boy, Ekalavya was refused training in archery by Guru Dronacharya. Not only that. Ekalavya had to pay the price—his right thumb as Gurudakshina—so that he could never compete with great archers from royal families.

It is important to recognize that a major development in the post-independent India is the mainstreaming of millions of people. They had their own set of values that may or may not necessarily match with the values of the upper middle-class and middle-class Indian society. In the process of mainstreaming, they brought with them not only their values but also their aspirations which were substantially influenced by the middle-class culture and values. What resulted is a value confusion.

To get to the heart of the problem, we would need to take a more objective look and may have to carry out intensive and detailed research; only that may help us take a rational view about the contemporary value crisis in Indian society.

Yet, another important question is whether this social crisis is the aggregation of individual dis-values or social dis-values? This is a point where two schools of philosophy come into conflict with one another. The socialists claim the need for correcting the social setting that can take charge of the individual, social and personal behaviours. In other words, the individual's ethics and values are determined by the social system. The contra-thesis is built around behaviour models of the individuals, aggregation of which leads to social values. This is a difficult equation setting us in an egg-and-chick dilemma. It is easier to put corruption, nepotism, violence, sexual harassment, etc. at the individual's lap; though it depends significantly on good governance. For example, the difference in the treatment of such aberrations in countries like Singapore as compared to India are the indications of societal aspect of dis-values. In absence of deterrents, such individual behaviours are fall-outs of organizational crisis as well. There are many other instances, particularly, in private organizations where corruption is the organizational practice. In Government, corruption is difficult to justify as an organizational practice at least at the policy level. The recent study (of Transparency International 2002) indicate health and education—both in the government—as most corrupt sectors. But it cannot be completely neglected; often it is practised as a group.

The values, ethos and morality are also culturally conditioned and culturally defined. Margaret Mead described that women in a New Guinea tribe are aggressive and provider where male tend children and do household chores, a set of values that would be unacceptable to the mainstream Indian middle class. Under the umbrella of liberation and personal freedom, promiscuity or multiple sexual relationships is no more seen as bad ethics in the western world. Such practices are not acceptable to the Indian population by and large. In order to develop a better understanding of the value crisis in the Indian society, it is necessary to carry out a serious research and exploration as to what are some of those values that indeed sustain the Indian society and are still valid for the future generations.

## VALUE CRISIS AND THE YOUTH

Although there is a popular cry about value crisis among youth, it is a debatable contention. In the absence of well-researched and documented evidences it is difficult to maintain such a proposition. The argument is not to deny the existence of crisis of values in the society at large and also among the youth. The question is whether the youth can be singled out for the value crisis and held responsible. We need a more balanced view of the social scenario. The values are inculcated largely by the role models—either in person or in imaginative identification. The role models provide direct experiences of living values. Guru in the old Gurukula system is probably the best example. The imaginative identification implies identification with such characters that were read in autobiographies, biographies, novels, etc.

The contemporary knowledge about value development is reasonably clear about the role of the role models particularly early in life. Thus, the values displayed by youth today is what are being inculcated by the adult, in general, and parents, teachers and other social role models in particular. With the changing Indian power structure and power scenarios, politicians and bureaucrats exert greatest influence on the youth. For, they are the power centres. The people, who dominate the current power scenario, provide very little role model or value-based behaviour for the youth to follow. Nearer home, the youth, today, have been built by the parents and teachers who are overwhelmed and attracted by the culture of the west, particularly consumerism, individualism characterized by self-seeking and self-centredness, gender discrimination, etc. The children and youth are exposed to those dis-values right from the beginning.

Two teachings of Gita are relevant and important in understanding this value development. Firstly, younger people imitate the behaviour of the older people (*Sl. Ch. 3*). Second, it is the continuous thinking about material objects and physical comforts that creates attachment and desire to get more. When that is restricted for various reasons, it generates anger, which leads to violence (*sl. 61 and 62 Ch. 3*). It is the same consumerist tendency provoked by a variety of advertisements that generates lust, leading to sexual promiscuity. Sri Aurobindo, in his 'Call to the Youth of India', pointed out the paradox that we immitated some of the western behavioural models, losing our own positive tradition and glory; on the other hand, we hardly ever inculcated the strengths of western values and ethics. For example, value of time and punctuality is one of the many such positive values that we rarely picked up. Similarly, an average western individual spends more time on reading, enriching and empowering himself or herself. Compared to that, our reading habits, our writing habits are rather poor resulting in poor empowerment and poor contribution in knowledge creation and creativity. Both youth and age are trapped in this new value syndrome/crisis. The youth cannot be singled out. The value crisis in the youth has to be seen in the larger social context of the adults, particularly the leaders of today.

We must also recognize that, like in all other societies, the new values are being added into the repertoire of the youth that was not there earlier. For example, today's youth are much more adventurous and entrepreneurial in life; they take risks. Youth are more open and courageous, they raise question to adults, parents and teachers. Compared to obedience, that was the characteristic of the previous generations, the new generations are more capable of articulation and expression of their ideas and feelings. In the analysis of value crisis, it is important that these new dimensions be looked into carefully.

It will also be necessary to work out a detailed research on new values that are necessary for living in the global society. It will call for a different set of values; the current set of values may not be adequate for the new role and the new living.

## VALUE, RELIGION AND SPIRITUALITY

There is a tendency to associate values with religion. This is not necessary, though religion and religious practices offer an important value paradigm. While religions differ in religious practices, there are certain values and ethics that are universal in nature. Also they emerge primarily from social structure and social processes. For example, value of time like punctuality, cooperation, honesty, compassion and concern for others, etc. are values that are independent of religious philosophy and religious practices. Alternatively, all such values are equally promoted by all religions.

Human values, however, need not necessarily be separated out from the religions and religious practices. It is important to mention that religion, particularly the concept of *Dharma,* offers a time-tested institution that has helped us learning to live together which is now contented as one of the pillars of learning by the International Commission on Education for the 21st Century. The root of the word Dharma is *dhri*, meaning holding or sustaining the society. The story of human civilization, as depicted by several historians, particularly CEM Joad, is indeed a story of human conception, faith and nurturance of God, a concept of perfection hidden in human beings. This is an interfaith concept. This interfaith concept of human being leads us to believe that purpose of education indeed is drawing out the best in the human beings (Swami Vivekananda). In the context of education in human values, the debate to be resolved is whether God is characterized by a set of values; if so, to achieve the full potential of the human beings, inculcation of values becomes necessary. This proposition might be uncomfortable for the atheist who are a small minority with powerful opinion. Large majority of people in the world are non-atheist and God-fearing. Thus, secular (but not necessarily religious) values can benefit a large number of people.

The other related issue is the spirituality. It is in fact here that a lot of debate arises primarily because it is contended that the concept of spirituality is anti-science. Also because it is related to religious principles and practices. Sri Sri Ravishankar, a saint of our contemporary times, deciphers the different religions and spirituality with a beautiful metaphor. According to him religion and religious practices is the skin of a banana; inside the skin is the beautiful sweet nutritious food, and that is spirituality. How true is it! In Bhagavad-Gita, Sri Krishna tells Arjuna that people can achieve or get Him (God) whichever way they worship; this implies that irrespective of religious practices, the spiritual achievement is possible.

In any case, 'spirituality' is derived out of the word 'spirit', one that inspires human beings to move forward. It is the spirit that led Tenjing Norgay and Desmond Hillary, belonging to two different religious traditions to conquer the Himalayas. It is the spirit that compelled people from different religious traditions, languages, countries and societies to conquer and cross the English Channel. It is the spirit, indeed the spirituality, that brought Hindus, Muslims, Buddhists, Sikhs, Christians together to fight the British rule for Indian independence. The spirit, however, can be negative as well. For example, for conducting a bank robbery or similar other act also requires spirit. Spirituality, however, includes only the positive spirit. That it needs nurturing is beyond question. The rich literature on possibility thinking (see Richard Schuller's *Tough Time Never Lasts, But Tough People Do*), revolves round the concept of nurturing positive energy and the spirit to conquer negative energy. Education in human values, as it accommodates the concept of spirituality within it, will essentially mean nurturing the positive spirit of the human beings that can be extended to serve and service others. Swami Vivekananda defined spirituality in terms of service to humanity. One of the five Islamic tenets is 'jakhat'—sharing personal resources for the benefit of others.

## CASE FOR VALUE EDUCATION

The important question then is, whether there is a case for value education at the college level, particularly since value crisis is a continuing universal phenomena. The case, I suppose is stronger now than ever before. For example, non-violence is a value. The effect of violence is essentially destruction of one or more parties involved in the violent activity. In the olden days of fist fighting, it would have taken days to neutralise one or the other. In the next phase of development with swords and other such instruments, it took hours to resolve a conflict. Today, the world can be destroyed in couple of minutes, if not seconds, in nuclear warfare. Similarly, the promiscuity in the olden days did not threaten the spread of AIDS as it is today. These are only illustrative. Value development and value inculcation is much more necessary today for the world to be a safe and a better place to live in.

The choice of the youth for such value inculcation is important. For, it is this youth today who will enter the workforce of the country tomorrow and will be the decision-makers in the government and in private. The value inculcation among the college and university youth is, hence, an investment of great importance. The debate often arises about the kind of values that need to be inculcated among the college and university youth. The commonly articulated values are value of time, attitude towards money and material possession, compassion for others, austerity, cooperation and sharing, leadership, respect for elders, respect for others' views, rationality and questioning and the like.

## VALUE EDUCATION PARADIGM

There are several interrelated issues in deriving a value education paradigm in higher education. These are value education (theoretical) framework, curricular framework, instructional methods and materials, value assessment and certification, etc.

### *Value Framework*

Axiology offers the framework of secular and non-secular values. There are universal and socially relevant local values. The universal values cut across all societies; the locally relevant values are locale specific. Values have also been classified as personality values and character values. The personality values are described in terms of presentation of oneself, values related to the management of the body, and character values as the values that define the psychology of the person.

In identifying the values relevant for the Indian youth, we need to identify both the universal (global) as well as the local cultural values. In the globalized world, where WTO and GATS will rule the market, the universal values like truthfulness and honesty, cosmopolitaness, cooperation, positive orientation of mind, empathy and concern for others, ecological concerns, etc. will assume new importance. Universal values like reading, scholarship and keeping oneself informed are becoming increasingly life-skills in the information age. Values that are locally relevant for the Indian youth are respect and care for elders, sexual relationships based on respect, love and affection, respect for women, tolerance and respect for other religions, appreciation and respect for cultural and social diversity, concern for the poor and the deprived, patriotism, etc.

Rather than approaching the issue of identification of values in a piece meal manner, it would be advisable to resort to certain frameworks that offer a logically organized structures. Various UN Charters and Declarations related to human rights, ecology and environment, women and children, etc. provide one framework for deriving global values. Indian Constitution, particularly, Article 51A, provides the framework for national values in three different categories. While one set of values is related to patriotism and nationalism, the second set of values is related to society and learning to live together, and the third set refers to individual growth and development like striving for excellence, scientific temper, humanism, etc.

Ashtanga Yoga comprises Yama (non-killing or non-violence, truthfulness, non-stealing, continence, and non-receiving of gifts), Niyama (cleanliness, contextual, austerity, study, and self surrender to God), Asana (posture), Pranayama (control of prana or breathing), Pratyahara (restraint of senses from objects), Dharana (fixing the mind on the spot), Dhyana (meditation) and Samadhi (super consciousness). Swami Vivekananda, in *Raja Yoga*, provided interesting analysis of all these eight stages, indicating that Yama and Niyama depict the fundamental values of life in relation to others. Asana and Pranayama relate values to physical life; this is equally extendable to the concept of Pratyahara. Dharana and Dhyana are the values of inculcating the power of mind. The contemporary literature, both on neuronal science (see *Mozart's Brain and the Fighter Pilot* by Dr. Rastak) as will as psychology of thinking validate and contribute substantially to this framework.

The *Sraddhatray Vibhag Yoga* and *Debasur Sampada Vibhag Yoga* of Gita offer meaningful paradigms. The *Sraddhatray Vibhag Yoga* deals with the three sets of human qualities, namely *Swattivik, Rajasik* and *Tamasik,* and then elaborates it further. The *Debasur Sampad Vibhag Yoga* deals with the qualities that distinguish between God and the demon that are resident in human beings in different proportions. Similar frameworks can be derived from the Holy *Quran*, *Guru Granthsahab*, Holy Bible and other such literature of wisdom.

The four pillars of learning proposed in the Report of the International Commission on Education for 21st Century offer an interesting paradigm. The first among the pillars is learning to learn implying learning as an endless process, it is a skill that can be continuously upgraded to optimise human potential, and remain informed. The second pillar is learning to do, implying practical application of learning and dignity and love of labour. The third pillar, learning to live together professes social, environmental and global values to be able to live together, in a world that is divided on several counts. The fourth pillar is learning to be—optimizing human potential. The Commission defines human living at physical, mental, intellectual and spiritual levels; accordingly, it defines the concept of learning to be in terms of all the four levels including also the spiritual dimension. It is indeed these dimensions of learning that make human beings different from animals, on the one hand, and from robots, on the other. The title of the International Commission's Report, *Learning: The Treasure Within* carries significant meaning. The basic purpose of education, in the context of our college and university education, is to search for the treasure within. Education in human values and ethics offers the major support in that search for the treasure within.

### *Curricular Framework*

The major question is whether value education should be subject-integrated part of the ongoing education, or it should be a separate course, or it should be inculcated through co-curricular activities. The debate takes serious turn when it is construed that values cannot be taught but can only be inculcated through value demonstration by the role models. This, I presume, assumes tremendous meaning. In the absence of a well-documented and articulated research, if we look at our daily experiences values are inculcated primarily through role models and experiences. Hence, value education programme must create opportunities for role modeling and experiential learning. Nonetheless, a theoretical backup to such experiential learning will be necessary and meaningful. There is wide divergence of views in this respect. Some recommend study of ethics supported by value-inculcation activities. Some propose a structured curriculum on values along with activities. International research documentation reveals existence of formal courses on human values. Several Indian institutions also offer moral education and education in human values as a necessary component of education; Sri Sathya Sai Institute of Higher Learning, for example.

In the contemporary scenario, a course is valued only when it is linked directly to job opportunities and prospects. It is difficult to predict whether a certificate in a course on values education will make much difference in the job market for a candidate. If so, there will be great risk on value education course getting into the conventional trap – just yet another course where students learn to write examination, but not master or appreciate the knowledge system. (see '*Surely, you are joking Mr. Feinman*' autobiography of the noble laureate physicist Richard Feinman). This will be self-defeating.

On the other hand, if value education is inculcated by integrating with subjects, it may get lost in the din of examinations, marks, distinction and the like, though there is a value content in every subject. For example, science not only teaches the content of science but also promotes values of questioning, experimenting, non-acceptance of authority without proof, searching for truth, etc. Similarly, literature has been described as the mirror of the contemporary society. It is fully potential to sensitize young minds about the contemporary social values. The literature is also potent in inculcating aesthetic values. On the issue of education in human values, the social sciences have always been in the forefront. The value content of each subject needs to be brought into the fore while teaching.

There is, however, hardly any substitute for co-curricular activities for value inculcation. The NSS, NCC, Red Cross, besides the normal sports and games, cultural activities, student union activities, provide opportunities of value inculcation. This needs to be strengthened.

This, however, does not foreclose the option for a curriculum framework combining theoretical framework with practical activities. As mentioned earlier (in my initial chapter in this book), such a framework can include courses on self, family , community living, Indian constitution and citizenship obligations, transition to world of work, leadership and Indian art and culture or aesthetics.

## METHODS AND MATERIALS

A related issue in value inculcation and value education is the relevant literature or educational material. Three different sets of literature or training material can be identified for education in human values.

First and foremost are the literature in print. Autobiographies and biographies of great men and women offer an important source of learning. As mentioned earlier, values are inculcated by the role models through practical demonstration of values being lived. Autobiographies and biographies are the direct documentation of values lived. So also the wisdom literature from different religious traditions that inspire people. A large number of values that have sustained our society through the corridors of time are derived from the religious literature. Atheists apart, the large majority of people who believe in God are guided by the religious dictums, basically providing a framework of personal and social values. The conflict today is largely because of poor education about the religions, and not because of the religious education. The interfaith research (see *Education for the Global Society: interfaith Dimensions* edited by Marmar Mukhopadhyay) stands evidence that almost all the religions propose the same set of values that lead to personal excellence and living together in harmony in the society. The third type of print material is the literature. Not only it represents the contemporary social values, but also certain ideals. For example, *Anandamath* of Rishi Bankim Chandra is a great inspiring literature on patriotism; similarly, Sarat Chandra's *Devdas* has caught the imagination of the young people on the value of love. There are some other interesting pieces of new literature emerging in the world scenario that are classified as personal development literature in the bookstores. Books like Richard Schuller's *Tough Time Never Lasts, but Tough People Do*, *You Can Win* by Shiv Khera, *Count Your Chicken before They Hatch* by Arindam Chaudhary, a large number of books by Dale Carnegie, Wyne Dyer, Deepak Chopra, and others also provide an important basis for learning human values.

The second set of material comprises films, videos, and CDs. In this medium, there are biographical films like Gandhi, Bhagat Singh, Joan of Arc, etc. A large number of other films particularly with important social communication, can make meaningful contribution in value development. Almost all films of Satyajit Ray, Mrinal Sen make important social communication having important value messages.

The third category of material is the case studies, episodes, incidences. The entire methodology of generating debates on values require such material. Obviously, case studies, episodes and incidences should be life incidences. There are several such life incidences documented under the title value vignette (see *Ethics and Values in Organisation* by S.K. Chakravarty). I have provided in the third section of this book a series of such kind of life incidences in the form of case studies, episodes and incidences. While we have been able to document a few of them, a large number of such incidences are not documented. Whenever I have shared such incidences with someone else, I have invariably been enriched with a reciprocal incidence. It is important to document such incidences, both by students as well as by teachers. As the students document such incidences, it gives us a glimpse how they look at the issue, as young persons.

There is a lively debate about the method of transaction of value curriculum. Without variation the conventional lectures on values have been discarded as possible methodology for value education and inculcation. The preference is much more on experiential learning. The main idea is for the students to debate on real-life situation captured in the value stories. The idea is not that the students need to agree with what the characters in the stories said or did. The idea is to generate a debate so that students can experience similar and contradictory views on the same subject. In that process, they will be able to take a decision after considering several different alternatives as well as the consequences—both positive and negative, both individual as well as social.

The other important methodology is field work. For example, when in NSS or Red Cross students work on construction of village or rural roads, cleaning ponds, educating the illiterates, nursing and helping the diseased and the disabled people, they learn a whole range of new values and life-skills.

The methodology followed by SPICMACAY to spread culture among the Indian youth is worth emulating. It invites an eminent artist who gives a discourse along with demonstration on a 'raga' or the musical traditions of India. In view of the recent developments in the information and communication technologies, we should seriously consider using interactive television for delivering the course on education in human values and life-skills. Department of Space has decided to launch a dedicated satellite for education with 72 channels, both interactive and non-interactive channels (see Mukhopadhyay, Marmar, Educating the Nation: Need for a Dedicated Satellite published by DECU, Ahmedabad). There are proposals for channel for the youth, sports, music as well as for conventional education. Such channels can be used for offering programmes of value education. A still better alternative would be to use multi-channel learning systems comprising both the conventional and unconventional methodologies including application of information and communication technologies.

Despite emphasis on experiential learning of values, the role of theoretical learning through reading and listening of lectures cannot be ruled out. The theories, be it on ethics or values, provide a theoretical framework against which the practical and applied values can be related. Thus the transactional methodology for value development has to be a multi-channel learning incorporating theoretical learning either by study of literature or listening to lectures and discourses, debating on cases and life incidences, and practising values in the field setting.

## ROLE OF TEACHERS

Questions are often raised about the role of the teacher; whether teachers are competent in transacting value education? The question is not whether we are academically competent or not. A more serious issue is whether we are morally competent? A much more fundamental question, however, is whether teachers are conscious that they are in the process of man-making or shaping of minds, and they are role models for students for positive or negative purposes.

Are they conscious or do we recognize the importance of transmission of values whether we teach English language or literature, or hard core science and mathematics? For example, in academic profession, continuous learning and reading is an important value; considering the declining study habits among the teachers, whether we have the moral right to teach the value of learning to learn? It is probably here that there is a need to train and develop the teachers not only in the areas of academics, but also in the areas of ethics and moral development. An important viewpoint is to make use of the teachers' participation in the in-service education programmes in academic staff colleges as an opportunity for moral development. The teachers can be offered a course in ethics; they can be called upon to debate on the life incidences that have important issues of values; they can also be involved in social and field work. It is only through this kind of practical and experiential learning that the teachers can be prepared to act as a facilitator in value education among the students.

## VALUES AND MANAGEMENT

Given the current practices and ethos in the colleges and universities, education in human values may generate a new value confusion or crisis. There will be a visible difference between the preached values and the practised ones. For example, the value education programme would teach against nepotism and partiality; whereas experiences indicate that in the same college students taking private tuition are favoured; candidates known to the selection committee members or are recommended by influential people are favoured for the job, and so on. Similarly, on inculcation of values of time and punctuality, it will demand the teachers to be punctual and be on time. We may not need many more examples to illustrate the gap between the preaching and practising of values in the colleges. It is another question whether one would welcome the transparencies and public-mindedness to this cleavage between the preached value and the practised value in the college.

Learning from the study of social change will indicate that a new kind of counter-veiling force will come into operation in the colleges and universities. It may be in the short-term, disturbing, for it will definitely upset the current equilibrium. In the long-term, I guess, it will be welcome. It will demand a major re-engineering of the college management for changing the college ethos. Today, the government is beyond audit, despite the fact that colleges are institutions of public expenditure and there is every reason to justify governance audit. The introduction of education in human values in colleges and universities will eventually lead to the demand for self-imposed practice of governance audit. This will be a boon in disguise

## CONCLUSION

Education in human values is purported to be introduced through the window of value crisis in the society at large. This appears too naïve. Crisis of social values is neither a contemporary phenomenon, nor necessarily an exclusive Indian crisis. The crisis of social values is universal today, and Indian society has experienced such crisis all throughout its life. Education in human values is not to tide over such crisis. Also, it is quite possible that, what we commonly call as value crisis may actually be a value transition – old values creating space for new values, indicating social resilience.

The basis of education in human values is much more positive. The total potential of human being is still untapped. Education in human values is an effort to explore the inner dimensions of human life that makes human beings different from animals and the robots. Education in human values is intended to complete the journey that began with a massive incompleteness of single cell amoeba to the completeness through self-actualisation of all dimensions of life, namely physical, mental, intellectual and spiritual.

# Section III

# Value Episodes

MARMAR MUKHOPADHYAY

# Madhu-Vijay

There was a loud bang on the swing door of Madhubhai, the head of the Department of Education. Vijay, a B.Ed. student rushed in shouting, abusing Madhubhai and his colleagues in filthy languages. What could be deciphered from the loud banging was a complaint against one of the teachers in the department. The only other person in the room was Kamal, one of Madhubhai's research fellows drafting together an important communication.

Madhubhai looked up intently at the boy, sat back, relaxed. Vijay got exhausted with his excitement and shouting. Madhubhai gestured him to take a seat. The boy sat down with a bang.

Madhubhai asked, "What does your father do?"

"I don't have one." replied the student angrily.

"How many brothers and sisters do you have?"

"Two sisters and a brother". Same angry response.

"How old are they?"

"Sisters are 20 and 17 years old and the brother is 11". Reluctance was evident in Vijay's face.

"What do they do?"

"Sisters sit at home, brother goes to a municipal school".

"Who earns at home?"

"My mother."

"What is she?"

There was silence. Vijay looked down and away, avoiding an eye-contact. Madhubhai persuaded.

"She is a maid-servant", Vijay said hesitantly.

The Madhubhai sat back, quiet, thinking, brooding. There was complete silence in the room. He picked up his telephone and dialed a few numbers. What could be heard from this side were:

"Rajanibhai, you needed a teacher of Biology, isn't it?'

"He is doing his B.Ed. here."

"No, no, don't worry. We will take care of that during the next GB meeting. Please engage him immediately – part-time, fulltime whatever way you can."

Madhubhai pulled out a slip of paper and wrote the address of a school and handed it over to the agitated student and said, "Go and meet the principal of this school tomorrow morning at 8.30. He will help you with a job. And, I assure you, I would look into your complaint."

Vijay walked out silently with tears in his eyes.

* * * * *

Kamal was intrigued at the whole incidence. He had known Madhubhai only as an internationally famous professor. He could not believe his eyes and ears that it could happen to Madhubhai; still bigger mystery was Madhubhai's behaviour. He could not resist his inquisitiveness.

He asked Madhubhai, "Sir, can I ask you something?"

"What?"

"What was it all? He abused you, insulted you; and you helped him with a job. He complained to you about a teacher, you did not talk about that. . . ."

Madhubhai explained: "You see, he is neither my boss, nor my equal or my subordinate. Had he been in any of these categories, I would have acted differently. He is my student. It is a different relationship. I need to understand him. What transpired in my mind was why should a student shout at me if one of the teachers in the Department is not able to teach well? His outbursts were clear indications of a deeper malaise than the complaint.

His complaint was that the teacher teaching Hindi does not know enough Hindi. Why does he have to be agitated on that and shout at me? My guess is: he did not have food to eat; he is in a hungry stomach. He feels ashamed that his mother is a maid-servant. His sisters are grown up; they must not be having enough clothes to wear; he must have locked them in the house; as an elder brother he is unable to see it; he is ashamed. I thought he needs support for his survival.

That is why I did not scold or punish him. I tried to understand his problem and give some help. I am sure this boy will change drastically. Of course, only if my assumptions are correct".

About two years later, Kamal was assigned practice teaching supervision duty in Rajanibhai's school. While moving from one class to another, a young teacher came and said, "Namaste"

"I did not recognize you."

"Sir, I'm Vijay. I am a student of your Department." He paused for a while, then hesitantly reminded, "You were with Madhubhai when I entered his office and misbehaved with him. I feel so sorry."

"Yes, now I remember the incident. How are you doing?"

"Madhubhai's blessings. I am a full-fledged teacher here; Rajnibhai is an excellent principal ..."

As a usual practice, before leaving the school, Kamal met Rajnibhai. While chit chatting, he asked, "How is your teacher, Vijay?"

"Oh, he is a good teacher; rather an asset. He is very hardworking and takes interest in various activities......."

Kamal thought, "Thank God, Madhubhai's assumption was correct".

# Soft Tissues under Hard Cover

Chetan had come to the department at 8 o'clock in the morning. That was his usual practice. At 4.45 p.m. he was called by the head (his teacher as well). He told Chetan, "You know, this book (a project of the department) is being printed in Satyen Press. The press person had telephoned me. The outstanding proof must be read overnight and cleared off. I suggest, you go to Dalapur (about 100 k.m. from the city) and complete this job overnight."

Chetan was a bit surprised, and tried to say something. Teacher said, 'Oh, you don't have money. Don't worry, take this money from me. (He took out money from his pocket and gave it to Chetan). You should start just now. There is a bus leaving at 5.15 p.m. for Dalapur".

Chetan said, "But I need to go home, I have been out since morning".

"No, no, you go ahead, I will send a message to your wife; and she will be able to manage for herself".

Chetan had to start, very unhappy, hungry, tired; he knew his wife would wait for dinner. Any how, he went, completed the work overnight, managing on seven cups of tea. He did not close his eyes even for a minute.

Next day, Chetan got back at 10.00 a.m., and went straight from the bus stand to the department and to the head. He reported that he had completed the work.

"Very good, I knew you would do it. Now, go home and take rest. Do not cycle, you have some money left from what I had given you yesterday. Take an auto-rickshaw, go now." said his teacher.

"Should I apply for leave...?"

"No, no, you are on duty. Do not worry now, you go and relax."

Chetan knew that his wife who worked in the same department would have left for office and the house key will be with the neighbour. So he took an auto for home. He had hardly got ready for bath, there was a knock at the door. He opened the door to see his wife standing. Chetan asked, 'What's the matter? Are you well?"

"Oh yes, I am absolutely fine."

"Then why have you come back at this hour?"

"Well, the Head told me, 'You know, your husband worked throughout night. He needs to relax. Go home and comfort him; see that he relaxes and sleeps well. So, I am here."

"But you already have used up so many leaves, why did you waste another?"

"My dear, I am not on leave, I'm on duty, don't worry, go and take bath", said his wife.

# Students: Self-seize

Setting: Amta Ramsaday College, 1963. Under the leadership of the students' union, about hundred students gheraoed Prof Santosh Das, 59, the principal of the college. Prof Das was an eminent scholar in history and economics. Among his many scholarly treaties is *Education of the Ancient Indian Hindus*.

It was middle of September. Time was about twelve noon. Students were shouting slogans, banging the table of Prof Das while he was seated on the chair. Some were dancing at his back. Some are sitting on the window blocking the air and the light. Prof Das was, at least apparently, unperturbed working on the files. The students blocked the entry of the files, and then teaching and non-teaching employees to Principal's Office. They also disallowed Prof Das going out not only for lunch but also to the toilet. After a mild effort to get up and realising that students do not want him to even move, Prof Das quietly sat down.

As entry of everyone in the college was forestalled by the slogan shouting students, Prof Das took to reading books. As onlookers into the whole episode, some of the more perceptive students were surprised to see the concentration with which he was reading, by turning of the pages and also the calmness that spread all over his face.

The sun started setting down on the west. The noise of the slogans steadily reduced; students were visibly tired. Prof Das called Indrajit, the leader of the union and said, "All of you look tired. Why don't you go, eat some food and comeback."

Indrajit asked, "Sir, why don't you talk to us about our demand? Then we can withdraw our Gherao."

Principal said coolly, "No. I don't negotiate under sieze. Nor, I am going to concede any of your demands since these are not just demands. You can hold on to your ghearo till you are convinced that these are wrong demands. So you can go, eat and come back."

A student retorted, "Principal is trying to befool us. He will escape the moment we go for food."

Prof Das was as cool as ever. He said, "I'll be the last one to leave the college today. You know that I was a freedom fighter. We spent many days walking on our stomach without food. I am old but some of my capacities are still intact. You are young, you are not used to hardships. You need food. Go and eat. If you still have doubt, fifty of you can go and have food and fifty can be here ensuring that I do not escape. When the first batch comes back and stays here, the second batch can go and have their food and comeback."

Indrajit understood the sincerity of the principal. He suggested that food be brought here and principal also shares. "You must also be hungry."

This disturbed Prof Das for the first time. He said, "you have gheraod me and stopped my movement out of the chair to punish me. My taking food will defeat your purpose. More than that, you know that the tiger never eats when it is in chains. I shall eat only when I go back home."

As a prestige issue, the students also decided to forego food.

Sun had already set in. It was dark all around except the light in the room of the principal. There was a dead silence; students were tired; Prof Das was engrossed in his reading. The clock in the room ticked on – 7.30, 8 o'clock, 8.30, 9 o'clock, 10 o'clock, 11 o'clock .....

All of a sudden, Prof Das stood up and raised his voice, drawing attention of the students outside the window and to the approaching jeep towards the college. He shouted, "This must be police jeep. You must stop it outside. If police enters my college and if I'm alive tomorrow, I shall rusticate all of you whose faces I have seen today in my room."

Indrajit said, "Sir, police is coming to rescue you from the gherao."

Prof Das retorted back, "If I had to be rescued by the police from my own students, I have no right to exist on this earth, and be called a teacher. If you want yourselves safe, go and stop the jeep outside and ask them to go back."

Students rushed out and stopped the jeep outside the gate. The police officers went back. Students were clueless. They were really in a Catch-22 situation. If they withdraw the gherao, they are defeated, if they do not, it seems to be an endless process.

There was a commotion in the small township that Amta was. It was past midnight. A gentleman appeared on the scene and asked for permission to see Prof Das. When Prof Das declined, students fervently requested for his permission to allow the guest to come in. Prof Das agreed. The guest was none other than the local police officer, in civil dress. Before Prof Das could say a word, the officer introduced himself as a local resident, and he has come at the request and insistence of other citizens of the locality and not as a police officer. He appealed, "I have something to say, Sir."

Prof Das intently looked at him. He said, "Sir, please forgive them and let them go home. It's past midnight, please go home and relax."

Prof Das responded, "How can I let them go. It is they who have gheraoed me; I have not gheraoed them or ordered them to be here. They had to decide themselves to be here or to go. I have no role. If they go home, I will also go home."

The police officer turned towards Indrajit and asked him to ask the boys to go home. Indrajit asked his followers to go back. They were literally waiting. So, quietly they started walking back to their homes.

Prof Das was still sitting on his chair. Indrajit came personally along with the police officer and requested him to get up and go home. Prof Das obliged. As he started walking back, police officer offered to escort him because it was past midnight. Prof Das refused; he insisted that if he has to be escorted, it can be done only by his students. Indrajit asked the police officer to return to his place and himself took charge of escorting Prof. Das.

Indrajit along with four boys rang the call bell at Prof Das' residence. As Mrs. Das opened the door, students touched the feet of Prof and Mrs. Das and left quietly.

# Kamal's Adventure

Professor Kamal, head of a major national institution was invited to a conference in New Zealand. The invitation was attractive to Kamal for more than one reason. First, this would have been his first exposure to an international conference on open learning; secondly, he has never been to New Zealand, he was greatly interested.

After joining this new institute, Kamal reviewed bio-data of all the academic staff. Evidently, they were a bright lot. He was unable to find an equation between their brightness and potentiality, and their performance. He was consistently getting convinced that the staff can perform at much higher level provided they are given the right opportunity, mentoring and encouragement. Just couple of years ago, the Institute organized an Asian conference. Kamal was invited as one of the speakers. He had noticed that the academic staff was busy in the organisational aspects of the conference including petty details like serving tea and coffee, managing delegate lunches, etc. He did not see any one of them making any academic contribution.

Kamal wanted to use this opportunity of New Zealand Conference to simultaneously build capacities in the faculty, and also give them an opportunity and an international exposure. He decided to test his hypothesis.

He called the faculty, just about 15 of them, for a meeting. He announced that there is an international conference in New Zealand on open learning. He also mentioned that he has received an invitation to address the conference. "But I thought I should share it with you and also open it up to you as well. Should anyone of you be interested in presenting a paper in the New Zealand conference, I shall be prepared to give you the details. You probably know that in order to participate in any conference, you have to first submit an abstract of your proposed paper. If the abstract of the paper is accepted, you are to submit the full paper and present it at the conference. So, those of you who are interested in participating in the conference, please prepare abstract of your proposed paper. For the first time, please submit it to me so that I may see its relevance to the theme of the conference." Kamal stopped at this statement to watch the reaction of the faculty members.

The very first reaction was an expression of awe. The senior most of the faculty members, Dr. Sumitra asked, "You mean, Sir, we too can present paper and participate in an international conference!"

Kamal responded, "Yes, that's exactly what I'm telling you and asking your interest."

The comparatively more vocal, Dr. Rajkumar asked, "But who would pay for our travel and stay?"

Well, if your paper is accepted, the institute will pay for both your travel and stay there; but you have to bring back a good name for the Institute. That's the deal," said Kamal with a smile.

There was a bit of buzzing and commotion. Kamal strategically allowed that. After a while, he asked, "Whatever you are talking to each other, can I also hear it?"

While the buzzing stopped and everybody was silent, Dr Rajkumar disclosed the secret discussion. He mentioned that so far the foreign travels were restricted to the head of the institution and the heads of the departments of his choices. The faculty is finding it difficult to believe the offer. He again asked, "You really want us to prepare paper and participate in the conference?"

Kamal smiled and reassured, 'yes', he meant what he said.

Days passed. He received abstracts of the proposed papers from four of the faculty colleagues. Kamal took trouble to correct, edit and modify the abstracts. The abstracts were sent to the conference organisers in New Zealand. Three weeks later, Kamal received the message through individual faculty members that all the four abstracts have been accepted for presentation. The faculty members were excited at the prospect of visiting New Zealand and presenting papers in an international conference for the first time in life. Kamal was both happy as well as in difficulty. He was not prepared for the total financial commitment because it meant both delegation fee and the travel and per diem expenditure for the four members. While he was sharing his difficulty with the Finance Officer, Chaudhry, he came up with an interesting formula.

Chaudhry said, "Sir, we can handle it. The Conference is in May. This is February. We will send the delegation fee from the current year's budget; and we have enough for that. The actual conference is in the next financial year. We will draw the travel and per diem expenditure from the next financial year's budget. I assure you, Sir, that this will not tax us."

Kamal agreed.

The next stage was actually preparing the papers. The faculty members worked very hard to prepare the papers. Because of lack of experience the papers were not of high-quality. Kamal reviewed every paper and helped in improving them. When the papers were ready, he called for a mock-conference where every paper had to be presented before the faculty members with Kamal himself acting as the chairperson. It was an interesting experience.

Faculty members started saying, "I'll say this first and then this....". Some started reading out the paper. Kamal stopped them and asked them to address the chair and the participants before presenting a paper. Further, he mentioned that a good presenter rarely, if ever, reads out a paper. It's boring. He asked each presenter to basically highlight the points and refer to the paper as and when necessary. He allowed them half an hour to prepare themselves for this exercise. With this preparation in a mock-session, Kamal asked them to prepare transparencies that can be used to present their paper by highlighting the main points as they had done just now.

All the four faculty members visited New Zealand and presented their papers. After coming back to India, they met Kamal and reported about the conference, their presentation, and other interesting incidences. They were evidently very happy. Kamal kept his feelings hidden; he needed to know exactly how did they fair.

During the next two three months, Kamal happened to meet a few internationally reputed experts in open learning from other countries who also participated in the New Zealand conference. Without variation, all of them appreciated Kamal's colleagues for their professional competence, commitment and understanding of the open learning system.

Kamal's happiness knew no bounds, though he himself missed the conference because organisers ran out of money to support his travel; and he refused to draw it from his own sources. For, it was meant for his younger colleagues.

# Swapan Kamal

"1969-70. Peak period of the Naxalite movement in West Bengal. The Communist Party of India had broken into—CPI and CPI(M). The ultra revolutionaries within the party constituted still a third party, though not recognised, CPI (ML). The new revolutionary party largely comprised of young people; found ready takers among the college youth except for the few ideologues who were in their middle ages. Burdwan district of West Bengal was an active centre of CPI (ML). Our college had a strong presence of all the three parties through their student-wings. There have been several instances of violence and killing of students. This is one of such but major incidences in the college. One of the students group affiliated to a particular political party had been threatened of dire consequences by another group of students, affiliated to rival political party. The battleground was ready and the battle line had been drawn up.

Students of the threatened group, in good number, were standing on the courtyard in front of principal's office. Teachers were standing on the elevated varandah of the principal's office just behind the students. The other group of students were approaching the college shouting slogans, displaying the bombs and country-made guns in their hands. While some students awaiting their opponents were courageous to face them, others were shivering. This was true for majority of the college teachers as well for more than one reason. First, they were not sure how many of the students would be killed or injured today. They were also not sure whether they will themselves remain unscathed.

Kamal, one of the youngest teachers in the college, jumped into action. He called upon Swapan, the youngest and Bikas (a local teacher) to come down to the ground ahead of the students in the courtyard. Swapan was hesitant, not sure, "what do we do? They are armed and determined to take revenge".

Kamal clarified, "The students will not able to hurl their bombs and open fire as long as three of us stand before them."

"But why?"

"Because, they respect us."

Without a further word, the lean and thin Kamal was already on the ground. Before other teachers could question Kamal's wisdom, Swapan and Bikas had already joined Kamal.

Five of the slogan-shouting students came forward to meet the three teachers, asking their comrades to keep quite and wait. They tried to persuade Kamal, Swapan and Bikas to withdraw from the scene. They refused. One of the students challenged, "Sir, three of you withdraw from this, let all other teachers come and protect the students behind you. We will take charge."

Kamal smiled and said, "We also know that, and that is why we three are here. We know you respect us, love us".

Just at that moment something dramatic happened. Bikas slapped hard one of the boys wielding a gun. Before Kamal could make out what has happened, he heard Bikas shouting, "You idiot, you have the courage to touch your teacher? Apologise to him." It was a strict order.

Swapan realised what had happened. During the argument with Kamal, one of the students had placed his hand on Kamal's arm. He actually did not recognise Kamal since Kamal taught in the morning section of the college, and the student belonged to the nightshift. The student leader joined Bikas asking the student to apologise to Kamal. The student took no time, kept his gun down on the ground, folded his hands and apologized.

Kamal, Swapan and Bikas continued their persuasion to withdraw. Finally, students withdrew with a threat for the future. "Let us see, how long Sirs can save you."

# On the Way to Ahmedabad

Sovan was a professor in an Institute in Delhi. He was invited to deliver a lecture in Ahmedabad. Whenever Sovan got a chance to visit Ahmedabad, he used to visit his teacher and some of his acquaintances in Baroda. This time also, he did so. The day before his lecture, he came to Baroda.

Next morning at about 8 O'clock, Sovan picked up a car to go to Ahmedabad by road. Bardoa-Ahmedabad road is very good. Good surfacing, wide road, car moves smoothly. After about 50 kilometers, Sovan noticed a large crowd on the road, and a growing traffic snarl. As the car approached nearer, he noticed police vans parked across the road; and the road totally blocked. The car stopped behind couple of other cars. Sovan stayed quietly hoping that the jam will be cleared soon. After about five minutes, when he was loosing patience, he got inquisitive. He got out of the car. He started walking towards the crowd to see what is the problem. He instructed the driver that if the road gets cleared, he should drive slowly at the left most lane so that Sovan can get into the car.

As he approached the crowd, he realized that the crowd was quite thick. He treaded through the crowd. A horrifying scene; he could not believe his eyes. At least 20 people were lying wounded, bleeding, shrieking or dead and motionless, seething in pain, crying for help. The road was full of powdered spices like turmeric and red chilly powder soaked in human blood. There was a major accident in which a bus and a truck loaded with spices had collided head on. The vehicles were on two corners of the road. Sovan quickly counted seven or eight of them were motionless. He thought probably they are dead. A few of them were moving very slowly but at least six of them were crying for help and moving their limbs severely out of pain and burning.

Sovan asked stand-by people in the crowd. "What is the problem? Why they have not been picked up and taken to hospital?" One of the persons responded that police is waiting for more police to come and pick them up and take to the hospital.

Sovan asked, "But why not we do it. If there is one vehicle, let them take as many as they can".

Sovan was about to put his left foot forward when the advice came from the crowd, "Don't get involved in these things. You will be unnecessarily harassed by the police and there will be police case".

Sovan was stunned. He didn't know what to do. On the one hand, there is a real practical advice, on the other hand, his conscience advised him that a quick help may save a couple of lives yet. He came forward and asked the cop standing there, "Can I come in and help you?"

The policeman welcomed. Sovan asked another constable to give a hand to lift one of the victims lying on the road with a definite sign of life. The constable came forward; they lifted the body and put him in the standing van. He now called upon the public, "Please can a few of you come and help us? They can still be saved." At this call and watching the policeman joining hands with Sovan, five/six young people came forward. When they started giving their help, Sovan said, Please don't waste your time on those who are already dead. Let us first pick those who are still alive and send them to the hospital. We will then clear off the dead bodies".

It took half an hour. With the support of the police and ten people joining hands, most or all of the persons lying on the street and still alive were sent to the hospital; the dead bodies were shifted to the side of the road. The road got cleared. It is only then Sovan noticed that his hands and shirt sleeves were full of bloodstains. He could not have got into the car in that condition. He looked for a tube-well – an unknown place. He was not sure where to find one. But local people came forward and guided him to the tube-well. They pumped water out for him. He washed his hands and went back to the car. In the meanwhile, police had cleared the crowd and the traffic started moving.

Sovan reached Ahmedabad for his lecture but his clothes

gave the impression of something massive to have happened. He kept quiet to himself, delivered his lecture and returned to Delhi by taking the evening flight with some bloodstains still on his shirt.

# Smile Priceless

Since the time Kanak came back from the office, he is tense, anxious, waiting for his elder brother, Samar, to come back. Today was the last date for depositing examination fees in the University. Kanak had borrowed the money from his friend and gave it to his brother so that he may save the year.

Kanak had just completed his B.Sc. and taken up a job as a school teacher. He was very impressed and proud of his brother. Samar was four years elder to him. Samar was an artist. He sang well, acted well, indeed, very well. But that was not what Samar made Kanak proud of. He was proud of some unusual human qualities of Samar. Samar was an artist at heart. He would reach out with joy and bliss wherever these are in short supply. And that made him popular wherever he goes or wherever he is. He was elected General Secretary of the University as an independent candidate, defeating both the politically affiliated students' wings.

But Samar seemed to have a lot of qualities with a bunch of bad luck. He taught Kanak mathematics in B.Sc. Kanak passed but Samar failed. In fact, since then Samar gave up his studies earning his living on private tuition and musical performances. Kanak had no doubt about his brother's scholarship and learning. Kanak only persuaded Samar to go back to the university after a lapse of eight long years. So Kanak had a stake - a proverbial obsession to see his brother completing graduation and post-graduation.

Samar would appear at BA honours examination in English. He was to pay his fees today. And today was the last day. Kanak knows his brother too well to trust him that he would be worried of a year. He was pacing up and down in the verandah.

Samar quietly enters the house. It was 9.15 in the evening. Samar was exhausted – probably walking for quite sometime. But Kanak cannot wait. He rushed to his brother.

"Have you paid the fees?" Kanak asked.

"Yes, yes, I have paid".

"Show me the receipt", Kanak insists.

Sister Dolly intervened, "Let him breath first. Wait, let him take water, have a wash, then you can talk about your studies".

"Chhordi, we are not talking of studies. Today was the last day for paying his fees. I want to know whether he has paid the fees. And I want to see the receipt", Kanak insists.

Samar takes the opportunity to go away. He enters the bathroom for a wash. Kanak now becomes apprehensive – praying his apprehension does not come true.

As soon as Samar comes out, Kanak rushed to him "Mejda, please show me the receipt". Samar uses all his skills to avoid the issue, but Kanak insisted. Dolly now joined Kanak "why don't you show him the receipt! He is worried?"

Samar reluctantly comes out with the truth. He has not deposited his examination fees.

"Look, I did stand in the queue with the form, I had still six/seven students before me. All of a sudden, I saw Didi standing alone in one corner and wiping tears in her eyes. You know Didi".

Kanak explains to Dolly "Chhordi, Didi is the pet name of Shefali – otherwise a very young student liked by all".

Samar continued, "I went to her, asked her what was the problem. First she won't tell me. I had to shout at her. Then it flashed – she was from a poor family and must not have been able to collect the money for the fees. On pursuing, she told me that she won't be able to pay the fees and hence, lose a year. Her mother has to wait for one more year for her to earn and get out of present situation. So I told, 'come on, this is no reason. I have enough money to spare. In fact, I have brought extra money knowing some would need it today. I had to tell a lie to convince her. I got a form for her, pressed Rs. 265.00 in her hand and dragged her into the queue in my place".

"You be here and go ahead. Let me see what was happening to Sarat and Kalpana. They too would be in difficulty today."

"So, ultimately you have not paid your fees and lost one year. Mejda, did you think of us, our dreams", Kanak asked.

"Yes, I thought all that. But, I could not have ignored it and lived a life so small and full of sense of guilt. Kanak, I wish you had seen the smile on Didi when I left. You can't have it for millions of rupees, I tell you."

"So what will happen now? Didn't you talk to Ramadi?"; Kanak asked.

Ramadi was the Vice Chancellor of the University, an erudite scholar of Sanskrit. Everyone in the University addressed her Ramadi.

"Well, I went to Ramadi only. I requested her to keep a date for me. First I had a good banging from her for being the student leader. On her insistence, I had to tell her the whole thing and seek her assurance not to talk to anyone. Didi will feel bad. You know, what Ramadi said? She said, "Samar, I believe in what you say. I am proud of you. I can't keep a date for you, despite this good act of yours. You leave the form with me and rush to get money. May be your brother can help you".

"I could not tell her that you had already borrowed and you cannot find any more. So I left the University, had a music session with Bijon. And that's it!"

Unusual calm descended on all the three. Samar broke the silence, "Come on Kanak, be a sport. I have lost eight years, one more so what. From this money, one student had to pass. So equation is alright. 'X" is to be replaced by 'Y'. Cheer up".

A month later Samar receives a registered letter from the University. With utter confusion, he opened it to find his admit card. He could not wait, shouted for Kanak, "see, here is my admit card."

"So some one did pay your fees", Kanak asked.

"But who could it be?", Samar questioned .

"Whom did you leave the form with?"

"Ramadi".

"So, she has paid your fees."

# Disclaimer: Gem of a Human Being

Chanchal came to know only today how he landed up here, though he has been here for more than five years now. It was in his farewell party that his head of the department, while appreciating his contribution to the department, mentioned, "but for Dr. Sharada Devi, a good friend of ours, we could not have Dr Chanchal here with us".

Series of scenes/pictures flashed through Chanchal's mind. He was back on time by more than five years when he first met Dr Sharada Devi in Regional College. Chanchal joined Regional College as a research assistant. He was posted at the College by its headquarters in Delhi. The college was clueless what to do with Chanchal, what to assign to him since there was no instruction from the headquarters to the college. And, Regional College never asked for a research assistant. One day, Principal called Chanchal in his office and asked him to assist Dr Sharada Devi. She was to organise and direct an in-service education programme for teacher educators.

Chanchal, by nature, is a serious and sincere young person. He took up the work with all seriousness. As the days moved on in the programme, Dr Sharada Devi involved him more and more in academic aspects of the workshop. Chanchal also gave a good account of himself. On the last day, after the closing session, one of the very senior participants left a comment in the ears of Chanchal, "Don't waste your time here. You are cut out to be much more." Without actually understanding what was hidden in the statement, Chanchal thanked the participant.

Next day, Dr Sharada Devi called Chanchal to her office. She repeated almost the same words, "Don't waste your time here . . . you should go to Baroda and do your doctoral studies with Prof Buch." She wrote Dr Buch's address in a slip of paper and handed over the slip to Chanchal. "Just write to Dr Buch a letter stating your intention of doing Ph.D with him. He is a very nice person. Just write to him and send it tomorrow itself."

For Chanchal, going to Baroda, doing Ph.D with Dr Buch was a dream. Once bitten, twice shy, Chanchal reminisced his ambition of studying in one of the Ivy League Universities in USA; securing a place also in Columbia University; all support guaranteed except travel; he could not manage enough money for the passage. Instead, he landed up in a rural College as a College teacher. He thought, this probably was one more game of fate. All the same, he wrote to Dr Buch, the very next day.

There was complete silence for several weeks. No response from Baroda. Chanchal was reconciled. For, he expected that, little realizing that greater trouble, greater frustration was just round the corner.

He received an interview call from Baroda. There was still two weeks before the interview. But he can't go. He decided to keep quiet and not inform Dr Sharada Devi about the interview call.

It was probably after two or three days of receiving the call-letter, Chanchal was walking through the corridor towards the library. He saw Dr Sharada Devi coming from the other end. Before he could skip and hide himself from her sight, Dr Sharada Devi saw him and called rather loudly. Chanchal came closer and saluted her.

She asked, "Have you heard from Baroda?"

"Yes, Madam," said Chanchal

"So, when are you going?"

"No, madam. I'm not going for the interview."

"Why?"

"I have some problem. I am not going to Baroda."

"Well, I know the problem. You haven't got your pay for the last two months. I found that out from our Accounts Section."

She opened her purse, took out some money, and offered to Chanchal.

"Keep this, go to the station and book your ticket."

"No Madam." Chanchal refused.

Sharada Devi put one of her rickety hands on the equally lean shoulder of Chanchal and pushed the money into his pocket with the other, with motherly care and affection.

"This is only a loan. You must return it whenever you can. But must go for the interview," Sharada Devi insisted.

Without giving the second opportunity she briskly went past Chanchal and entered Principal's office. She was beyond Chanchal's reach.

* * * * *

Chanchal woke up when he was called upon to address his farewell function. He was still negotiating with the mystery—"How did Dr Buch know the role of Sharada Devi in his coming to Baroda?" During the last five years, Dr. Buch has never taken her name. He decided to pursue Dr Buch and crack the mystery.

Dr Buch told, "She wrote to me about you with all superlatives. Why?"

"She never told me, even when she helped me buy the ticket to reach here for the interview that she actually wrote and recommended me to you," said Chanchal.

"She is like that. Never claims credit. Prefers to remain behind the scene. Gem of a human being."

# 'I Primarily Read Radhakrishnan'

"I had applied for admission to the post-graduate program in Kolkata University. I did not get either interview call or notice for deposition of fees for the admission. I came to know from some friends that the last date for deposition of fees is just three days away. I decided to rush to Kolkata and meet the head of the department. I set off the very next day for Kolkata. I reached the university department at about three o'clock in the afternoon. I sought an appointment with the head, Prof. Kamalakanta. I was lucky. He agreed to meet me after half an hour. I waited.

When I entered his office after half an hour, I found a fair plumpy gentleman in the late fifties comfortably couched in his chair, eyes soaked in some file. Without looking up at me, he asked, "Yes, what can I do for you?"

I said, "I had applied for admission to the post-graduate programme; I have neither been given admission nor have been called for interview. I am very keen to study."

Prof asked me, "What's your name." Still head down on some paper.

As soon as I told my name, he remembered to have seen my application. He said, "You are from . . . university. That is not equivalent to our university. Standard of your university is very low compared to ours. Also, our curriculum is much richer; and you shall not be able to cope with it."

I was desperate. I said, "I have really studied well. I shall be able to cope with the course of this university. You can test me, Sir."

He probably did not expect such an arrogance from a student from a lowly placed university. The Professor looked up and took a good look at me from toe to top. "Are you really sure? You're prepared to take an oral test right now?"; he asked.

I had very little choice. I agreed. Prof asked me only now to sit down. I sat on the chair just opposite him, and prepared mentally for the test. I had absolutely no idea what kind of question and from which kind of subject he will ask.

Professor asked a number of questions on philosophy of education. I guess I successfully defended myself by answering all the questions correctly. There was a smile, for the first time, on the face of the Professor. He said, "You seem to have studied well." I must say when he smiled, he looked so generous and fatherly.

I said, "Sir, what you asked me is only the first unit of the course; there are six other units in this course."

Professor was inquisitive, "What are some of the other units of the course?"

I quickly rattled out all the other units from the course. He now accepted that the course that I have done was really good. His next question was on the books that I have read on the subject.

"I read Ross, Rusk and several other books. I have also read Brubacher. But I read more of philosophy books than just philosophy of education."

"That's interesting. Who guided you to read philosophy? If I remember correctly, you are originally a student of science."

"Yes, Sir. I am a student of science. My father guided me; his contention is philosophy of education is derived from philosophy per se. Unless I read philosophy as a subject, I shall not be able to appreciate the philosophical basis of education."

"So, what books did you read in philosophy?"

"I primarily read Radhakrishnan."

The name had an electrifying effect on the Professor. He almost jumped out of his chair. "Do you know Dr Radhakrishnan was my teacher; I have studied Philosophy directly under him?" The Professor went into reminiscence about his days as a student of Dr Sarvepalli Radhakrishnan. One could easily notice the great pleasure, pride and satisfaction on his face.

Without a further word with me, he picked up the telephone and dialed the registrar of the University, and told him that he was sending the papers for extending equivalence to .. University with Kolkata. In response to the query of the registrar, he mentioned, "I have tested the candidate. He is very good; the curriculum prescribed in the course is equally rich."

I was granted admission.

# You are Like My Children

The Professor used to teach, besides one of the regular papers in the postgraduate programme, a special paper called Educational Classics. Because of heavy administrative load of the University, he was unable to take the classes in Classics which was offered by seven students. We were getting worried as the examination was nearing.

One afternoon, he called me and asked me to inform all the students to come to his residence on Saturday afternoon. He said, "I'll take the classes on Classics at home on Saturday from three to six in the afternoon."

All of us gathered together little before three in the afternoon in Professor's house. Before he entered, we were contemplating and chatting with each other regarding the tuition fees that we may have to pay for this coaching at home. This, we understood was a common feature. However, we became quiet as soon as he entered.

We were all seated on the floor, on mattresses covered neatly with white bedsheets. He also came and sat on the floor at his designated place. He started teaching Plato's Republic in classical style. He would read line by line, and explain. But something better was still in store.

A young man (probably a servant) came with seven plates in a tray. Each plate contained some food items – some fruits, sweets and biscuits. He also served us with water. Professor instructed us to eat and listen to his teaching.

This went on every week till he completed teaching the two prescribed Classics, Plato's Republic and Rousseau's Emile.

At the end, one of us took the courage to ask for the amount to be paid as (private) tuition fees. He laughed loudly to his heart's content, almost unstoppable. "You are like my children. Where is the question of fees?"

His laughter, instead of anger gave us some more courage; someone said, "Sir, we ate so much all these days ...!"

"So what? When you are at home, you are my guest. I must treat my guests the best I can. This is our Indian custom and culture. And, how can you study if you are hungry?"

Professor appeared to be still amused with our foolish questions. He came to the door to see us off like all other days, except a word of blessing, "Wish you all the best in the examination".

# List of Contributors

Dr. A.K. Merchant, Director of Baha'i Office of External Affairs in India.

Prof. Amlan Datta, Former Vice-Chancellor, Viswa Bharati, Shantiniketan, West Bengal.

Prof. Anil Bhattacharya, President, All India Federation of University and College Teachers' Organization, Kolkata.

Dr. Arati Sen, Professor and Former Head, Vinaya Bhavan, Viswa Bharati, Shantiniketan, West Bengal.

Prof. Bart J. McGettrick, Professor of Education, University of Glasgow, Scotland.

Dr. Jaya Indiresan, Former Senior Fellow, Higher Education, National Institute of Educational Planning and Administration, New Delhi.

Prof. K.P. Pandey, Former Vice-Chancellor, Kashi Vidyapith, Varanasi.

Dr. Karan Singh, Eminent Scholar and Member, Rajya Sabha, New Delhi.

Dr. Madhu Parhar, Reader, STRIDE, Indira Gandhi National Open University, New Delhi.

Prof. Marmar Mukhopadhyay, Joint Director, National Institute of Educational Planning and Administration, New Delhi.

Dr. R.P. Sharma, Former Dean, Faculty of Education, University of Delhi, Delhi.

Sadanand Ward Mailliard, Founder, Mount Madonna Center near Santa Cruz, California.

Prof. Syed Mahdi, Vice-chancellor, Jamia Millia Islamia, New Delhi.

Prof. Udai Pareek, Former Professor, Indian Institute of Management, Ahmedabad.

Dr. Uma Jain, Director, Academy of Human Resource Development, Ahmedabad.